ALIEN PLOTS

Liverpool Science Fiction Texts and Studies
General Editor DAVID SEED

Series Advisers I.F. Clarke, Edward James, Patrick Parrinder
and Brian Stableford

ALIEN PLOTS

Female subjectivity and the Divine in the light of James Tiptree's 'A Momentary Taste of Being'

INEZ VAN DER SPEK

LIVERPOOL UNIVERSITY PRESS

First published 2000 by
LIVERPOOL UNIVERSITY PRESS
Liverpool L69 7ZU

© 2000 Inez van der Spek

British Library Cataloguing-in-Publication Data
A British Library CIP record is available

ISBN 0-85323-814-6 (hardback)
ISBN 0-85323-824-3 (paperback)

Typeset in 10/12.5pt Meridien by
XL Publishing Services, Lurley, Tiverton
Printed by Bell & Bain, Glasgow

Contents

Acknowledgements

Many people accompanied and supported me on the long and winding road of writing this book. I can mention only a few of them. My academic supervisors Rosi Braidotti, Toine van den Hoogen and Anne-Marie Korte time and again challenged me to transgress my own limits of thinking; Anne-Marie not only as a supervisor but as a true friend for years on end. Several other people also critically read (parts of) the manuscript. First of all I have to name David G. Tomas, who kept sending his valuable comments on content and style from across the Atlantic with unflagging interest. Sarah Lefanu, Maaike Meijer, Liana Borghi and Christien Franken offered many creative suggestions about the interpretation of Tiptree's text.

The Dutch network of female researchers in religious studies (OPP) always provides fruitful surroundings for developing new questions and ideas, in particular its annual study weeks at the beginning of January. Of its participants I want especially to name Maaike de Haardt, whose genuine interest in my work is very encouraging, and Jonneke Bekkenkamp, my colleague in religion and literature in Amsterdam.

I wish to express special gratitude towards the women of *De Zolder* (The Attic), Christien Franken, Geertje Mak, Jann Ruyters and Denise de Costa, for their stimulating mix of knowledge and gossip, the food and cigars, and above all, their friendship. Some people who were helpful in the prehistory of this study have to be recalled as well: Grietje Dresen, Herman Wegman (who died too an untimely death), Theo de Wit. Furthermore, the residency on the *bioapparatus* at the Banff Centre for the Arts in 1991 offered a great opportunity for starting up my project, as did the two years' research appointment at the Department of Women's Studies of the Arts Faculty at Utrecht University.

In the final stages of writing this book, life sometimes was almost too full to grasp. My mother and my dear friend Betty died, while little Frederiek and Noraly entered my life. With his wit and care, Anton Simons has helped me to keep my emotional sanity and intellectual imagination. I cannot thank him enough (he prefers a bottle of Scotch, anyhow).

Introduction

Why and how I read 'A Momentary Taste of Being'

In this book I weave together a perhaps somewhat unusual variety of topics, texts and genres. They reflect fragments of myself that I seek to unite in a momentary tale of being: cultural critic, scholar in religious studies and in women's studies and bookworm, who alternates bursts of passionate science fiction reading with indifference to the genre. That is, at times I am thrilled by its daring and imaginative worlds, while at others I suddenly find myself bored with or even chafed at what I then experience as science fiction's artificiality and complacency. Yet some authors never fail to rouse my excitement and admiration. James Tiptree, Jr is the most persistent of them.

As a theologian, I have always considered modern literature an important resource and challenging dialogical partner for posing questions about the meaning(lessness) of life. It was not until some ten, twelve years ago, however, that, to my great surprise, I found such qualities in science fiction. A previous interest in utopic literature and the discovery of messianic themes in television serials like *Star Trek* and *V*, watched on lazy Sunday afternoons, gradually converged on the reading at random of loads of science fiction. Its alternative worlds, extrapolations, fantastic imagination, and speculative vein became an acquired taste to me: and indeed, food for religious studies in a double sense. First, there is science fiction's either intended or subliminal transformation of mythological and religious themes and images. Think in particular of the battle between good and evil, end time myths, stories and figures of Fall and Redemption. On another level, science fiction's best writings are of interest to the theologian because of their critical and visionary qualities. In its imagination of, literally, new worlds, science fiction may shatter the apparent naturalness of the existent and suggest the myriad horizons of the possible.

'Theology' and 'religious studies' will be used interchangeably in this book. In my perception, the distinction between evocation in the former and explanation in the latter is not so much a matter of rigid fences but of emphasis and intention. In a similar way, strict divisions of labour between theology and 'secular' disciplines dealing with the meaning of life, such as philosophy and the arts, are untenable and unfruitful. As Mary McClintock Fulkerson states:

Theology as 'discipline' is neither the study of revealed truths, nor the correlation of the sciences of modernity with the contents of Christian faith. If there is one clear lesson from the turn to discourse, it is that the project of separating out the signifiers of theology from the signifiers of other disciplines—of culture, of secular knowledge— is a fundamentally ill-conceived one.[1]

As I understand it, theology/religious studies is a critical discourse on images, stories, concepts and theories and on disciplinary and spiritual practices both inside and outside religious traditions, which give shape, value and direction to existential questions and to people's orientation towards dimensions of reality which are qualified as transcendent.[2] By way of a supplement to this description I would like to quote Grietje Dresen. As early as 1981, when feminist theology was still considered a queerer fish in women's studies than nowadays, Dresen explained in an article for a Dutch interdisciplinary journal on women's studies why it was not only legitimate but even *fun* to be a theologian. Written in a personal style—it was titled 'Mijmeren' [*musing*]—the conclusion of Dresen's essay nevertheless also stands as a witty and pertinent theoretical statement which remains as relevant today as it was then:

> [I]t is a privilege to be a theologian. Thinking of old about love, pleasure, desire, pain, death, power, fear and liberation—even before this gained popularity. And thinking about something that is a mystery. Try to find that in mathematics or psychology. Immediately some statistics are conjured up. Sometimes theologians attempt to do that too, but it always goes wrong—'Do you believe in the Divinity of Christ the Human Being?'—yes, no, don't know—strike out whichever is not. Some people, in other words, are not divine then?
>
> We reflect, in particular, on the historical representations of the divine. On images and imagination. And why people need those: because it is frightening without them, or hopeless, or empty, or boring. Stars for people, people for the stars. Because sometimes struggling people feel strenghtened by these images: as *models* [voor-beelden].[3]

More recently she summarized her 'musing' as follows:

> Theology as reflection on the believing, or as I would prefer to say *receptive* attitude to life, shares with for instance philosophy the quest for meaning, the longing for wisdom. Theology, however, does not limit its attention to what people can think up themselves, but, in my view, builds in more room for the non-rational, for what people do not have in their own power but what approaches *them*.[4]

As a feminist theologian I am especially interested in how *women* think about love and death, suffering and well-being; how they give expression to a quest for meaning and wisdom; and how they imagine the divine. I want to reflect on how our struggles to come into being get represented, to see what is inspiring and what is impeding them/us in our quest to become subjects who imagine, hope, believe, speak, desire and write in our own ways and on our own terms. That is, neither as failed men or their indistinct shadows, nor as True Women, but as women telling as yet unheard—and never definite—stories about how they experience, interpret and envisage reality. Stories of multiple kinds, be these theories, liturgies, narratives, discussions, or 'musings'. Consoling stories with a beginning and an end, just as well as disruptive and stumbling stories of which you cannot make head nor tail.

Science fiction stories, too. More and more during my reading up on science fiction I became acquainted with female-authored texts, including those of James Tiptree, Jr. It is one of her texts, 'A Momentary Taste of Being', published in 1975, that I have decided to put in the centre of attention. To avert any misunderstandings from the outset, the goal of this book is not to provide a general insight into Tiptree's work by means of an exemplary discussion of 'A Momentary Taste of Being'. I intend to offer an investigation of the various ways in which this particular text may interact with feminist and other critical theories on the issues of female subjectivity and the meaning of the divine in a postmodern context. Instead of producing an overview of recurring themes and motives in Tiptree's writings, I have chosen to experiment with a practice of multiple readings of only one text. I found many of Tiptree's texts to be so provocative in their ambiguity, philosophical wit and literary interplay, often deceptively hidden in the corners of seemingly trivial stories, that for me it would be impossible to deal with them in general. I have no pretensions, therefore, to making claims about Tiptree's oeuvre, even though at times during this study I will not hesitate to make cross-references to her other stories.

From Tiptree's writings, I selected for in-depth exploration the one most intriguing from the perspective of religious studies. The core of 'A Momentary Taste of Being', as I shall explain below, is a radical reshaping of the conventional figure of the *alien encounter*. In my interpretation, this encounter, as it is textually organized, mediates both a vision of the divine and of female subjectivity. To anticipate more detailed explanations, it concerns a multiple and highly ambivalent vision of the divine, while (female) subjectivity appears as a difficult and painful process of continuous splitting and reassembling. It is not a story, in short, for those who believe in the promises and practices of New Age, with its creed of all-encompassing holism, its consecration of a psychology of personal growth, and its therapeutic ideas of evolution and progress in which suffering and evil are mere moments of ignorance that have to be overcome, and will be overcome, in the New Age for which this world is heading.[5] Instead, 'A Momentary Taste of Being' evokes a view of life subversive of wholeness, (self)affirmation and progress. Some would even go so far as the editors of *The Encyclopedia of Science Fiction* did as to call it, besides Tiptree's 'finest and most intense longer story', also 'one of the darkest genre-SF stories ever printed'.[6] As I hope to demonstrate during this book, Tiptree's text does contain more traces of lightness than thus suggested. These, however, just shimmer through the wastes of being; the wastes are highlighted in the text. And for that very reason it is a challenge for theologies that attempt not to resort to convenient harmonization of contradictory, violent and unsettled existence in our postmodern worlds of technoscience capitalism and global migration.

One of the burning questions for contemporary theologies is not only how, but *if* we can still speak of God at all. As the editors of a collection of Dutch essays, *Echoes of an Embarrassment*, recall, many modern people experience the impossibility of 'fill[ing] the image of God with meaning'.[7] For these people the image remains empty and finally obsolete, for it is without any obvious function. Nevertheless the editors wonder if the modern human being has not arrived at a dead end with his proclaimed atheism and his desire to exclude every sacred dimension of reality. Is the human being as self-sufficient as he claims to be? Do not the very failures of modernity indicate the limits of human complacency? The authors of this book, however, reject both religious regression and modern adjustment. Instead, they commit themselves to the thought experiment whether the *failing* of names for the sacred could not imply a new opportunity for the sacred.

Many feminist theologians would agree with this experiment insofar as they seek to rethink the meaning of the divine, which is a theological interpretation of the sacred. Because of the oppressive or even misogynist implications of traditional God-language, they put a high value on a *via negativa*, speaking about the divine in terms of what it is *not*, about the ineffable and unfathomable. On the other hand, they understand the self-sufficiency and godforsakenness of the modern human being as constitutive in the first place for *his* being in the world, the experience of modern *man*. It is in the interest of women, who always had a passive or marginal role in the naming of the divine, to be able to explore affirmative ways of imagining the divine as well. In my discussion of the divine in the light of 'A Momentary Taste of Being', I aim to strike a balance between negative and affirmative God-talk.

Interwoven with the project of women's naming of the divine is a search for reformulations of female subjectivity. Of course feminist theologians share this interest with other feminist theorists. It is only more recently, however, that we have begun to be involved in the theoretical conceptualization of subjectivity in order to connect it to the more pragmatic modelling of female subjectivity in (church) political, social and liturgical contexts. The principal concern is the tension between a deconstruction of the subject and the striving for subjective agency for women. On the one hand feminist theologians assent to the critique of the subject as a discrete, autonomous and self-conscious agent whose identity rests upon a permanent essence or substance, whether it be a 'soul', or 'reason', or a 'true self'. A critique which, as Paula Cooey rightly points out, challenges not only 'conventional notions of knowledge, moral responsibility, and individual immortality', but also 'concepts of a transcendent reality, symbolized primarily as a super subject who stands over against the world as its author'.[8]

This critique, on the other hand, need not result in the by now infamous notion of the 'death of the subject'. The subject is decentred and derived; it is at the mercy of barely comprehensible or controllable libidinal, social and cultural drives and forces, and its identity is always forged out of differences. It is not possible to speak of a natural female identity or an authentic female experience, be it either of the self or the divine. And yet, the disappearance of a stable and unified subject does not preclude *any* kind of subjectivity, of some sense of self, however provisional, divided and fragile. I suggest to understand instead subjectivity as a process, as a never-ending dynamic of being subjected to the power of language, the social, the unconscious, and, simultaneously, as the search for the articulation of one's desire, experiences and views on one's own terms. The interpretive dialogue with 'A Momentary Taste of Being' is intended as a contribution to this search.

I hope the reader will at least bear with me in the various explorations of Tiptree's story, and even enjoy this expedition. The study is designed as a serial. To a certain extent it in fact resembles the soap opera in its circular movements around a group of more or less allegorical people entangled in odd plots. In four subsequent chapters I will present a reading of Tiptree's text departing from different possible narrative viewpoints.[9] Each of these readings brings about not only another dimension of the text but also another story about truth and reality. In its investigation of possible narrative perspectives, this study also resembles a detective story. Yet, while cherishing the fun as well as importance of detection and speculation about the meaning and interconnection of textual signs, I consider neither the modern private eye, who seeks to solve the mystery of crime, nor the traditional priest, aiming for the confession of sin, to be credible role models. None of the versions of truth and reality, I will therefore conclude, can be qualified as definitely *true* on textual grounds, although this does not exclude the possibility that one may be considered to be *preferable* to another on ethical grounds.

Furthermore, different theoretical perspectives will be brought to bear on each of these narrative viewpoints with the objective of illuminating their particularities. The various interpretations of the narrative text, in turn, will also shed light on the theories that are used. Text and theory are brought into a dialogical relation with each other. This method rests on the supposition that there is no rigid, hierarchical distinction between theory and literature, according to which theory would contain a truth-revealing quality with respect to the literary text. Instead, both are forms of discourse, of which the specific conventions and styles reflect and produce different insights that might illuminate as well as criticize one another.[10]

An important device in this interaction between theory and textual interpretation will be the generation of *specular figurations*: imagery, metaphors, myths and cultural expressions (including literary and cinematic texts) highlighting and commenting on each other—both inside the narrative text and between narrative and theories—so as to make new meanings emerge and to revise old ones. As we shall see, Tiptree's text simultaneously affirms and frustrates a linear view; it has a plot which is at the same time a non-plot, the end of the story may suggest the future as well as the past. In an analogous manner, this study both affirms and escapes linearity. On the one hand it is inevitably subjected to the linearity of any more or less scholarly book: the structure of introduction, chapters and conclusion; and the necessity to present a coherent vision. At the same time, however, the use of specular figurations also undercuts, or at least moderates, the dominance of the linear organization of meaning, and hence of the possibility of any synthetic conclusion. In my view, this is valuable because linearity, no matter how indispensable for not getting lost in the chaos of reality, also precludes the richness and colourful abundance of chaos and multiplicity. The analogy between Tiptree's text and this study is also the first example of a specular figuration: the two texts, or discourses, are connected to each other in such a way that a particular image or myth in one text is looked at through the—reflecting, distorting, or enlarging—mirror of another. Nonetheless it is my belief that the string of associations, quotations and relations has to be bound as well lest it be mere playfulness. As the reader is actively involved in this process, not only as an interpreting reader but also as someone writing beyond and behind the text, she has to make decisions about the perspective of the specularity. In my project, once again, this perspective is a contribution to a critical feminist discourse on female subjectivity and her relation to the divine.

The following contains, first, a brief introduction to the life and work of James Tiptree. What I consider to be, from my field of interest, the most poignant issues of Tiptree's fiction will be illustrated by just a few telling examples. This introduction is not intended as a detailed context for the discussion of 'A Momentary Taste of Being', but rather as a roughly designed backdrop. Next comes a synopsis of 'A Momentary Taste of Being', to refer back to during this study, followed by an explanation of the central figure of the text—the alien—and, finally, the itinerary of this book.

Who is Tiptree, what is she?—James Tiptree, Jr

This is also the title of the chapter devoted to James Tiptree, Jr, or Alice Sheldon-Bradley as her real name was, in Sarah Lefanu's pioneering book on feminism and science fiction, *In the Chinks of the World Machine.*[11] When I stumbled across this study, I was engaged in an initial exploration of female-authored science fiction, having only a cursory acquaintance with the work of Ursula Le Guin and Joanna Russ. I am still very grateful to Lefanu for introducing me to the bio- and bibliographical phenomenon Tiptree is.

Within the science fiction community, Tiptree's work is generally acknowledged as belonging to the best of the genre. During the 1970s, many of her stories had won Hugo, Nebula and Jupiter Awards, which are special awards for science fiction writing. Recently, authors have begun to emphasize the importance of Tiptree's work for the development of feminist science fiction. They express their appreciation by dedicating books to her memory and, since 1992, through an annual James Tiptree, Jr Award for science fiction and fantasy, which has been funded by the sale of cookery books whose titles are a pun on one of Tiptree's stories (such as *Her Smoke Rose Up From Supper*). However, insofar as Tiptree's name is known to people outside of a science fiction milieu, it is most likely to be associated with the confusion created by the disclosure of her 'true' sexual identity.

Sheldon's desire to lead a secluded life seemed to be best secured through the adoption of a male pseudonym, which she picked from a pot of jam, while her husband added the Jr for fun. A male name provided the additional advantage of being taken more seriously by publishers. Hence, for years, she maintained contact with editors and fans only by correspondence, the return address being a post-office box in Virginia. She even participated under her male pseudonym in a written symposium on women in science fiction, which was published in the magazine *Khatru* in 1975.[12] Her contributions provided, as Lefanu puts it very well, 'the positively bizarre experience of reading the words of a woman, writing about the politics of being a woman, who is masquerading utterly convincingly as a man'.[13]

Until her cover was blown by an astute editor a year later, speculations on her identity abounded. Robert Silverberg's introduction to Tiptree's collection of short stories *Warm Worlds and Otherwise* became notorious in this respect. It was titled 'Who is Tiptree, What is He?', a title which was, as we have seen, adopted with considerable irony thirteen years later by Lefanu. Silverberg brushes aside the suggestion that Tiptree might be female as simply 'absurd, for there is to me something ineluctably masculine about Tiptree's writing'. He compares Tiptree to Hemingway, both of them sharing

> that prevailing masculinity ...—that preoccupation with questions of courage, with absolute values, with the mysteries and passions of life and death as revealed by extreme physical tests, by pain and suffering and loss.[14]

After Tiptree's true identity was exposed as that of a frail sixty-year-old woman, Silverberg had to admit that this had completely called into question the notion of what is 'masculine' or 'feminine' in writing. For this very reason Ursula Le Guin, in the introduction to Tiptree's collection *Star Songs of An Old Primate*, compares her to Virginia Woolf's Orlando, who also embodies an 'unanswerable criticsm of the rational and moral fallacies of sexism, simply by being what and who she is'. Yet Tiptree even surpasses Orlando in that she upsets our sense of what reality is 'by being a fictional character who writes real stories'.[15] Her masquerade imperils, as Le Guin points out, both theories about femininity and authorship and assumptions concerning the existence of the writer *per se*.[16]

I certainly would agree about this last point insofar as it implies that priority is given to the reading-process of the narrative texts, in the sense that speculations about the author's *intention* be avoided. Nevertheless, I think it is important not to ignore either the position or the figure of the author altogether. Tiptree's case is illustrative of the fact that there is indeed an author's *effect* on the interpretation of the text. In addition, I agree with Nancy Miller that the postmodern declaration of the death of the Author in favour of the proclamation of the primacy of textuality, 'does not necessarily work for women and prematurely forecloses the question of identity for them'. As she explains,

> women have not had the same historical relation of identity to origin,

institution, production, that men have had, women have not, I think, (collectively) felt burdened by too much Self, Ego, Cogito, etc.[17]

For women the question is rather how to *become* a writing subject and create a female writing identity in and through the texts that are written. In Sheldon/Tiptree's case, it is important to call to mind that when she started writing in the late 1960s, the science fiction scene was still very much male-dominated. Women have had to fight their way into this masculine milieu and its narrative worlds of 'hard science' and technology. The use of a male *nom de plume* of course is a classic aid for women writers, offering protection and access to 'institution and production'. On the other hand, these writers are banished to anonymity through the adoption of official male identities, which prevent their voice from being acknowledged in public as *female*, let alone feminist. Illustrative in this respect is that Tiptree's advocacy of the concept of 'mothering' during the course of the *Khatru* symposium aroused such discontent with the other contributors that the result was not a stimulating feminist debate on motherhood, but, instead, Tiptree was asked to leave the panel because of 'his' masculine ideas. (I will return to Tiptree's idea of mothering in Chapter III.) It is important, therefore, that Tiptree did become known as a woman after all, since her female writing identity thus turned out to be able to disrupt fixed and essentialist views about what femininity is and should be.

While I will shortly present a brief outline of Alice Sheldon's remarkable life, I will do so having taken note of Maaike Meijer's warning that the 'autobiographical reduction [of fiction] leads to passive voyeurism, to gawping at another woman's life'.[18] What matters is 'not what precedes a literary work, but what comes after it', in other words, the *reader*'s active confrontation not with the life of the author but with her work. A genre like science fiction may be the best witness to the inadequacy of simple biographical reduction. How could the life of a twentieth-century writer provide the basis from which the fictional life of—say—a three-eyed, green-furred alien on the planet Andromeda could be explained? Such a strategy might find credibility within a framework provided by a psychocritical interpretation in which the work of an author is considered to be a reflection of the author's unconscious wishes and fears. Yet here too life and work risk to be uncritically reduced to one-dimensional reflections of each other, without it either being acknowledged that *new* meanings and narratives get realized in the text or that the reader's own projecting activity is involved in it. The production of surplus meaning asserts even a source of pleasure in one's engagement with a work.

Nevertheless I do think some knowledge about the author's biographical background can be valuable. The same can be said about the knowledge of the text's historical and cultural context of production. From a feminist viewpoint, as Annelies van Heijst has rightly pointed out, the postmodern taboo on correlating author and text, life and work, prevents the recognition of new articulations of female subjectivity. When the dividing lines are maintained less rigidly, one can say with respect to some writers that:

> the fictional literary work plus the stories about their personality offer very real subject positions which cannot be found yet in the supposedly 'real' reality. Subjectivity thus gets into existence in the process of writing and reading, and the unending re-telling of the story about the 'self', like a continuing story.[19]

In the case of Alice Sheldon/James Tiptree, some knowledge of Sheldon's unusual life can increase the reader's sensitivity for certain obsessions, struggles and desires in the text. Never, however, in order to reduce the three-eyed, green-furred alien to 'actually her mother', or 'in fact one of these exotic creatures she met in her youth'. It can only be understood as a function in the *story* about the 'self', that is, a story that is a co-creation of James Tiptree and the reader of her texts.

Alice in jungleland

Alice Sheldon-Bradley was born 1915, in Chicago, as the only child (after nine miscarriages) of Herbert Bradley, a lawyer and explorer, and Mary Hastings Bradley, an explorer and writer of 35 books on travelling, mountain gorillas, women's rights and a variety of other issues.[20] The weight of Mary's intellectual and personal power pressed so hard on Alice's shoulders that she would not be able to write while her mother was actively working. Mary Hastings died in 1977, at the age of 92. That one of her books is titled *Alice in Jungleland* already displays much about Sheldon's childhood. She spent a great deal of her childhood in Africa, India and South-East Asia on expeditions with her parents. The most vivid description of this extraordinary period of her life and its profound effects on her later being is to be found in Tiptree's own words:

> She found herself interacting with adults of every color, size, shape, and condition—lepers, black royalty in lionskins, white royalty in tweeds, Arab slavers, functional saints and madmen in power; poets, killers, and collared eunuchs, world-famous actors with headcolds, blacks who ate their enemies and a white who had eaten his friends, and above all, women; chattel-women deliberately starved, deformed, blinded and enslaved; women in nuns' habits saving the world; women in high heels committing suicide, and women in low

heels shooting little birds; an English-woman in bloomers riding out from her castle at the head of her personal Muslim army; women, from the routinely tortured, obscenely-mutilated slave-wives of the 'advanced' Kibuyu, to the free, propertied, Sumatran matriarchs who ran the economy and brought six hundred years of peaceful property to the Menang-Kabau; all these were known before she had a friend or playmate or her own age. And finally, she was exposed to dozens of cultures and sub-cultures whose values, taboos, imperatives, religions, languages, and mores conflicted with each other as well as with her parents. And the writer, child as she was, had continuously to learn this passing kaleidoscope of Do and Don't lest she give offense, or even bring herself or the party into danger. But most seriously, this heavy jumble descended on her head before her own personality or cultural identity was formed. The result was a profound alienation from any nominal peers, and an enduring cultural relativism. Her world, too, was suffused with sadness; everywhere it was said, or seen, that great change was coming fast and much would be forever gone.[21]

To escape parental influence and the feeling that she would never be able to live up to their standards and expectations, Alice asked to go to a Swiss boarding-school. She found it hard to fit in, an experience which continued when she went to study at Sarah Lawrence College. While still at college, she married William Davey, 'a beautiful but absolute idiot',[22] whom she had met only three days before and who turned out to be an alcoholic and debauchee. They were divorced in 1938.

For various years Alice Bradley worked as a graphic artist and painter in Mexico City and Chicago, until 1942 when she enlisted in the U.S. Army Air Force. She became the first American female photo-intelligence officer and was stationed in the cellars of the Pentagon, charged with the interpretation of high-altitude photographs of the Far East for use in bombing sorties. In 1945 she joined the Air Staff Post-Hostilities Project, the aim of which was to seize and transfer to the United States as much German secret scientific research and personnel as possible, including atomic physicists, lest they fall into the hands of the Soviet Union. The head of the project, Colonel Huntington D. Sheldon, became Alice Bradley's second husband. They never had any children, as Alice became infertile owing to a bad case of peritonitis, 'contracted in the middle of the Mojave Desert one August'.[23]

Right after the war she joined Friends of Democracy, a little counter-espionage organization, which specialized in infiltrating fascist groups.

I came to the conclusion that there was about a ten percent hardcore paranoid component in this country: those whose natural idea of government, whether impassioned or lethargic, was fascism. I still do believe that; they smolder there like an ember. Reagan started out from a point further toward the middle, but he attracted in his following, of course, a lot of what is politely called the extreme right.[24]

In 1946 both Alice and Huntington left the military and settled down in New Jersey to run a custom hatchery. But in 1952 they were called to Washington to help staff the new Central Intelligence Agency. Alice's assignment was to evaluate captured German air photography of the USSR. For a while she also 'played games on the clandestine side for a bit',[25] about the exact nature of which she has always remained secretive. However, she began to feel herself increasingly at odds with clandestine militarism, 'destabilizing other people's governments, and influencing elections, to actual assasinations and military operations like the well-named Bay of Pigs'.[26] Finally, after three years, she wrote a two-line letter of resignation. 'I used the techniques the CIA had taught me, and in half a day I had a false name, a false bank account, a false social security card, and had rented an apartment and moved in. I was somebody else'.[27] Briefly separated from her husband by this event, she was soon reconciled with him, and they lived together until their deaths.[28]

After this episode, Alice Sheldon entered a whole new part of her life when she returned to college, where she had to start right from the beginning. She managed to receive her Ph.D. *magna cum laude* in experimental psychology from George Washington University in 1967, at the age of 52. Her research involved the behaviour of rats when they are confronted with a novelty: wild animals avoid novelty, while animals in a safe environment will be attracted to the novel stimulus.[29] This pattern of behaviour is, according to Sheldon, very similar to that of human beings. A few years after her doctorate she unfortunately had to retire from academia. She could not cope with the monster classes of students she was supposed to teach and the prospect of writing grant proposals while only conducting research on the side. Her health was also declining, 'I just burned out. I was too old'.[30]

Her experiences in the psychology laboratory are echoed in her story 'The Psychologist Who Wouldn't Do Awful Things to Rats' (1976). Even the drawings accompanying the text, picturing rats performing all kinds of activities, seem to been have taken from her dissertation. They bear the signature of Raccoona Sheldon, Alice Sheldon's second pen-name. Tiptree's first science fiction stories were, in fact, written during her Ph.D. exams to burn off nervous energy. To her surprise, they were published.

The first one was called 'Birth of a Salesman' (1968). James Tiptree, Jr. was also born at that moment.

Alice Sheldon-Bradley wrote over fifty stories and three novels as James Tiptree, and about ten stories as Raccoona Sheldon. In May 1987, when her husband was in the advanced stages of Alzheimer's disease, and her own health was very precarious, she shot him dead and then turned the gun upon herself.

Tiptree's fiction

Of course I was fascinated by the extraordinary life this woman led, including the masquerade of a male writing identity, and the turmoil produced by the disclosure of her female identity. But I was also attracted by the catchwords employed by Sarah Lefanu for characterizing Tiptree's work: 'Sex, death and violence are major themes in Tiptree's work' but it is 'specifically the male sexual drive, that Tiptree associates with violence and death'. 'The mad destruction of our home planet is a constant theme in Tiptree's work'; '... the glorious indifference of the universe to the vicissitudes of life'; '... the notions of nature and nurture, of free will and determinism, that recur in her stories'. 'Immortality, transcendence, but at what cost?'; 'Loneliness is as common a theme as violence'; 'Tiptree's characters, whether human or alien, long to be elsewhere'.[31]

Highly intrigued, I started looking for her scarcely available volumes of short stories and novels in Dutch librairies, and soon placed orders in women's and American bookshops, wrote to established as well as obscure documentation centres, and slowly gleaned bits and pieces of material by and about Tiptree. Her writings turned out to be amongst the most unruly, obsessive and disturbing, yet witty and sardonic texts I had ever read. They were clearly guided by some feminist interest, but what a complex, unorthodox and at times uncomfortable feminism!

Lefanu is right in asserting that, paradoxically, 'Tiptree's feminist vision in fact appears at its most powerful and complex in some of the stories that have a male narrator, or where the authorial voice is mediated through a macho world view'.[32] The narrative strategy employed in these latter stories is that 'machismo itself becomes the protagonist. Tiptree appears to allow this, and then subverts it: this is what makes it a feminist story, as much as what "happens" in it'.[33] In what may be Tiptree's most well-known story, 'The Women Men Don't See' (1973), the masculine narrator, Don Fenton, sees the two women whom he is stranded with in the interior of Mexico after a plane crash depart with a shipload of aliens.[34] As Lefanu points out, Tiptree plays cunningly with the possibilities of the science fiction genre here. Fenton remains stuck in the conventions of male-dominated science fiction: he gets out his gun when the aliens arrive, prepared to defend the women against the 'unknown monsters'. 'The ending reverberates with the echoes of decades of pulp science fiction; only this time the women are no man's property and have chosen to remain unrescued.'[35] It is not revealed, however, what the aliens are like, whither the women go, and what their future will be. The important point is that suddenly alienness and alienation get defined from a different perspective: the women's desire to escape the power men exercise over women and everyone and everything that is vulnerable makes *men* appear as the aliens of this world. The alien as a metaphor for the cleavage that separates men and women is a leitmotiv in Tiptree's work.

Sometimes there is even mention of the sexes as two *races,* such as in the horrifying 'The Screwfly Solution' (1977), in which millions of women are raped and killed, both by men they trusted before and, more systematically, by movements named for instance Sons of Adam.[36] 'Man's religion and metaphysics are the voices of his glands. Schonweiser. 1878' is written as an aside in the text.[37] Yet this seems less an ontological statement than an expression of deep compassion for the actual fate of many women in a world in which sexual violence and misogyny are pervasive. In many stories women are represented as in pain—victims of men's drives and fears, muted by a history of exclusion, suffering from their bodies which fall short of public standards of femininity. The way out is seldom found in representations of transformative social female agency, but rather in fantasies of a disembodied existence somewhere in the vastness of the cosmos, a refuge into madness, or a lonesome survival in the wilderness. As Ruth Parsons, one of the women men don't see, explains, 'What women do is survive. We live by ones and two in the chinks of your world-machine.'

However, the concern for and partiality towards women in Tiptree's stories do not imply a defence of either women's moral superiority or their innocence. What is at issue is the fact that male violence is more physical, more effective and more large-scale. Alice Sheldon's black views in this respect are reflected in Tiptree's and Raccoona Sheldon's narrative texts:

> By 'superior male violence' I refer simply to the fact that few men are afraid of walking past a solitary woman on a dark street; that people aren't installing bars and alarms and deadbolts for fear of women breaking in and killing them. And history shows us few examples of women personally raising and leading a gang to butcher or bomb their neighbors, or conquer the world. In brief, war ...
>
> Women are the faceless figures, arms loaded with infants, scattering under the male splendor of the dive-bomber, or hauling

their children through the barbed-wire. Women are the meat in the minefields. The body count. Women in war are, in short, boring. No glory, no triumphant combat ...

Of course, women too may be loaded with hidden hate and do terrible things to prisoners or their own children. And there was always Lucrezia Borgia. But women's evil is typically small-scale, secret, or indirect, like witchcraft and such, which man-the-hero can sweep away with a blow.[38]

At the same time, however, Sheldon is self-conscious about the fact that neither reading nor writing about violence is innocent in itself:

I think that for all of us the sense of being in contact with something that has the potential to do—or maybe ... has done—real evil, gives a little thrill to reading. Some people seem to have projected that onto Tiptree. Maybe I did a little too.[39]

The tension in Tiptree's writings between the fascination for evil and violence on the one side, and the anger and pain about women's suffering on the other, forms a great part of my own fascination as a reader. What remains so disturbing about the writings, however, is the vacuum in the middle: the absence of unconventional *affirmative* representations of female subjectivity. Yet it does not mean that female subjectivity is absent from the texts altogether. In the first place, of course, it is established in the writing and reading process of the narrative texts themselves. At the level of representations, female subjectivity seems to have often been displaced by male narrators and protagonists. Not every one of Tiptree's male narrators is masculinist nor does the authorial voice always convey a machismo world view. In several stories, including 'A Momentary Taste of Being', the male narrator or point of view gives evidence of such ambiguous views and feelings that one cannot but sense the female voice beneath them. In these texts, the male perspective may be less a cunning contrivance for feminist purposes than an unwitting dispersal, division or displacement of female subjectivity.

Another reason for my desire to pursue a more in-depth investigation of Tiptree's work is that I found that it dealt with all the issues traditionally mediated by religious symbol systems, notwithstanding the fact that Sheldon calls herself a 'lifelong atheist'.[40] Suffering and salvation, pain and pleasure, flesh and spirit, evil, community, the place of humankind in the cosmos, death, (im)mortality and transcendence, and the relationship of human beings with otherness/the Other. But what little solace do the visions of transcendence in the stories actually offer! Disembodied existence beyond the stars, fusion with aliens, transformations into the posthuman ...[41] Yet these writings appealed to me, and so strongly, precisely because of this tension between a relentless quest for meaning and a deep sense of the lack of any secure foundations to rely on. The stories are pervaded by desire as much as melancholy, by vitality as much as horror, by a modern sense of godforsakenness as much as a postmodern longing for a new sensitivity to the sacred.

The latter tension has been elaborated most explicitly in the posthumously published story 'Second Going' (1987), a parodic allusion to the second coming of Jesus Christ at the Last Judgement. The aliens who visit the earth—the fact that they call themselves Angli and that their names sound remarkably like those of the archangels is called 'just one of those cosmic coincidences'—bring along with them a group of incarnated dead gods. At the humans' request, the Angli present a procession of creatures resembling animist totems, fertility goddesses, the Greek pantheon, 'the inevitable old male of unlimited power and authority, whether Zeus, Jove, Wotan or Jehovah', Persian, Indian and Chinese deities, and a 'culminant patristic deity [who] repeatedly incarnated himself in his own son' and still has a few believers left. The deity the Angli worship at present is a huge female figure in veils leading a beast on a chain, who they name The Law of Cause and Effect. After this figure nothing seems to appear any more except that a few people suddenly shiver as though a cold wind has passed and, far away, one lightning bolt flashes: the shadow of the God to Come: 'Though what it will be we know no more than you ...', the announcer says. It seems that the Angli have brought with them this 'whole evolution of orphaned, unemployed gods, doomed with no people' in order to find somewhere in the Universe a race in want of gods. But in the end the aliens and the gods go away again, leaving the humans 'looking up at the sky that would be empty for ever ...'.[42]

Does 'A Momentary Taste of Being' display shadows of a 'God to Come'? And what senses of the human play a role in it? How do the sexes relate to each other? How is feminity organized in the text? Let me further introduce this story now.

Synopsis of 'A Momentary Taste of Being'?[43]

The physician Dr Aaron Kaye and his sister Dr Lory Kaye, a biologist, are crew members of the Centaur, a spaceship on a mission sponsored by the United Nations. The Centaur has been roaming the universe for ten years in search of a planet with a potential for lodging the billions of inhabitants of an overpopulated and devastated Earth. Lory has returned to the mother ship from a two-year exploratory mission to a finally discovered planet with promising atmospheric conditions. The other members of the scout mission decided to stay behind on the paradisaical planet. Lory has brought with her an alien life-form, described as a sessile plant-thing. Lory is interrogated twice by the ship's security officer, Frank Foy. During the first session the sensor bank to which she is wired shows some anomalies in the physiological reactions accompanying her verbal responses. Unfortunately, part of the computer data has accidently been erased. For the time being, Lory is given the benefit of the doubt and the anomalies are attributed to the excitement at the planet's suitability for colonization.

The scoutship China Flower with the alien sealed inside, was at first berthed in one of the corridors of the mothership. After the mysterious collapse of one of the crew members, lieutenant Tighe, on the deck in front of the scoutship, the China Flower is undocked and fastened to the mothership with a cable. Strangely enough, although Tighe's vitality is diminishing every day and he cannot possibly leave the isolation ward, other people start to spot Tighe for short moments at different places on the ship. There is no rational explanation for this.

During her second interrogation, Lory explains that she welded shut the cargo module in which she transported the alien, not because she suspected that the creature might be harmful, but simply because she was afraid that it might grow towards the light, or even become mobile. In addition, she now sheds light on some events on the Edenic planet. There had been a fracas between commander Kuh of the China Flower and his crew over the taking off of space suits and the wisdom of camping outside the scouter. In the end Kuh had decided to resolve the tension by commencing colonization, while entrusting Lory with the task of conveying his report on the planet to the Centaur. After feeling initial relief upon hearing this explanation for the discrepancies in Lory's earlier account, Aaron starts to wonder why his sister originally tried to cover for the commander, knowing her to be a rather intolerant person with respect to human imperfections.

After the interrogation of Lory has been settled, a general meeting is organized where photoshots of the planet are displayed. These show an incredible beauty, especially of multi-coloured mountains covered with the alien vegetation; a sweet wind is blowing. There are shots of Kuh and his crew, bare-headed and smiling. The people on the Centaur are deeply impressed. The captain of the ship, Yellaston, tries to avoid premature euphoria, drawing upon the complicated history of colonization on Earth. Since the shots of Kuh and his crew were taken a year ago there is no certainty whatsoever of their present well-being. Nevertheless, people are getting very excited and hopeful. However, Aaron approves strongly of Yellaston's decision not to send the green signal to Earth until the Centaur arrives at the planet.

Some people obviously are not able to bear the severe strain of awaiting the two years until this arrival. The Russian officer Timofaev Bron from Omsk misuses the ship's communication equipment to send the green code to his government. In response Bron's nearest collegue, Don Purcell from Ohio, also finds a way of sending a positive signal to his own government. Aaron fears complete anarchy now, but

Captain Yellaston re-establishes order by announcing that Bron's and Purcell's independent actions should be considered as mere confirmations of the official transmission of the green signal to Earth as a whole.

Then the planetary life-form is examined. For this purpose the China Flower is brought back aboard into one of the corridors. The examination is conducted under decontamination seal by a special team, but the entire operation is displayed on viewers to the other crew members. Finally the port of the module in which the alien has been confined is opened. A beautifully multi-coloured, hypnotic light: the alien's bioluminescence, flows outside.

This unleashes an enormous turmoil. Nobody is carrying out their tasks any more, they are all staring at the glow. The examination personnel start to take off their helmets, the people who were watching the operation on the viewers force their way into the corridor. Aaron Kaye feels a longing for the marvellous light as well, but he resists. Lory, in exultation, makes fierce efforts to pull her brother with her towards the port of the module. He manages to sedate her, after which he drags her with him, shuffling on his knees along a thick cable that will lead them away from the light towards the inboard lock. Other people attempt to come to the lock: Yellaston, Tim Bron and Aaron's assistant, Bill Coby. The Captain mutters that the red signal should have been sent. Despite the drug Lory manages to flee from the lock. After reaching the gyro chamber of the communications room, she destroys the ship's entire transmission gear.

Aaron tries to lead Lory to the clinic, starts to question her about what really happened on the planet with the China Flower crew. She admits that there had not been any fight between Kuh and the others, who were all 'gentle and happy' after being in touch with the beauty and the light of the planet. They just watched while Lory worked for days to get one of the alien specimens into the scouter. Then, again she runs away, but Aaron does not chase her any more. In his clinic he encounters a weakened Coby, who mumbles fragments of an amazing hypothesis that the people of the Centaur have been used as sperm's tails in a peculiar cosmic process of sexual intercourse. At that moment Aaron is too occupied to pay any attention. He sets off with the intention of reviving people as far as possible, sealing off the corridors and depressurizing the China Flower in order to kill the alien. Carefully he moves through the ship, well aware of the lure of the alien's radiance. Suddenly Lory reappears; her face is ecstatic. When he yells at her that he is going to vent the air, she starts running towards the hatch of the China Flower. It turns out that Ray Bustamente, the ship's electronics officer, is already in the scouter, ready to leave. Lory reaches out to get her brother on the China Flower with her. But the scouter is too fast for the both of them: Lory is blown back to the ground next to Aaron while the China Flower takes off and disappears for ever.

The last part of the story features Dr Aaron Kaye recording. He has started drinking.

He is surrounded by 'ghosts' now, huge more or less transparent and floating appearances that show resemblance to the ship's crew members. They do not communicate; they are just there, growing. Finally the creatures move out into space. The people of the spaceship themselves are only functioning in a vegetable-like way. Aaron speculates, acknowledging Coby's hypothesis, that the crew members have been used as gametes, as half of the germ-plasm of whatever creatures of some race. Tighe and Tim Bron have already died, soon more people start dying.

He goes on doing his rounds, helping his mates as much as possible, while Lory assists him insofar as her condition allows it: she too has reached the zombie-like state. The communications system is beyond repair. Aaron Kaye is alone now, he doesn't dream any more.

The alien encounter

A videoscreen comes to life, showing spinning stars. A space suit occults them; when it passes, three small yellow lights are moving toward a blackness—the helmet lights of the team going down to *China Flower* far below. Aaron's gut jumps; an *alien* is out there, he is about to meet an *alien*. (A134)

As in many science fiction stories, human contact with the alien is the pivot on which 'A Momentary Taste of Being' turns. For the most part, however, the alien in these stories is an *intelligent* creature, with whom some communication, friendly or hostile, is established. In contrast, the alien the crew of the *Centaur* comes in contact with is merely a faint shadow of this conventional alien.

No brain. It's a sessile plant-thing. Like a cauliflower, like a big lichen; like a bunch of big grapes, she [Lory] said. All it does is metabolize and put out a little bioluminescence. (A84)

Apparently botany is the science that offered Tiptree the model for representing the alien life-form. Lory makes a reference to a common myxomycetes, the *Lycogala epidendron*, called Coral Beads, a fungus that has a motile phase.[44] Photoshots show that the unknown planet is covered with miles of specimens of these 'vegetables', producing a gorgeously colourful scene,

like a flower-painted textile. Its terrain seems old, eroded to gentleness. The mountains or hills are capped with enormous gaudy rosettes, multi-ringed labyrinths ruffled in lemon-yellow, coral, emerald, gold, turquoise, bile-green, orange, lavender, scarlet—more colors than he [Aaron] can name. The alien vegetables or whatever. (A94)

Night-shots give an impression of its bioluminescence: 'Weird auroral colors, apparently flickering or changing continuously' (A95). The first speculations state that the alien life-forms obtain nourishment from the air, constantly moving their fringed 'foliage'. A number of types of air-borne cells 'resembling gametes or pollen' have been examined. It is suggested that although the dominant plant-like forms apparently reproduce by broadcast methods, 'they may represent the culmination of a long evolutionary history' (A96). After a tentative identification of over two hundred forms ranging in size from metres to a single cell, however, no 'self-motile life of any kind has been found' (A96).

After the actual encounter of the crew with the alien life-form, botanical associations recede to the past. Aaron Kaye, following his assistent Coby, now sees the alien life-form as reproductive material for some other alien creatures.

> Maybe they live in space, I think so. The, their zygotes do. Maybe they aren't even intelligent. Say they use planets to breed on, like amphibians going to the water. And they sowed their primordial seed-stuff around here, their milt and roe among the stars. On suitable planets. And the stuff germinated. And after the usual interval—say three billion years, that's what it took us, didn't it—the milt, the sperm evolved to *motility*, see? And we made it to the stars. To the roe-planet. To fertilize them. (A158–9)

So the identity of the alien life-form seems settled; Aaron speaks of 'Coby's final solution—hypothesis, I mean' (A158). Earlier, Aaron had already declared himself in favour of 'Occam's razor, the best explanation is that requiring fewer unsupported postulates, or whatever' (A108).[45] It made his colleague Bruce Jang, a Chinese–American engineer, teasingly reply that Aaron was actually citing 'the law of parsimony', and that 'old William ended up proving god loves us'. Yet Aaron also appears to be well aware that any reductive or decisive explanation of the 'alienness', of the strangeness and incomprehensibility of the alien, falls short. Indeed, the allusion to the fourteenth-century nominalist William of Ockham would seem to undermine any suggestion of a 'final solution'. The nominalist assumption that universal concepts are just names or signs (*nomina*) for individual things, and therefore have merely subjective meaning, is reflected in Aaron's observation on the crew's responses to the alien life-form:

> It may be of great scientific interest that they all saw it different, the egg-things I mean. Don said it was god, Coby saw ova. Ahlstrom was whispering about the tree Yggdrasil.[46] Bruce Jang saw Mei-Lin [his lover, crew member of the *China Flower*] there. Yellaston saw death.

> Tighe saw Mother, I think. All Dr. Aaron Kaye saw was colored lights. Why didn't I go, too? Who knows. Statistical phenomenon. Defective tail. My foot got caught ... Lory saw utopia, heaven on earth, I guess. (A160–1)

Although the alien 'egg-things' themselves are very real, there is no final truth or positive knowledge about their meaning. The people on board have widely divergent models for interpreting them. Or rather, what they try to name is an *experience* of the alien to which the visible 'eggs' and radiant light refer. Their diverse responses to the life-form suggest that the alien is not a passive object of knowledge but a meaning-generating actor itself. It influences people and compels them to invest its alien matter with names. Moreover, the alien does not just generate meaning, first and foremost it generates *desire*.

'It's that light, it's doing something to us!' (A140), Aaron realizes when the module is opened, and finds himself torn between fear and desire. One moment he wants to shut the light out, but during the next:

> The beauty of it floods Aaron's soul, washes all fear away. Just beyond those bodies is the goal of man's desiring, the fountain—the Grail itself maybe, the living radiance! (A141)

Thus Aaron, and notwithstanding the fact that he will later claim that all he saw was 'colored lights', formulates a double dynamic of desire between human and alien. The alien light generates and directs desire; it is both fountain and goal; the Grail, in other words, is origin and end of the quest. But is the Grail really found, does the alien light offer actual fulfilment, or do we observe in Tiptree's story what Salman Rushdie describes as the postmodern 'elevation of the quest for the Grail over the Grail itself'?[47] But then again, what *did* the people of the *Centaur* experience through the alien light? Many different, and even contradictory things, as Aaron recalls: god, reproductive material, the principle of life, erotic love, death, the maternal, utopia. But why did Aaron himself, unlike his sister, not yield to the lure of the alien light? In particular, is their diverging relation to the alien elucidating with respect to the meaning of sexual difference?

I too am fascinated by the alien. By the alien *in* the story, as well as the alien that *is* the story. Their alienness fuels my desire to create meaning while, on the other hand, it encourages me to face and name the limits of meaning. My aim, therefore, is not to domesticate either alien or text but to explore their boundaries, to find out where they still move on familiar grounds and where they stop making sense (to me). Moreover, I seek to add my own naming of the alien to the story by interpreting the alien as a reference to the *divine*. The question accompanying this experimental interpretation is how the divergent namings affect an understanding of the divine, and what could be its significance from a feminist theological viewpoint?

The remaining question, finally, is the meaning of the 'momentary taste of being'. Tiptree's text is headed by a quotation taken from Edward FitzGerald's rendition of the *Rubáiyát* (quatrains) of the eleventh-century Persian poet and astronomer Omar Khayyam:

> … A momentary taste
> of Being from the Well amid the Waste—

The whole stanza reads as follows:

> A Moment's Halt—a momentary taste
> Of BEING from the Well amid the Waste—
> and Lo!—the phantom Caravan has reach'd
> The NOTHING it set out from—Oh, make haste![48]

The stanza illustrates in exemplary fashion the tenor of the *Rubáiyát*, which gives expression to a religious and moral scepticism, by urging the reader to enjoy life, as death will put an end to everything. 'A Momentary Taste of Being' can be read as a narrative representation of this particular quatrain in the idiom of the science fiction genre. However, Tiptree's text is not so much a twentieth-century affirmation of the *Rubáiyát*'s tragic hedonism as an ironic reversal of it. Here the momentary taste of being appears not as an exuberant defiance of death, a feast of sensuality in honour of life, but as a devious *part* of death. In this story the reader is faced with the darkness of the human condition as it is experienced in a post-Enlightenment era after the death of the metaphysical God. What we shall encounter in this text is human insignificance on a cosmic scale, a tragic yearning for wholeness and communion, violent sexuality. And yet, 'A Momentary Taste of Being' also encourages the reader to search for the traces of hope in the fissures of the text.

Preceding the actual reading of 'A Momentary Taste of Being' in this book, there is a background chapter situating this project in the inter-mingling discourses of literary theory, (feminist) theology, and (women's) science fiction. In Chapters II–VI the discussion of 'A Momentary Taste of Being' occupies centre stage. In Chapter II the manifest narrative viewpoint of the story, Aaron Kaye's, is taken as point of departure. A series of dreams by which Aaron is haunted form the first key for unlocking the text. By turning this key it will be become possible to give an interpretation of the pervasive—predominantly phallic—sexual imagery of the text.

In Chapters III and IV the monopoly of Aaron's viewpoint is changed for the subliminal perspective of desire for the alien. I shall argue that the alien life-form can be interpreted as a sign of the maternal figure or function as it is conceived of in psychoanalytical thought and cultural theory, in particular that of Julia Kristeva. In the light of this assumption, then, 'A Momentary Taste of Being' will be interpreted as a mother/daughter narrative in science fictional guise. I explore two possible versions of such a mother/daughter plot. In Chapter III, 'A Momentary Taste of Being' is read as a *choric* fantasy. The *chora* is a notion derived from Kristeva to designate the maternally connoted dimension of the construction of the subject, which stands in a dialogical relation to the paternally connoted symbolic. Reading Tiptree's text in the light of Kristeva's theory will allow me not only to discuss the narrative text but also to develop my own contribution to the feminist reception of Kristeva's theory of the maternal.

The second mother/daughter version, the focus of attention in Chapter IV, is embedded in a reading of 'A Momentary Taste of Being' in connection to the Judeo-Christian textual heritage. In Tiptree's text, as in many science fiction space travel stories, one finds all kinds of thoroughly revised, not to say distorted, versions of basic biblical motives, such as the Exodus and the quest for the Promised Land. These revisions will provide the setting for an elaboration of the alien as a sign not only of the maternal but also of the divine. Kristeva's theory of abjection and the fantasy of the archaic mother, and especially the way it links these notions to the history of Judaism and Christianity, serves as an important frame of reference in this reading.

In Chapter V, finally, it is Lory's narrative viewpoint that will be taken as point of departure. It is the least manifest viewpoint and has to be distilled from the text with some effort. The uncovering of Lory's submerged story is embedded in the interpretative framework of the apocalyptic imagination of science fiction. I will pay ample attention to various theoretical perspectives on the apocalyptic orientation of science fiction. These perspectives offer a framework for the assessment of the particular, feminist apocalypse of 'A Momentary Taste of Being'. This implies consideration of possible revisions not only of *imagery* of the biblical Book of Revelation, but, equally important, also of the *structure* of apocalyptic imagination in Tiptree's text. In close connection to this interpretation, I seek to envisage in what ways apocalyptic thinking might and might not be a valuable feminist resource.

The various readings of 'A Momentary Taste of Being' will converge, in Chapter VI, on some tentative conclusions about feminist postmodern understandings of female subjectivity and the divine in the light of Tiptree's text. These will allow me, finally, to sketch the contours of a momentary taste of being which is as terrifying as it is joyful.

I. Seed-beds: Crossing Theology, Feminism and Science Fiction

The greenhouse of interdisciplinarity

A variety of concepts and metaphors are used when people try to explain that their research is involved with different discourses simultaneously. Webs, fields or networks of connections are rather popular, just as intersections, interdisciplinarity and the construction of conversations. Although interdisciplinarity seems the most academic label, it most aptly addresses the approach of this study. What does it mean to be or to move *inter* disciplines? And which disciplines are involved when a science fiction story is read by a feminist theologian?

In an article called 'Science Fictions', Corinne Squire energetically argues for linking feminist psychology to science fiction. In particular her ideas about interdisciplinarity wonderfully apply, *mutatis mutandis*, to feminist theology as well. Feminist theologians frequently express a desire to be more interdisciplinary, without it always being clear what this 'vague yet ubiquitous concept' signifies. 'Does it mean adding one discipline to another, obliterating the boundaries that separate them or falling into the cracks between them? Is it a viable aim?'[1] Squire makes the remarkable suggestion to turn to science fiction's interdisciplinary 'gossip status' for orientation. Squire derives the idea for this qualification from a male protagonist in the science fiction story 'The View from Venus', written by Karen Joy Fowler. This person explains that the difference between female and male writers, 'between Jane Austen and Joseph Conrad', is the difference between gossip and insight.

Rendered freely, this translates into the hardly innovative thought that female authors merely conjecture, they work with intuitions, associations and suspicions, while their male collaegues boldly analyse reality, formulating their insights with razor-sharp wit. In other words, women have subjective and men have objective views. A familiar cliché. But notice the female protagonist's riposte, 'I'm not sure a clear distinction can be made between the two. Who knows more about people than the gossips?' And who could tell us more, I would add by extension, about God and the divine than the storytellers of all religions?

The most obvious parallel science fiction offers to both psychological and theological women's studies' interdisciplinary status is its ambiguous scientific character. Science fiction hovers between science and fiction, between science and non-science. Similarly, neither psychology nor theology can make simple claims to producing 'hard knowledge', and feminism further attenuates their claims to scientificity. From an academic scientific point of view, therefore, both science fiction and feminist theology (but to a lesser extent, probably, theology *per se*) may be seen as 'gossip', as intuitive, speculative hearsay. I want to argue against this biased opinion of lower literary and academic genres.

Science fiction writers, to turn to Squire again, openly accept the ambiguity of their scientific status. For them, as for writers of other genres of popular fiction, the exclusion of science fiction from the literary canon is the most pressing disciplinary issue. Why is the mainstream science fictional writing of Borges and Burgess seen simply as literature, 'while the literariness of sf is ignored because it is popular—"gossip", again, rather than literature?'.[2] This is even more complicated for feminist science fiction writers, as they also have to define their relationship with feminist theory as well as with mainstream science fiction. The latter sometimes marginalizes women's contribution to the genre, again, as a soft, gossipy form. The example of science fiction suggests that interdisciplinarity does not automatically match the ideal of the so-called democratic, boundary-free space between disciplines. The greater prestige of the literary canon frustrates efforts of science fiction to exceed the confines of popular literature. The result is that, as Squire points out, science fiction is either ignored or assimilated wholesale into the literary canon.

The problem of literary canonization has been thoroughly tackled by Maaike Meijer in *De lust tot lezen*, an innovative book on the politics and erotics of reading by the example of Dutch female poets.[3] Against the myth of the One Literature and One Literary History which could encompass everything ever written if only it were Good Enough, Meijer introduces a multifarious literary system, consisting of a diversity of, partly overlapping, literary circles. There are dominant and non-dominant circles, 'counter-literatures', so to speak, which may show an 'upward mobility' themselves. Each of these circles has different authors, texts and reader's expectations. And every literary circle has its own development, with its own avant-garde, canon and pulp section. Literary theory, moreover, does not hold an 'objective' outsider's position but is itself part of these circles.

The recognition of the plurality of the literary system exposes the traditional canon of white male writers as one literary circle among others and questions its self-evidency. It likewise questions, I would like to stress, the great divide between 'real literature' and 'genre fiction'. In the classical sense, the established literary forms such as the epic, tragedy and comedy were considered as genres with strict rules, which had to be meticulously observed. Today genre fiction is often equated with popular literature, and hence as 'not literature' covering mere formulaic stories for the simpletons of the earth. Generic writing in this view implies the uncreative following of a set of rules and conventions by writer and reader. However, once the anxious high/low division of culture is abandoned, it may become obvious that not only popular literature but mainstream literature as well can be conceived according to genre. Genres—popular and literary—are forms of discursive practices, in a similar manner, I would say, as theology is understood as discourse. Their conventions, or codes, are no natural laws but social constructions liable to change and heterogeneous readings. As Helen Carr argues,

> Each genre—whether the sonnet or sci-fi, revenge tragedy or soap opera—has grown out of specific social situations and conditions of literary production. Norms and expectations are not inscribed for ever within the text, but are always dependent on the readers' knowledge of the codes ... Genres represent a set of conventions whose parameters are redrawn with each new book and each new reading.[4]

The way I see it, the process of canonization is always an attempt to screen off one allegedly superior group of texts from another that is considered inferior, alien, or non-serious. The suggestion, however, that there are many canons makes the walls of the castle crumble, and alien elements can creep in to pollute the common ground inside. In an analogous way, the 'purity' of a particular academic discipline, that is the need to establish clear-cut boundaries, can be challenged by non-canonized, 'gossipy' knowledge. However, this does not necessarily bring about an interdisciplinary sanctuary; as in the case of science fiction and the literary canon, 'alien' knowledge runs the risk of being either ignored or simply incorporated without being really digested.

Nevertheless I agree with Squire that the struggle of a new or less powerful field to enter into 'interdisciplinarity' with an established field always problematizes the latter, and by its very doing so may produce 'a frail but autonomous new discipline'.[5] At times, mainstream literature, non-feminist science fiction, dominant psychology and traditional theology may value positively the proficiency of female-identified 'gossip'. Of course this is an ongoing process, as Squire rightly recalls, for gossip that assumes the place of insight, also attains its canonical authority. Thus marginal fields are being assimilated in the canon and margins are being remade over and over.

Interdisciplinarity is not simply a method of doing science; it defies a disciplinary division of reality. One of the implications of the secularization has been the end of an overall view of reality. The heavenly canopy was replaced not by a secular canopy but by the fragmentation of knowledge and the coming into existence of various parallel and overlapping discourses and disciplines. An interdisciplinary approach, then, seeks to breach narrow compartmentalization without falling into a nostalgic regression to a holistic worldview. Such a crossing of disciplinary boundaries is, even though not always a smooth process, crucial to women's studies. That which Teresa de Lauretis calls the 'technology of gender', the social-symbolic construction of sexual difference, takes place in all parts of reality.[6] Technologies of gender point to the seemingly incessant drive to impose an ordering through assigning masculine and feminine categories, where the masculine term is always normative and more highly valued. The critical study of these 'technologies', as well as the envisioning of new ways of understanding sexual difference, cannot stop short before conventional borders. The exchange and testing of divergent ideas, methods and perspectives is able to enrich and transform both the traditional disciplines and feminist knowledge. In this sense, feminist theory is to be understood not as a circumscribed discipline but rather as a field of interest in which aspects of various disciplines converge in the investigation of a particular question from a feminist viewpoint.

My study fits in with this approach. I will be reading James Tiptree's 'A Momentary Taste of Being' in the intersecting contexts of theological, literary, cultural and philosophical theories. It is an exercise in interdisciplinarity, in which science and fiction, 'high' and 'low' cultures, gossip and insight, traditional and feminist knowledge are struggling for recognition and empowerment as scientific discourses, sometimes clashing with each other, and at other times producing innovatory views. As in a greenhouse, experiments of cross-fertilization may alternatively turn out to be sterile or fruitful. To adopt a more contemporary and better fitting simile: the greenhouse effect of increasing conversational heat may even produce at times what look like monstrous mutants. However, these transformations need not be inevitably fatal: alien and scary at first sight, on further acquaintance they may turn out to be promising new life-forms.

Reading women's (science fiction) texts as a feminist theologian

In a parodic turn of the classic definition of theology as systematic reflection on God and religion by means of the Judaic-Christian tradition, Catherine Keller calls theology 'the systematic fixation upon the one God's one end for one history, revealed and sealed in one book'.[7] This theology, however, is coming to its end. We are facing the question of how to imagine divinity in a postmodern context, where sure foundations have become contingent foundations, pluralism has replaced the homogeneous religious and cultural signifying system, and universalist claims must make way for partial perspectives.[8] Many theologians rack their brains over this question; I concentrate on those who take as their explicit point of departure the critical feminist reflection on experiential, representational and theoretical aspects of sexual difference, in its interwovenness with other differences. A large number of feminists have turned from the One Book that narrates One History to *multiple* textual sources to find different narrations of different histories about life. Consequently, the Bible has no longer a privileged and unique status. In her book on the biblical *Song of Songs* as well as Adrienne Rich's *Twenty-One Love Poems* as sources of theology, Jonneke Bekkenkamp argues that,

> [t]he value of a text ... depends on the function we assign to it. It is possible to read the Bible 'as literature' and literature 'as Bible', that is to say, as a spiritual authority. Our assessment will be in accordance with the different expectations projected by us on a text.[9]

What function do I assign to 'A Momentary Taste of Being', what expectations do I project on the text? Is it a spiritual authority to me? In a sense, yes, except that the very idea of authority has turned highly disputable in the postmodern era. You could say that Tiptree's story has authoritive value to me insofar as it provokes either urgent questions or inspiring visions for the interpretation and creation of reality. I do not conceive of any (literary) text as 'sacred', as is suggested in Carol Christ's famous pioneering study *Diving Deep and Surfacing*.[10] Christ's interpretations of texts of Kate Chopin, Margaret Atwood (*Surfacing*), Doris Lessing, Adrienne Rich and Ntozake Shange have laid the base for what could be called a feminist theological 'canon' of literary texts. The literary texts function as a mirror and model for the reader's own quest for subjective becoming, spiritual renewal and ethical values. I want to go a bit further into this book, on the one hand because it is a trend-setting and important study in this field, while, on the other hand, it allows me to sharpen my own view.

Crucial to Christ's approach is the notion of *story*: women need stories to give sense to their lives. Following Stephen Crites and Michael Novak, Christ explains that stories create a sense of self and world. Experiences and stories stand in a dialectical relation to each other: 'Stories give shape to experience, experience gives rise to stories'.[11] The depth or 'sacred' dimension of stories reveals the 'powers of being larger than the self' that provide orientation in people's lives. 'These powers may not be named divinities and they need not speak out of whirlwinds for their presence to be felt'.[12] Rather they are grounding forces, not only of life but also of death and destruction and finally transformation. 'They sometimes provide revelation when the self is at loss—when she does not know where to turn'.[13] Women's new naming of these forces beyond the traditional language is not just a matter of words but of obtaining subjectivity by those who were not allowed to have one before.

Christ does not claim that a sacred dimension in a literary text is a self-evident characteristic of a text or a group of stories, nor does she justify it by the author's intention. As Bekkenkamp also emphasized, it is the reader who relates to it in this particular way.

> What is common to all these stories is not their genre but their function in providing orientation to life's flow. Indeed the same story may be sacred to one person but not to another. Classic myths that were revelatory to the ancient Greeks became simple adventure stories for Christians, while Biblical stories are not revelatory for post-Christians.[14]

In my understanding, what Christ's view of story comes down to is an interpretation of literary texts as *myths*—stories that provide (women with) a sense of self and world and orient them toward the great powers of life and death. They are read as affirmative stories in which oppositions are not only mediated but even, in what I interpret as a radicalized form of Lévi-Strauss's structuralist view of myth, reconciled into a unity. Christ believes that 'women's quest seeks a wholeness that unites the dualisms of spirit and body, rational and irrational, nature and freedom, spiritual and social, life and death'.[15] Poems and fiction of female authors can be understood to reflect this quest, turning thus into what Bekkenkamp consents to as stories of identity and coherence, 'stories that [women] can read with a "believing" attitude, without the need of decoding and translating them first'.[16]

Although myth-making is a powerful faculty of the imagination, and thus an indispensable part of any religious orientation, in my view a postmodern theological reading of literature—and of a mythologizing kind as science fiction in particular—acknowledges and destabilizes the mythical orientation in one and the same movement. This means that my own appeal to literary texts at least partly differs from the story-and-religion stance. These differences may have to do with the various religious, cultural and academic contexts and communities in which a theologian is developing her view. Views which can never be universal and disinterested but are necessarily partial and situated. Christ's model of the spiritual and social quest which is reflected in women's writings seems to originate in what could be called a pedagogical–religious concern. This means that literary texts fulfil a pedagogical and consciousness-raising function: the reader detects a fundamental orientation toward grounding powers in the text and interprets this as a dimension of women's—the protagonist's as well as the reader's—process toward social and spiritual well-being and wholeness. The function of the theologian, as Christ seems to envisage and perform it, is to further illuminate in what manner the chosen texts can support women in this process of transformation and identity seeking. With the aid of the literary text the theologian offers moral support, political inspiration and spiritual guidance.

While my intention is certainly not to repeat classic—and gendered— oppositions between religion and theology, faith and reason, vision and analysis, or others of the kind, I do believe a theologian who is primarily involved in theology practiced as an interdisciplinary cultural science might want to highlight different aspects and dimensions of literary texts.[17] She problematizes the assumed referentiality of the text and, moreover, she complicates the category of 'woman's experience' instead of taking it as an evident point of departure. Rather than understanding a text as a model for the acquisition of a subjective and cultural wholeness beyond dualisms and attributing religious revelatory power to it, her option would be, with a felicitous expression of Donna Haraway, 'a powerful infidel hetero-glossia', or, 'an imagination of a feminist speaking in tongues'.[18] To render this pentecostal imagery into more pragmatic language: the reading of literary texts becomes a creative undertaking of sustaining differences. This does not imply a simple plea for inclusionary practices, which, as Mary McClintock Fulkerson rightly points out, are basically more liberal than liberating:

> It is not just that we (women) are different, and that the variety of subjects who represent different races, classes, and sexual preference need to be assembled in the creation of theologies that will reflect a rainbow of multiplicity.[19]

Sustaining differences, in other words, does not mean that who and what is considered other is benevolently allowed a refuge under the same big umbrella of 'woman's experience', but that differences, insofar as they are unbridgeable, are to be respected and investigated instead of forced into identity. Sustaining difference *creatively*, at the same time, demands that common grounds and affinities are found as well, in order that cultural, political and spiritual transformations become possible.

Yet another aspect of sustaining differences is of equal importance—the insight into the 'differences within'. Here I am referring to the various interwoven levels of sexual difference described by Rosi Braidotti in *Nomadic Subjects*.[20] It concerns different structures of subjectivity as well as different moments in the process of becoming subject. The first level Braidotti distinguishes is the *difference between men and women*. It contains a critique, initiated fifty years ago by Simone de Beauvoir in *The Second Sex*, of Man as the universal signifier and the devalorization of women as other, as non-man. At the same time, moreover, the analysis on this level seeks to redefine sexual difference in terms of positivity and to elaborate alternative forms of female subjectivity. Level two, then, refers to the *differences among women*. As Braidotti points out, the political and theoretical emphasis since the 1970s has been shifting from the asymmetry between the sexes to the embodiment and experience of sexual difference by real-life women. The central issue here is how to create, legitimate and represent a multiplicity of alternative forms of feminist subjectivity without falling into relativism (or, in keeping with McClintock Fulkerson, liberalism). The third level of sexual difference highlights the *differences within each woman*. It rests on a post-psychoanalytic view of the corporeal subject, that is, it conceives of the subject as a multiplicity in herself, structured by both consciousness and unconscious, and in an imaginary relationship to variables like class, race, age and sexual choices. Let me recall my own kindred description of (female) subjectivity as a process, a never-ending dynamic of being subjected to the power of langauge, the unconscious, the social and, simultaneously, as the search for the articulation of one's desire, experiences and views on one's own terms.

From this perspective, woman's experience can no longer be understood to signify a prelinguistic self-authenticating experience of the self and of the divine which is allegedly found in literary texts. I think also in theological discourse we have to focus on, in the words of historian Joan Scott, 'processes of identity production, insisting on the discursive nature of "experience" and on the politics of its construction. Experience is at once always already an interpretation *and* is in need of interpretation.'[21] A feminist theological reading of Tiptree's text or any female-authored stories, poetry and other imaginative texts relies on the textual organization and mediation of female experiences of difference. That is to say, of the experience that neither self nor divine are present and accessible in a 'true' form. Self, world and divine are constituted over and over again through multiple and never conclusive stories. A feminist theological reading of women's texts is actively engaged in the creation and negotiation of meaning in these stories.

Tales of suffering and passion
Examples of compelling experiments with such an approach are the Dutch study *Leesbaar lichaam* (*Legible body*) by Annelies van Heijst and especially Paula Cooey's *Religious Imagination & the Body*.[22] Both studies focus on

female-authored literary (and other) representations of the female body as a source for reflection on women's experiences of difference(s).[23] Novels, according to Van Heijst, are part, together with popular culture and religious and philosophical traditions, of a culture's iconographic and narrative repertoire. They are publically accessible stories which can have a function in people's orientation to questions of meaning and morality. Van Heijst reads the Dutch novels *De verliezers* (1960), by Anna Blaman and *Het perpetuum mobile van de liefde* (1988), by Renate Dorrestein, as modern *Passions*, tales of suffering and passion. In these passions, the female body is the pivotal figure. How do these authors in these particular—very diverging—literary texts conceptualize and represent the body, and which relations between corporeality and the making of meaning are suggested by them?

> In what ways do they construct the area of tension between meaning and meaninglessness, sense and nonsense? How do they signify the transience, vulnerability, and imperfection of the human body? How do they appraise the non-controllable forces of life: *fatum*, this fusion of chance and fate.[24]

Cooey's study has likewise staged the interaction of the female body as a material locus and as a nexus of discursive and representative practices. An interaction which is 'a testing ground or crucible, indeed in some cases a battleground, for mapping human values, as these are informed by relations of and struggles for power'.[25] Also in this study the vulnerability and (self-)violation of the female body, and the concomitant fragility of female subjectivity, are at the centre of attention. In addition, Cooey considers the significance of the body as site and sign of religious imagination; she investigates what role the body plays in the imagination's appropriation and, to a lesser extent, generation, of religious symbols and images.

Cooey's conception of religion is rather pragmatic than essentialist. 'As with all concepts, "religion" is best understood as a heuristic device.'[26] Her use of the concept, in effect, very much resembles my own in that religious imagery is part of a symbol system which gives shape, value and orientation to existential questions, and seeks to extend and transcend the limits of human existence. As Cooey has it, religious traditions provide a context for 'the sociocultural transfiguration of human pain and pleasure in ways that continually recreate and destroy human subjectivity, the world within which it emerges, and the transcendent realities with which the subject seeks relation'.[27] Religious imagery, then, is found in its traditional, confessional surroundings but can also be newly signified as well as joined with 'secular' imagery in fairly unconventional imaginative practices.

As particular instances of this kind of religious imagination Cooey highlights contemporary art and fiction by women; besides the paintings of Frida Kahlo, she discusses the Argentine prison narrative and poetry of Alicia Partnoy and novels by Paule Marshall, Maxine Hong Kingston and Toni Morrison. The work of Morrison, in particular, offers Cooey the opportunity to develop a 'theological anthropology' in which notions of sin and evil, love, anger and mercy are connected to visions of embodied female subjectivity. She performs an imaginative interpretation of Morrison's textual representations of women's subjectivity, as it is taking shape through female sensuality and against the background of the interwoven contexts of white racism and black Christianity—a religious imagination faithful, according to Cooey, to both its African and its biblical roots. For instance, Cooey interprets the figure Nel Wright, from the novel *Sula*, in the light of traditionally male-identified concepts of an autonomous self, while she understands Sula Peace to typify her counterpart, the deconstructed subject. 'Their very significant differences require one another, and the relation is one of irony; in dialectical fashion they form a coherent whole.'[28] Yet Cooey finds a third, and more hopeful, alternative subjectivity represented by Pilate Dead in *Song of Solomon*; 'a renegade who embodies love, a love that frees both self and other', and who 'especially in its fierceness and its mercy, illustrate[s] a subjectivity that gives life in the midst of bondage, pain, and death'.[29]

For two reasons my own project of reading Tiptree's 'A Momentary Taste of Being' shows great affinity with Van Heijst and Cooey's appeal to women's literary texts from the viewpoint of a critical theology of culture.[30] For one thing, Tiptree's writings can be characterized, for an important part, as tales of suffering and passion related to the (corporeal) *condition féminine*, implicating a strenuous search for female subjectivity. Furthermore, speaking from a methodological angle, these two studies, in their quest for meaning amidst pain and brokenness, do not seek conclusive religious and feminist models in the literary texts. In their approach, the women's writings we feel attracted to and inspired by certainly can be read as stories that offer orientation, not so much, however, as sacred stories which reflect unity and identity but as texts which help to throw open the very notion of identity and investigate the meaning of difference. Stories then may express a *desire* for unity but a postmodern reader cannot grant this desire lasting fulfilment. After all, one result of the loss of a transcendent guarantee, in the epistemological as well as in the theological sense, is that what look like grounding forces from one perspective may turn into the abyss of being from another. In my view, narrative and imaginative attempts to make sense of human existence by confronting these perspectives with each other, without dialectically pacifying them, are indispensible for survival. *Women's* survival and well-being also depend on the possibility of making sense in our own ways.

Science fiction as feminist theological site

Science fiction texts do not as yet appear prominently in feminist theological 'canons' of women's literature. The selection of writings seems to be made mostly on intuitive and heuristic grounds, in particular the predelection for an author or a group of authors, or a virtual spiritual dimension in a book. The main criterion of interest is whether a reader recognizes a text as being able to provide orientation in (her) life. There is little reflection, therefore, on the generic specificity of literature and what it may have to offer a feminist reader. Science fiction, moreover, with its connotations of masculine technology and galactic imperialism, is least likely to obtain feminist theological interest. Yet I want to argue that it is a genre outstandingly well-equipped for a theological reading from a feminist perspective.

It is not as if connections between science fiction and religious *themes* have been unnoticed. Tom Woodman, in his article 'Science Fiction, Religion, and Transcendence', for instance, as well as the contributors to *The Transcendent Adventure*, discuss a large variety of ways in which the religious theme occurs in science fiction.[31] They range from struggles between church/belief and science, a critique of science as religion, moral and ethical questions, Christian apocalyptic imagery, the future of churches and religion on Earth, extraterrestrial religions, speculations about the nature of God and being, to computer gods, cosmic gods and goddesses and mystic visions in outerspace. In addition, the writings which are referred to range from serious extrapolations and speculations to dystopian criticism and hilarious satire. Particularly noteworthy, however, is the *structural* analogy between religious aspirations and science fiction with which Woodman concludes his overview. The bulk of science fiction writings is formulaic, according to him, and meant to entertain us and soothe us with predictable futures and safe horrors. The best science fiction, on the other hand, offers much more than food for the psychologist or the sociologist: it can help 'shatter the complacencies of our present views of reality, and make our imaginations enjoyably receptive to new visions of the future'.[32] Hence the idea of *transcendence* is introduced, as it 'creates a common ground between aesthetic criteria for evaluating science fiction and a degree of theological interest that goes beyond the purely diagnostic'.[33] Nevertheless it is exactly science fiction's ambivalent character, even displayed by the finest elaborations of the genre, that I appreciate. That is to say, while a science fiction text may match the criterion of transcendence Woodman proposes, its extravagant imagination will also always reveal something of the obsessions, anxieties and desires that lie stored in the reservoir of twentieth-century culture's unconscious. Its impurity might even display the genre's very potential, as Sarah Lefanu advocates: 'Its glorious eclecticism, with its mingling of the rational discourse of science with the pre-rational language of the unconscious'.[34] Borrowing from other literary forms like horror, fairy-tale and mythology, science fiction, she asserts, 'lets writers defamiliarise the familiar, and make familiar the new and strange'.[35] Here we are reminded of the inter-disciplinary 'gossip-status' of both science fiction and (feminist) theology defended at the beginning of this chapter. The very fusion of insight and intuition, of knowledge and belief often produces further-reaching new views of reality than mere rational knowledge.

Woodman's employment of the notion transcendence, to continue, is clearly not meant in the metaphysical sense but rather resembles the way various feminist theologians conceive of transcendence as an activity in place of a substance or essence.[36] Transcendence points to transformation, to the power to cross over, make new connections; it indicates an imaginative movement from the existent to the possible. The transcending faculty of science fiction simultaneously refers to the rupture of fixed views and the vision of future—in the sense of as yet unimagined—possibilities. The genre's fantastic and speculative mode, resting on the crossing of the boundaries of space and time, offers an enlargement of the imagination. Feminists, moreover, have opened up science fiction's potential for the crossing of the boundaries of sex and species, which offers the means for deconstructing fixed identities and envisaging unthought and unexpected relations. The latter especially has not escaped feminist theological attention altogether.

In a short article by Robert Pielke, it was claimed that many of science fiction's symbols and mythic imagination have a 'panentheist and non-dualist' character, displaying a remarkable similarity with the rejection of traditional theism in feminist theology.[37] With a truly futuristic panache, Pielke suggested that feminist theologians start to write science fiction and science fiction writers adopt the insights of feminist theology. Setting aside Pielke's assertions concerning content of science fiction and feminist theology, methodically, the proposed connection of both discourses surely offers possibilities for bridging the gap between conceptual and imaginative language.

A similar analogy between theological language and the imaginative power of science fiction has been expanded on by Sallie McFague. Her argument for a metaphorical theology is based on the assumption that metaphors may be able to express something about the transcendent or sacred dimensions of reality without immobilizing reality by truth claims.

Science fiction, or speculative fabulation in her terms, is therefore an
obvious resource for metaphorical theology, 'for it opens the imagination
to think what has not yet been thought'.[38] More specifically, McFague puts
science fiction, and in this case Ursula Le Guin's *The Left Hand of Darkness*,
forward to elucidate the meaning of contemporary 'Goddess religion' in
the US represented by women such as Starhawk, Carol Christ and
Zsuzsanna Budapest, in relation to the Christian tradition. McFague
proposes to conceive of so-called the*a*logians as fantasy writers, who are
not so much predicting alternative futures for religion as presenting an
alternative way of seeing the limitations and possibilities of the Christian
tradition. From this perspective, not only a novel like Le Guin's but also
the writings of Goddess religion can be seen as experiments in thought and
imagination in which conventional views of sexual difference are upset.
While Le Guin's book questions assumptions about sex and sexuality,
theologians of the Goddess challenge the patriarchal model of divine–
human relationship. Both 'question the present in the light of future
possibilities' by painting 'a new world—a world radically different from
the one we know, giving us alternatives, some of which are dark, while
others pose possibilities for a richer, more humane life'.[39] Speculative
fabulation can be seen, according to McFague, as the 'creative negativity
of dialectical questioning' in the search for renewal of the tradition in which
one stands. It is capable of 'opening up the conventions of a culture, its
paradigms which are unquestioned, its models which have become
absolutized and irrelevant'.[40]

I very much appreciate McFague's experiment of introducing science
fiction to enrich the theological discourse. Nevertheless my own method
of working obviously differs from it. For McFague, speculative fabulation
is a model for discussing the value of post-Christian the*a*logy or Goddess
religion as a critical and imaginative impetus to the Christian tradition.
'The revolutionairies have posed the question; it will be up to the reformers
to see if the Christian paradigm has any resources for answering it', is how
McFague words her programme. In my study, however, science fiction will
not function as a model for metaphorical theology nor as a resource for
revitalizing the Christian paradigm. Instead, the imaginative world of
James Tiptree *itself* is read as a theological site. That is to say, as a cultural
site of questions, desires and visions which have traditionally marked
theological discourse: suffering and salvation, evil, love, the relation of
flesh and spirit, death and immortality, the meaning of the cosmos, human–
divine relations, the ineffable, and so on. Indeed, among the multiple
idioms involved in this process of making meaning, traditional religious
language is found as well. Basic elements of Judeo-Christian imaginary are
echoing in Tiptree's texts, as we shall see. This, however, is hardly to be

understood as a fortification of the Christian paradigm but rather as a corroboration of Grietje Dresen's observation that,

> [f]or centuries women and men have used religious symbolical language to express the fact that they do not entirely control their lives ... this language is not gone from body and mind overnight. More insight in the Christian background of our Western pattern of life, moreover, produces more insight in the present crisis as to the interpretion of reality.[41]

Furthermore, I read Tiptree's texts with a critical feminist commitment. I listen to the many voices expressing and evoking women's experiences of difference—and the joy and pain they cause. To whom, or rather, to which aspect of subjectivity, the multiple voices in Tiptree's stories belong, and what they (don't) speak, shout or murmur about, is what the following chapters are all about. Here I want to recall that these voices do not just sound in a fictional world but, more particularly, they are the resonances of a *science* fictional world. The crossings of the boundaries of space, time, sex and species, which form the ingredients of science fiction's speculative writing, take place in imaginary settings that are fundamentally informed by the twentieth century's scientific and technological developments. It does not deliver scientific stories, but science and technology form, as Teresa de Lauretis puts it, science fiction's 'diffuse landscape'.[42] With this, the second major reason for paying attention to science fiction as theological site has been indicated. It may encourage feminist theological reflection, which is now almost entirely lacking, on the implications of late-twentieth-century technoscientific existence for both the meaning of female subjectivity and the sacred. In the following, I shall briefly discuss the impact feminism has had on science fiction's writing and reading practices, in order to provide a background against which to situate the work of James Tiptree.

The feminist transformation of science fiction

Many literary historians mark Mary Wollstonecraft Shelley's *Frankenstein: or, The Modern Prometheus* (1818) as the first modern science fiction novel.[43] On the one hand, this can rightly be dismissed as a founder myth, just like other views privileging one individual as 'the first science fiction writer', like Edgar Allan Poe, Jules Verne or H.G. Wells.[44] At the same time, however, I think that highlighting Mary Shelley's particular role in the development of the field displays a pertinent gender awareness. In the creation of Frankenstein's monster, the increasingly complex web of science and technology, social and cultural power relations, and the meaning of sexual difference in modernity are foreshadowed. Shelley's novel is written in the style of the Gothic fantasy. Ellen Moers has also distinguished a particular *female Gothic*, horror and ghost stories written by woman writers, in which socially constricted women act out a strong desire for physical and moral heroism.[45] Notwithstanding its male protagonist, the obsessions with creation, reproduction and maternity justify an understanding of *Frankenstein* as—among many other things—a contribution to the female Gothic. Between Mary Shelley and the next major science fiction writers, Jules Verne and H.G. Wells, is a gap of almost three-quarters of a century. Verne and Wells produced quite differently oriented writings, which had a great impact on what Anne Cranny-Francis indicates as two distinct strands of science fiction. With technological adventure stories like *Journey to the Centre of the Earth* (1864) or *Twenty Thousand Leagues Under the Sea* (1870), Verne established 'a toys for the boys strand of science fiction, totally preoccupied ... with technology and with little interest in the social implications of that technology'.[46] This strand dominated the science fiction pulp magazines that started being published in the US in the late 1920s and early 1930s, in particular *Amazing Stories* of the maligned editor Hugo Gernsback, who nevertheless is said to have introduced the name 'science fiction'. As in Verne's literary universe, women were almost entirely absent in the writings of these magazines, or they appeared as the stereotypical background figure of the beautiful daughter of the professor.

It was not as if Wells made an issue of an alternative representation of women and technology—though as a member of the Fabian Society he supported women's rights—but he did use science fiction to speculate about the transformation of his own society, the English class society of the turn of the century. In works such as *The War of the Worlds*, *The Invisible Man* and *The Time Machine*, called 'scientific romances', Wells employs pseudo-scientific novelties to produce fictitious situations in order to explore his own environment. In this, he follows in Mary Shelley's tradition of socially and politically conscious science fiction. Cranny-Francis thinks this strand of science fiction is not revived until the 1960s. However, while this by and large applies to the United States, in my view this tends to ignore European science fiction writing. Unlike the American contributors to the subculture of SF pulp magazines (or 'fanzines'), the contemporary European writers of what, in retrospect, can be called science fiction, were individuals, participating in mainstream literature. They were not driven by technological romanticism, like the writers and readers of the fanzines, but by the anxieties of the interbellum period. In Czechoslovakia, in 1921, Karel Capek's play *R.U.R.* (Rossum's Universal Robots), to which we owe the word robot, was performed for the first time, while in the Soviet Union, Yevgeni Zamyatin wrote—though was not allowed to publish—the mathematical dystopia *We*. In Britain, Olaf Stapledon followed directly in the footsteps of Wells with his cosmological novels and philosophical inquiries *Last and First Men* (1930), *Starmaker* (1937) and *Sirius* (1947).

An interesting point from a feminist viewpoint with respect to Wells is made by Robin Roberts.[47] According to her, Wells' *The Time Machine* reveals how the male science fiction tradition builds on Victorian female dystopias like *The Coming Race* by Edward Bulwer-Lytton or *The Revolt of Man* by Walter Besant. In these misogynist dystopias a male explorer/narrator visits an all-female world, which is pictured as an apocalyptic or regressive society. Ironically, the woman ruler is first supplied with social, economic and political dominance, in order to show next that female rule only leads to abuse of power or degeneration. In *The Time Machine* resonances of the female dystopia clearly sound in the depiction of the degenerated Eloi as stereotypical feminine. The Eloi, in this manner, are not opposed so much to their oppressors, the bestial Morlocks, but rather to the time traveller.

> At the same time, Wells points to hard science as salvation. Women and science are irreconcilable, as Weena's fear of matches and the Eloi's neglect of the museum of natural history show. Again, the male scientist–explorer is the hero. His chivalry, bravery, attractiveness to women, and most important, his scientific knowledge make him putative master of his future Earth.[48]

Roberts does not only point out the echoes of the female dystopia in Wells' work, but also describes its legacy in the American pulp science fiction and fantasy magazines of the 1940s and 1950s, in particular as regards its cover art. Along with spaceships and alien planets, many covers of these magazines picture nearly naked, gigantic and powerful female aliens, who appear to be the literally enlarged descendants of the women rulers of the Victorian dystopia. Always represented as dominating a human male— crushing him, carrying him, mesmerizing him—these huge figures are unconcealed projections of male anxieties about both the sexual allure and the maternal power of women. Anxieties which are also reflected in the tension between these covers and the content of the stories in the magazine. While the women on the covers are pictured in the height of their formidability and demonic strength, the texts defeat the visual images of female strength, by having the women eventually destroyed by their own sexual desire or reproductive powers.

Surprisingly, however, these female images of the pulp magazines can also be seen, according to Roberts, as material for later feminist revisions of science fiction. It is taken for granted that the *only* readers of magazine science fiction were adolescent males, but this is not true. Many of the first authors of feminist science fiction, like Joanna Russ, Ursula Le Guin, Suzy

McKee Charnas and Joan Vinge, acknowledge that they were introduced
into science fiction through the pulps of the 1940s and 1950s. Moreover,
several of them started their publishing careers in the SF magazines. To
female readers, Roberts argues, these images of powerful female aliens, as
well as the stories inside the magazines, meant something different than
to male readers. Primitive as these images may have been, even so they
offered young women in the socially restricted post-World-War-II period
some identification with strong and independent women. And some
decades later women writers draw on the radical potential of these female
aliens for creating feminist heroines.

> Male readers might be drawn to pulp science fiction by Oedipal fears,
> but women readers could produce resistant interpretations of the
> same texts, and some of those readers could then produce texts that
> developed this resistance more explicitly.[49]

While Cranny-Francis seems to be guided by a desire to entirely separate
culturally and politically critical science fiction like Wells' from the popular
SF of the pulp magazines, Roberts' view shows that a more ambivalent
stance is possible as well.

It is not as if Cranny-Francis' qualification of American science fiction
until the 1960s as predominantly 'macho genre' cuts no ice at all. The
major preoccupations of the SF community of writers, readers and editors
were scientific speculation inspired by military technology and space travel,
followed by the encounter with the monstrous alien, as the projection of
xenophobic fears, racial prejudices and cold war paranoias. No interest was
shown in non-stereotyped representations of women, or in experimentation around personal and political relations between the sexes. And yet,
it seems artificial to posit such a radical watershed between the science
fiction from before and after the 1960s as for instance Cranny-Francis does.
Also in the magazines, like *Astounding/Analog*, and the increasing amount
of hardcover SF of the 1950s, occasional stories were published with self-
reflective or satirical, stylistically inventive and socially and politically
investigative qualities.

In any case, it is true that the 1960s marked the start of a 'new age of
science fiction'.[50] Besides the transition from Space Age to Information
Age, the 1960s, as we all know, marked the time of student radicalism,
civil rights and other progressive movements, experimentation with drugs
and lifestyles. Together with the 'rejection of bourgeois 'rationalism' and
the exploration of the fantastic and the bizarre, [and] the freeing of pop
culture from the stranglehold of modernist legitimation', as Cranny-Francis
puts it, these developments meant an innovatory impulse to science
fiction.[51] American writers like Philip K. Dick, Kurt Vonnegut Jr and Robert

Silverberg and the Pole Stanislaw Lem wrote novels, in which they reanimated the critical technological tradition of Mary Shelley and H.G. Wells of 'transforming pulp into philosophy'.[52] One of the most famous— and by hardcore SF fans maligned—experiments of renewal was the transformation of the British magazine *New Worlds*, due to the arrival of the new editor Michael Moorcock in the mid-1960s. The *New Worlds* writings, known under the name New Wave, were characterized by a great interest in style and the move from 'outer space' to 'inner space': the conventions of space travel became metaphors for mind travel. Also many American writers contributed to the magazine, among them Pamela Zoline with her hilarious but chilling story about a suburban housewife falling into an entropic depression, 'The Heat Death of the Universe' (1967).

Together, the political and cultural changes of the 1960s and 1970s in the US and Britain, and the developments in the genre itself, prepared the ground for feminist writers to enter the science fiction field.[53] Except for stories like Zoline's, not many of the New Wave works can be caught showing feminist awareness, but the interest in psychic processes and sexual and life-style experimentation, and the preoccupation with ontological and ethical issues by Dick, Lem and others prepared the way for the exploration of the meaning of sexual difference from the late 1960s onwards. The most significant of these explorations have been written, not surprisingly, by women. The most well-known of these women writers who started publishing in the late 1960s and the 1970s are probably, besides the already mentioned Le Guin, Russ, Vinge and Charnas, Kate Wilhelm, Kit Reed, Vonda McIntyre and James Tiptree, Jr, but many others should be included.[54] To these American writers, British women like Tanith Lee and Josephine Saxton must be added. Sarah Lefanu states that there is no justification for delineating a British from an American feminist science fiction. 'The feminist texts ... of the 1970s sped back and forth across the Atlantic.'[55] On the other hand, as the reading and publishing market for all SF in the United States is traditionally much bigger, it is no surprise there are far more American writers.[56]

As remarked before, quite a few of the feminist authors were readers of science fiction before they started writing it themselves. Their involvement in the women's movement and/or acquaintance with the developing field of feminist theory encouraged them to criticize misogynist and reactionary tendencies in science fiction as well as to actively transform the genre from within. By doing so, they drew on the possibilities opened up by the strand within science fiction that 'rather than celebrating imperialistic and militaristic glory, is subversive, satirical, iconoclastic'.[57] But it has worked the other way around as well. Aldiss calls the early and mid-1970s a time of 'considerable maturation in the SF field'; and he is admirably willing to credit female authors for their share in this process.

> In the seventies there was a great influx of women writers. The revolution they began is still under way and having an effect on the kind of genre we now enjoy. By the end of the seventies it had become clear that SF was no longer a kind of juvenile men's club. Women were to be seen at the bar. SF's unexpressed half was beginning to speak out. Angrily, skilfully, persuasively, sometimes—as in all new causes—with ill-considered over-emphasis, but in many instances speaking with a new voice, a new intonation.[58]

During the 1980s and the 1990s, in which postmodernism and cyberpunk have deeply influenced the genre, these feminist voices continue to sound. Many women from the beginning are still active in writing science fiction, while interesting new authors like Octavia Butler, Joan Slonczewski, Rhoda Lerman, Pat Murphy and Gwyneth Jones (to name just a few) have entered the field. Also women like Marge Piercy, Margaret Atwood and Doris Lessing, who are well-considered mainstream writers, have demonstrated how not to be afraid of writing science fiction. Scholarship of feminist science fiction has kept pace with the increasing amount of fiction. This comprises, besides a variety of book-length studies, a large number of contributions on female writers and feminist science fiction in scholarly journals on science fiction, like *Foundation*, *Extrapolation* and *Science Fiction Studies*, as well as in journals and volumes on feminism, cultural studies, literature or philosophy. Now let me introduce some of the major issues concerning women's science fiction writings.

Narrative and language
A few years ago, Marleen Barr put forward the idea of a 'supergenre of feminist fabulation', as an 'umbrella term for describing overlapping genres'.[59] It comprises, besides feminist science fiction, also feminist fantasy, feminist utopias as well as feminist postmodern writings by male and female authors, all kind of fictions, that is, in which worlds are created which are discontinuous with patriarchal master-narratives. I think Barr's proposition is two-edged. On the one side, writings are being related to each other in unexpected ways, and demarcation lines between genres, as well as between high and low literature are crossed.[60] In her study *Alien and Others*, Jenny Wolmark, however, rather strongly attacked Barr for this attempt at 'rescuing' (feminist) SF from marginality and contempt, which she considers in fact a conservative reinvention of the canon.[61] Although I don't think this entirely does justice to Barr's intention to create greater utopian possibilities, it justly points to the problem of subsuming

feminist science fiction in a supergenre. It obscures the important fact that feminist science fiction not only disrupts patriarchal master-narratives but also explores the meaning of technoscientific existence for the female subject.

Science and fictions together produce the stock narrative devices of the genre—time and/or space travel, parallel worlds, entropy, the alien encounter, (nuclear) catastrophe and post-catastrophical worlds, cosmic and artificial intelligence, cyborgs (human–machine hybrids) and so on. Feminist writers use these conventions to question dominant cultural constructions of sexual and other differences and to explore new representational possibilities of female subjectivity. Moreover, one of science fiction's other specifics is that it is future-oriented. Precisely the genre's preoccupation with the future offers feminists the basis for the interpretation of subjectivity and identity as a *process*, of an always incomplete becoming. In my understanding feminist science fiction comprises all those stories and novels written by women who have been inspired by the revitalized women's movement of the last decades to explore what science fiction has to offer.[62] I consent to Lefanu's opinion that writings exploiting to the full both science fiction's literary and political possibilities are the ones 'questioning not just an apparent reality but its very construction'.[63] On the other hand I find it important, with Wolmark, not to ignore

> texts that are resolutely realist and conformist, but which are equally oppositional because they contain an explicit critique of the unequal power relations experienced by women within the dominant culture.[64]

To some extent feminist science fiction always finds itself in the tension between realism and conformism, in the sense of following the genre's conventions, on the one side, and subverting them on the other. The difference between more 'radical' and 'conformist' feminist science fiction may be interpreted as respectively practices of deconstruction of conventions and bending conventions to one's will. This applies in particular to the narrative convention underpinning a great deal of science fiction texts: the structure of the *quest*.

In the linear quest narrative, which dominates nineteenth- and twentieth-century Western writing and popular literature in particular, temporal succession is equated with material consequence. Events take place *because* time goes on. Narrative is the meaningful arrangement of events according to temporal patterning, the dynamic of the quest and the organization of a plot. As the word quest already indicates, the motivation of narrative plotting is Oedipal *desire*: the desire for knowledge and cognition, but also for happiness, beauty and salvation, as it is structured in Western twentieth-century thought on the basis of the Oedipal scenario of father–son rivalry and the desire for the (absent) mother.[65] Feminist theorists, however, like Teresa de Lauretis, Marianne Hirsch and Anne Cranny-Francis, have questioned the neutrality of desire as metaphor for the narrative dynamic.[66] As Cranny-Francis wonders,

> If narrative is envisaged as motivated by desire—as dynamic of signification, as Eros, in its plastic and totalizing function—will it matter if the writer or the reading position produced is female or male?[67]

I think it *does* matter, just as sexual preference, ethnicity, age and cultural background matter for form and content of desire. For instance, the description of desire in narrative as an unsatisfiable 'human' drive to seduce and to subjugate the reader, as given by Peter Brooks in *Reading for the Plot*, appears to be based on a masculine sexual and psychological model, as both Cranny-Francis and Hirsch convincingly argue.[68] But then the question rises what alternatives female 'human' desire has, as the traditional option of yielding and subjugation is no longer acceptable to feminist writers and readers. The search for the expression of their own desire, experience and vision in any case brings us into a liminal position, at the same time inside and outside a particular generic discourse. There they are involved in (narrative and subjective) 'reconstruction on the basis of another pattern of coherence; not the temporal logic of traditional narrative, but contradiction'.[69]

To return to feminist science fiction, texts that, according to Lefanu, question not only an apparent reality but its very construction, are likely to contradict the conventional linear narrative structure most consequently. These, in other words, are the most postmodern texts of feminist science fiction. Through the fragmentation and non-centredness of the narrative structure, in which not one but many possible plots emerge, the constructiveness of sexual subjectivity and social identity becomes manifest. A by now classic example is Joanna Russ' *The Female Man* (1975), in which four parallel worlds intersect with each other as well as with four modalities of female subjectivity, including the author's. A less well-known example is *The Book of the Night* (1984) by Rhoda Lerman, in which the powerful awakening of female sexual desire causes a breakdown of linguistic, natural and temporal order, which is expressed in the co-existence of the tenth and the twentieth centuries on one island, and the transformation of a young girl into a cow. The complex pleasure of these texts differs from the more elementary enjoyment feminist revisions of the quest narrative offer, in which the undermining of sexual and racial stereotypes nevertheless leaves the conventional structure of story-telling and plotting intact.

Hardly without exception studies of feminist science fiction emphasize the importance of language—and hence narrative structures—in women's exclusion from or access to knowledge and power. They seem to agree on that a real challenge to the linguistic structures on which patriarchal society rests requires experimental narration. Lucie Armitt puts it, somewhat sternly I must say, like this:

> Without such writing we can only go halfway towards a new language, a new reality, and indeed a new future. At its best science fiction must shake us from our complacencies. For women this is no luxury.[70]

In my opinion, however, it would be a mistake to try to draw a too strict line of demarcation between 'deconstructive' and 'conventional' feminist science fiction. In the inscription of different—that is to say, non-white, non-male, non-American, or even non-human—subjects in the genre *all* of these writings inevitably oscillate between affirming and disrupting the conventional narrative structure. Sometimes the characters in a conventionally structured story are so 'alienating' that this structure is unexpectedly disrupted and remains open-ended after all. Octavia Butler's novel *Dawn* (1987), for instance, may look like a bizarre version of a traditional Harlequin (Dutch: *Bouquet*) romance plot, as Lies Wesseling claims.[71] In my reading experience, however, the amalgamation of human beings and triple-sexual, genetically engineered Oankali, extraterrestrials who take care of the remnants of humankind after a nuclear war, is so prominently transgressive that narrative closure ultimately fails.

The technoscientific context
In the above-sketched issue of narrative strategies one of the central questions concerning the intersection of feminism and science fiction has become visible: what are the possibilities and the restrictions for the exploration of female desire and speculative visions in a traditionally male genre? Following these considerations in the linguistic area—the *fiction* part, as it were—the question arises in what ways women writers move about the genre's *scientific* landscape.

Traditionally, women's science fiction writings have been less involved in speculation concerning the natural and technological sciences. They rather put an emphasis on sciences like psychology, anthropology and ecology—often opposed to masculine destructive abuse of technology—and even parapsychology. It has been equally traditional, however, at least in American science fiction until the late 1960s and early 1970s, to defend a hierarchical split between writings of which the horizon is masculine 'hard', objective science and writings dominated by feminine 'soft' science, that is, subjective and easier to master. The last type of writings was often considered not to be genuine science fiction and, in consequence, its authors, who were predominantly women, were not thought of as serious SF-writers.

A radical subversion of these categories of hard and soft sciences and their valuation is suggested by Robin Roberts. I want to expand a bit on her views, as they diplay an original yet rather problematic outlook on feminism and science (fiction). Roberts' viewpoint is that feminist science fiction writers undermine the historical distinction between science and *magic*. It is an accepted tenet of science fiction that science and magic cannot be decisively separated; the statement of John Campbell, the editor of *Astounding*, that 'science is magic that works' has gained even a legendary status. According to Roberts, however, hard (male) science fiction writers relate differently to the magic/science opposition than female writers. The first ones 'usually reveal that what seemed to be magic was really science', whereas the 'depiction of magic as a science seen from an uninformed point of view allows women science fiction writers to draw on a long tradition of feminine power, the tradition of witches and magic'.[72] Roberts here refers to the European tradition of midwives and female healers who were condemned and persecuted as witches during the Inquisition, and have been shut out from the status of knowledgeable subjects since. Witches are recurrent figures in nineteenth- and twentieth-century science fiction, revised as female aliens, woman rulers of a utopian society or survivors of a post-catastrophical world. But while male writers mostly characterize them as horrific, magical and evil, feminist writers depict them as symbols of strength and empowerment, whose alleged magic powers represent an alternative, legitimate science that is valorizing for women.

Much as I appreciate that Roberts tackles the issue of the gendered relations between science and magic and hard and soft sciences in science fiction and its reception, she seems to reinscribe the very dichotomy she wants to undermine. While referring to deconstruction and post-modernism as means to criticize patriarchal myths, Roberts' study at the same time seems to be constantly on the verge of revitalizing deterministic notions such as 'female values' and the reduction of feminist science fiction writing to representations of 'feminine strength'. Moreover, Roberts tends to romanticize the meaning of alternative science, which is particularly manifest in her discussion of *Frankenstein*. She justly recalls Frankenstein's affinity with the alchemists, the 'feminine' coded vitalist science that was opposed to the rationalist 'masculinist' science of the nineteenth century. It is ignored, however, that Frankenstein found out next that, as Nell

Tenhaaf puts it, 'it was a grave error to mix post-Cartesian rational knowledge and technical skills with the discovery of the vitalist life-force itself'.[73]

To a certain extent the romanticizing of alternative science and female power to ward off what Roberts calls the 'dangers of present patriarchal science', reflects a tendency in feminist science fiction writings themselves. Nevertheless the reading of other stories—or even the re-reading of the same[74]—reveals also quite different elaborations of and attitudes towards science and technology. As will be seen in my first reading of Tiptree's 'A Momentary Taste of Being', I consent to Natalie Rosinsky's assumption in *Feminist Futures*, that many feminist science fiction texts are affected by post-Einsteinian physics, characterized by the principle of uncertainty and a dynamic phenomenological and narrative view of the universe. '[W]e have indeed begun to realize that the universe is figuratively made of changing stories *about* atoms, rather than literally *of* such illusory, discrete particles themselves.'[75] Rosinksy brings in the 'new physics' as an analogical model of feminist science fiction's 'fluid reconfiguration of perceived physical reality, validating temporal simultaneity and spatial relativity'.[76] To a certain extent, I would say, this applies to all contemporary science fiction. The specific contribution of feminist texts is that they employ these views to experiment with the instability of boundaries of sex and species, staged against the indefiniteness of the cosmos, to envisage transformation and alternative subjectivies.

Besides the structural affinity with theoretical developments in post-Einsteinian physics, feminist science fiction shows still another elaboration of the meaning of science and technology that radically diverges from a masculine technological science/female magical science opposition. In her famous, politically both visionary and realistic, essay 'A Cyborg Manifesto', Donna Haraway calls feminist science fiction writers like Russ, Tiptree, Butler, McIntyre, including some male writers like John Varley and Samuel Delany, 'theorists for cyborgs'. This does not imply that they legitimize a robotization of the human; rather it means that by situating their works of the imagination against the horizon of the late twentieth-century Western world, these writers become 'our story-tellers exploring what it means to be embodied in high-tech worlds'.[77] Their literary visions account for the pleasures, the power and the suffering, the affinities and the atrocities originating in a society that is dominated by micro-electronics and biotechnologies. In particular the impact of reproductive technologies and genetic engineering on sexual and social relations turns out an important issue for speculation and extrapolation.

In feminist science fiction's re-examination of relations of sexual, racial and technological dominance the *cyborg* is a central image along with the *alien*. Both 'creatures' represent a blurring of the boundaries between what is considered self and other, same and different, and help to provide narrative situations in which definitions of what it means to be human are examined and put at risk. In conventional male-authored fiction, the alien remains a being 'out there', the Other of American SF, as Ursula Le Guin has described it: 'the sexual Alien, and the social Alien, and the cultural Alien, and finally the racial Alien'.[78] In women's writings the alien often gains a remarkable intimacy, as sexual partner, or even as bodily interiority—the alien as part of the female subject herself, as the procreative result of inter-species mingling. Similiar (con)fusions are expressed in the cyborg: it literally embodies the fearsome/attractive uncertainty about the ontological status of *both* human and cyborg. If the cyborg is an interface between human organism and technological devices and cybernetic steering systems, where does the human stop and technology begin? The perspective of such instability may lead to nostalgic re-assertions of essentialist (that is, resting on a monolithic essence defined once and for all) notions of the human, as well as the masculine and the feminine. On the other hand, however, the very instability suggested in the figure of the cyborg may be also taken up as an opportunity to deconstruct essentialist accounts of sexual difference as cultural fictions.

This second stance is characteristic for the imaginative explorations of technological existence and the cyborg image by feminist authors like Gwyneth Jones, Rebecca Ore, Elisabeth Vonarburg, Marge Piercy and, earlier on, James Tiptree, which allies their writings to *cyberpunk*. Technology provides the environment in which both cyberpunk and feminist science fiction deal with the central questions of difference and identity in Western post-industrial and postmodern societies. Cyberpunk, the dazzling stories of authors like William Gibson and Bruce Sterling, in which high-tech near futures are inhabited by male and female cyborgs and mostly male console cowboys 'jacking into' the electronic hyperworld of *cyberspace*, has had a great cultural resonance. Also the cinematic worlds of *Blade Runner*, *The Terminator* or *Videodrome*, and phenomena like interactive *virtual reality* games, reflect the drives of cyberpunk. Except for Pat Cadigan, not many women write 'classic' cyberpunk, in which the 'consensual hallucination' of cyberspace is the major point of reference.[79] Female authors utilize the image of the cyborg—as either replica or hybrid—rather than the image of cyberspace to examine technologically informed power relationships. This is not fully surprising since precisely the image of cyberspace, with its solitary disembodied hero at the controls, is strongly inscribed with the masculine, and not leaving much space for a transgression of gendered identity. In his compelling study *Terminal Identity*, Scott Bukatman finds that the postmodern master-narrative of dissolution that is operative in cyberpunk fictions, with its experiences of 'bodiless exultation in cyberspace', is very often counterbalanced by a nostalgic or aggressive desire to re-establish a solid masculine subject.

> The fusion with machines represents something other than a postmodern celebration of dissolving borders and boundaries, because they are often as much attempts to reseat the human (male) in a position of virile power and control.[80]

Could this be one reason that, as Wolmark demonstrates, writers and critics do acknowledge cyberpunk's literary debt to mainstream writers such as William Burroughs and Thomas Pynchon, and New Wave science fiction writers such as J.G. Ballard and Samuel Delany, without crediting the influence of feminist science fiction. Wolmark quotes Delany, though, who ascribes this disregard to 'patriarchal nervousness' and even argues that without feminist science fiction there wouldn't *be* any cyberpunk. As Wolmark summarizes,

> Cyberpunk narratives focus explicitly on the destabilising impact of new technology on traditional social and cultural spaces: in so doing they provide a peculiarly appropriate response to the complex conditions of postmodernity, particularly the collapse of traditional cultural and critical hierachies, and the erosion of the distinction between experience and knowledge which has provoked the decentring and fragmentation of the subject.[81]

These are also key issues in feminist science fiction, which thus has provided cyberpunk with a conceptual vocabulary, 'without which we wouldn't be able to read it'.[82]

Feminist writers seeking to deal with technologically informed relations on the whole do not tend to merge with 'mainstream' cyberpunk. They seem to prefer to create their own cyborg narratives in order to maintain a critical stance towards technology's transformative value with respect to alternative views of sexual difference and subjectivity. As Bukatman rightly observes,

> [r]eading SF through the matrices of feminist science fiction and theory, one encounters another set of human–technology relations in which the techno-organic fusion produces something other than cyberpunk's ambivalent euphoria.[83]

Not coincidentally, I would say, it is an example from the work of James Tiptree, Jr that Bukatman resorts to for illustrating this proposition. In this story, 'The Girl Who Was Plugged In' (1973), an ugly and wretched girl's brains are used, for commercial reasons, to make an articifically bred beautiful female body move by remote control—a true science horror tale of suffering.[84] The girl, P. (for Philadelphia, meaning 'Christian fraternal love'), becomes an amalgam renamed Delphi who leads the life of a puppet-on-a-string movie star, while the remains of P.'s grotesque body, still housing her brains, will rest forever in a neurological lab deep below Carbondale, Illinois. To some extent, her new existence as a cyborg offers her a certain kind of happiness. The Delphi incarnation is admired for her beauty, while she also falls in love. Yet her fate is to remain P. Burke the monster, 'down in a dungeon, smelling Electrode-paste. A caricature of a woman burning, melting, obsessed with true love.'

In stories like these, not only the point of divergence between cyberpunk and feminist science fiction becomes manifest, but also that between postmodernism and feminism: the conception of subjectivity. Feminism and postmodernism have a lot in common, as has already been suggested at various places in the argument so far. They both stress the blurring of traditional boundaries between high art and popular culture, the dominant and the marginal, same and other, and also between conceptual categories like nature and culture, representation and simulation, biology and construction. To a certain extent, they have a common concern for the myriad ways in which social relations are globally redefined by the new technologies, although this particular point has not been dealt with sufficiently until now. Postmodernism and feminism, finally, are both emphatically involved in the undermining of a liberal-humanist construction of a stable 'self' outside, or prior to, power and language. The motivations for and the orientation for this preoccupation, however, reveal the dissonance between postmodernism and feminism. In summary, while in postmodernism the loss of a unified and autonomously acting human subject is digested, and either celebrated or mourned, feminism seeks a subjective identity and active place in history for women which have been denied to them until recently by the dominant culture. The subjectivity feminism envisions is not an updated female version of an isolated individual ego, though, but an identity in relationship, which is not fixed yet which makes social agency possible.

What postmodernist science fiction like the writings of cyberpunk often seem to lack, to draw a conclusion, is an awareness of the gendered character of both technology and visions of technologically mediated subjectivity. In feminist cyborg science fictions, on the other hand, the examination of power relations in a high-tech culture is guided by the search for figurations of female subjectivity and sexual difference which move out of the traditional binary divisions of the masculine and the feminine. Rather than celebrating the fusion of woman and machine, they picture the complex—and in stories like 'The Girl Who Was Plugged In' even tragic—entanglements of female desire and pain brought about by this fusion.

Utopia/heterotopia

Women's explorations of the representational possibilities and the expression of female desire in the imaginary worlds of science fiction bring me to the last issue I want to raise in this contextualizing chapter. Is feminist science fiction involved in utopian writing? The answer clearly depends on how utopian writing is interpreted. In the first place, of course, it refers to a long narrative tradition in which an imaginary ideal world is constructed: the dream of 'elsewhere'. In *Writing History as a Prophet*, Lies Wesseling states that science fiction has become 'the modern avatar of utopian thought'. The alternative worlds of utopian fantasies, 'radically other than the empirical reality and yet similar enough to invite comparison', are continued in science fiction in futurological and cosmological variants.[85] And in technological variants, I would add. utopian fantasies usually diverge more strongly from the known world than their counterpart, the nightmarish dystopia, in which either contemporary social-political developments or unconscious collective fears are looked at with the help of magnifying glass or distorting mirror.

As regards feminist science fiction, many of its writings overlap with a tradition of female-authored utopias from the nineteenth century onwards until the creation of what Tom Moylan, in *Demand the Impossible*, calls the 'critical utopia' which emerged in the counterculture of the 1960s and 1970s.[86] This overlap has been extensively mapped in a series of studies.[87] They point out that feminist science fiction writings of alternative worlds— all-female utopian worlds as well as dystopian patriarchal societies—have become more and more sophisticated and open-ended, both in terms of narrative structure and the picturing of social relations. It is a feature of the postmodern development of the genre, that feminist science fiction, as well as the SF genre in general, increasingly includes utopian and dystopian elements in the same text, 'in which they critically voice the fears and anxieties of new and fragmented social and sexual constituencies and identities in post-industrial societies'.[88] According to Teresa de Lauretis, all science fiction has moved beyond the alternatives of utopian and dystopian fantasies insofar as these are understood as future visions of what people hoped or feared. The fictions of the genre have become 'ambiguous, puzzling, unfamiliar maps of heterotopias', in reference to Foucault's concept of the heterotopia as a single real place in which several sites are juxtaposed that are in themselves incompatible.[89] In the utopia or dystopia there is still an (imaginary) common locus of all things, as found in the convention of the visitor/narrator of the utopia. In the heterotopia, on the contrary, the adventure is not the protagonist's but the reader's, as she/he has to make some sense from a disorder of fragments.

> In the best of SF, the reader's sense of wOnder as awe, marvel, portent, revelation is replaced by a sense of wAndering through a mindscape both familiar and unfamiliar. Displaced from the central position of the knowledgeable observer, the reader stands on the constantly shifting ground, on the margins of understanding, at the periphery of vision: hence the sense of wAnder, of being dislocated to another spacetime continuum where human possibilities are discovered in the intersection of other signs with other meanings.[90]

De Lauretis felicitously describes what I experience in the adventure of my reading of Tiptree's 'A Momentary Taste of Being', in which I am constantly accompanied by a—sometimes frightening, sometimes liberating—sense of wAnder. I would not say, however, that it fully replaces my sense of wOnder, for wonder may be the very motive for reading science fiction in the first place, as Damon Knight suggested as early as 1967, in *In Search of Wonder*. Science fiction often resembles the language of dreams: startled by the flood of uncoordinated familiar and unfamiliar images and illogical events one wanders through the imaginary landscapes seeking for meanings that constantly threaten to slip away but nevertheless do not cease to fascinate the reader. Sigmund Freud gave us a framework by which to read dreams in his *Traumdeutung*; I hope that the framework explained in the introduction, the interpretive dialogue between narrative texts and theoretical perspectives, allows me to make sense of both the unintelligible and the seeming familiar in Tiptree's science fiction.

The urgent question underlying the interpretative labour is whether there is a utopian horizon left in science fiction's heterotopias such as Tiptree's 'A Momentary Taste of Being', as the envisioning of what is not yet is especially important to women. Is the heterotopia, in other words, a mere jumble of relations among the most divergent sites or does it still refer to the *eu*-topos, the *good* place, too? I think that the vanishing of utopias as alternative paradigms of community-building does not preclude any type of utopian writing in feminist and postmodern science fiction. The utopian dimension, however, often is detectable as desire and hope rather than as optimistic projection of an alternative world. It means that the deconstruction of old forms is very important and that experimental and provisional sketchings of new social relations and subjectivities prevail over clear-cut representations. This certainly applies to the work of James Tiptree, Jr, and in particular to her story 'A Momentary Taste of Being'.

II. Sexual Universes

The chaos and tumble of events. The first sentence of every novel should be: 'Trust me, this will take time but there is order here, very faint, very human.' Meander if you want to get to town.

Michael Ondaatje[1]

Multiple knottings, must not be able to untie these in a hurry.

Aaron Kaye (A135)

Introduction

In this first of four readings in successive chapters, we will follow the viewpoint of the main protagonist, Dr Aaron Kaye. As in so many travel stories in and outside science fiction, the ship's doctor is the person through whose eyes the reader is informed about the adventures of the ship and its crew. The text of 'A Momentary Taste of Being' is divided into four parts, in which the events are chronologically told, as outlined in the synopsis in my introduction. Although Aaron is the focalizing agency throughout the story, only in the last part, in which he is logging the most recent events, is he the narrator as well. The first three parts are told by an external narrator, an impersonal agency. They are introduced by a dream of Aaron's, the meaning of which is not directly explained in the text and seems to escape Aaron's comprehension, at least up to the story's conclusion. Hence they form an invitation to the reader's interpretative capacities.[2] Significantly, the last part, containing Aaron's monologic recording, does not begin with a dream: 'I don't dream anymore' is both Aaron's last sentence and that of the text. Its meaning is twofold. First it simply expresses Aaron's loss of hope and illusions for his own future and that of humankind. But it also explains that by now the subtext, encoded in the dreams, and the principal text match each other. Or, differently put, the events and processes in outer space and Aaron's subconscious somehow mirror each other. The repressed gradually though ineluctably manifests itself, dream by dream. Eventually, Aaron has decoded his dreams, understanding that the repressed has returned with a vengeance.

In the following I will take the route of the subsequent dreams, understood as junction points between outer and inner space, between main text and subtext, so as to unravel the narrative dynamic and make suggestions about the interpretation of the text. An important task in this process involves making an assessment of the function and effect of the male focalisator, taking into consideration both that Tiptree projects herself as a feminist writer and my own feminist bias. As I explained in the introduction, male protagonists pervade Tiptree's work. They are sometimes downright sexist he-men, yet in other stories are far more ambivalent figures. Aaron Kaye is one of the latter. What kind of masculinity does he represent and how does it relate to the overall tenor of the text? In particular, we want to know what visions of sexuality and reproduction emerge from the text when Aaron's perspective is followed. In exploring these questions, I shall have recourse to various heuristic keys, of which the concept of the *grotesque*, and the model of *entropy/dissipation* are the most important. I shall illuminate the meaning of these concepts during my experiment of dream interpretation.

Aaron's first dream: monster genitals

> ... *It floats there visibly engorged, blue-green against the blackness. He stares: It swells, pulsing to a terrifying dim beat, slowly extrudes a great ghostly bulge which extends, solidifies ... it is a planet-testicle pushing a monster penis toward the stars. Its blood-beat reverberates through weeping immensities; cold, cold. The parsecs-long phallus throbs, probes blindly under intolerable pressure from within; its tip is a huge cloudy glans lit by a spark: Centaur. In grief it bulges, lengthens, seeking release—stars toll unbearable crescendo* ... (A65; italics in the original)

The grotesque
With this unsettlingly grim representation of a cosmically enlarged male organ, the contents of Aaron Kaye's first dream, the unwary reader is introduced into the text. The tone is set, it seems. And indeed, the grotesque character of the image points to a leading streak of the text, though it is not the only one. What is meant by the grotesque and what does it convey in 'A Momentary Taste of Being'?

Originally the name 'grotesque' referred to ornamental paintings, dating from the time of the Roman emperors, which were excavated at the end of the fifteenth century in Rome. They were called *grottesca* after the Italian *grotta* (= cave, or grotto), and showed hybrids of human, animal and vegetable figures. During the following centuries the notion came to refer to many kindred and derived matters, no longer only in the visual arts but also in literature. Today the understanding of the grotesque is largely defined by the two rather divergent views of Wolfgang Kayser and Mikhail Bakhtin.[3] For the former, the grotesque more or less coincides with the uncanny (*Unheimliche*). The deformed and bizarre creatures of the grotesque are interpreted as a play with the absurd and as horrific manifestations of the Freudian unconscious (the *Id*), directed toward an exorcism of the demonic. Thus, the grotesque is an expression of angst.

Bakhtin, on the other hand, strongly emphasizes the grotesque as an expression of vitality, which has its origin in the popular culture of the middle ages, above all in its festivals like carnival. His view of the grotesque is motivated by a materialism in which the regeneration and fertility, and hence unfinishedness of the body are pivotal. In this manner, the body is posited as the opposite of the classical/classicist body. As the Dutch Bakhtin scholar Anton Simons puts it,

> The body … is not merely the smooth surface we see beaming on the beach and in playboy magazines. It is a 'drama' of countless events. It is highly unlikely that these events are really concerned about the skin by which they seem to be bounded. Myriad exchanges take place between my body, the external world, and the body of the other.[4]

In the grotesque body the openings and bulges are the very spots where the boundaries between two bodies, the body and the world, and the old and the new body (death and birth) are overcome. The picturing of the grotesque body, therefore, is characterized by the exaggeration of openings and bulges: the mouth and the anus, the phallus and the (pregnant) belly, the ears, the nose[5] and the breasts. In addition to the exaggeration, the language of the grotesque is marked by the 'debasement' of the lofty and the sublime, which in the carnavalesque culture is part of the reversal of hierarchical relations. It is expressed in the reversal of 'low' and 'high' parts of the body and corporeal functions—the buttocks are represented as a 'reversed face', which is clearly expressed in the Dutch word for pudding face: *blotebillengezicht* (bare buttocks face).

Whether one follows Kayser's demonic grotesque or Bakhtin's irreverent laughter, finally, in either case, the grotesque *effect* is the result of a 'violent *linking* of heterogeneous elements, which are derived from very differently assessed layers'.[6] These linkings cause confusion—either a pleasant or terrifying one—in the reader, who is in the dark about how to judge or understand an image or text.

Confusion about the grotesque, however, should not but in fact does conceal an important point, put forward by historian Margaret Miles: the gender assumptions embedded in grotesque art and literature.[7] Twentieth-century analysts such as Kayser and Bakhtin fail to notice that the *female* body is an essential instead of an accidental aspect of the grotesque. The conversion from high to low, from the spiritual to the material and corporeal, requires woman's body as a catalyst. It is the female body, and not the male's, that is traditionally associated with materiality, sex and reproduction, which are the most prominent features of the grotesque. It would be naïve simply to celebrate this movement into matter since it ignores the historical depreciation in Christian religion of the grotesque as a signal of the 'insidious omnipresence of evil, the confusion of an orderly creation by an irreducible undertow, a bleeding of "high" into "low" which is both achieved and demonstrated by erratic matter's insubordination to form'.[8] The most erratic matter is woman's body, which recalls Eve's sin and symbolizes humanity's existence in a state of sinfulness and punishment. Thus, in the Christian West Eve became the prototype of the grotesque figure.

> Figured as Eve, the perversely bent rib, every woman was seen as essentially grotesque, though the revelation of her hidden monstrosity could be prevented by her careful adherence to socially approved appearance and behavior. The function was to identify, define, and thus to stabilize a feared and fantasized object. Grotesque figuration contributes the bonus of laughter, permitting relief of tension; the simultaneously feared and desired object becomes comic.[9]

Its bodily functions make woman's body grotesque 'by nature', for pregnancy, birth, menstruation make the body the opposite of the Western ideal of the closed, smooth and impenetrable body which represents individual and autonomous being. The 'leakiness' of the female body threatens this male fantasy.[10] Miles cites Bakhtin in saying, 'Birth and death are the gaping jaws of the earth and the other's open womb'.[11] Horror is warded off by its debasement to ridicule—or its celebration in carnavalesque transgression.

Miles admits that male as well as female bodies have been subjected to grotesque figuration in art and literature. However, when male bodies become grotesque they assume 'feminine' connoted characteristics: they merge and fuse with the world, 'they lose form and integrity, become penetrable, suffer the addition of alien body parts, and become alternately huge and tiny'.[12] In addition, male and female grotesque images differ in their social meaning and value. This may be illustrated by an example which is directly linked to our reading of 'A Momentary Taste of Being'. Miles distinguishes three major rhetorical and pictorial devices of the grotesque—caricature, inversion and hybridization. Caricature now isolates and fetishizes parts of the body, in particular sexual organs. Especially in a society in which female beauty is identified with being slim, soft and small, caricature featuring monstrous size of women or female bodily parts—breasts, vagina, uterus—is likely to display fear and hence contempt of women. On the other hand,

[m]assive male sexual organs are figures of pride, self-assertion, and aggression; massive female genitals, however, are likely to represent women's dangerous propensities for threatening men's self-control, autonomy, and power.[13]

I think that we only have to contrast the cross-culturally pervasive fantasmatic image of the *vagina dentata*, the toothed vagina that bites (off), to Aubrey Beardsley's *fin de siècle* monster-penises to grant Miles' point. But then an urgent question comes to the fore: what about Tiptree's monster penis at the beginning of 'A Momentary Taste of Being'?[14] What does it mean when a *female* author pictures (Earth as) a gigantic male organ? Which real or fantasmatic horror is kept at bay in the ridicule displayed in the monster-penis of Tiptree's story?

First it is important to observe that female-authored literary and visual texts do develop their own forms of the grotesque. In their elaborations of the grotesque, twentieth-century female authors often incorporate the issue of the social organization of sexual difference in a more articulate and self-conscious way than their male collaegues.[15] Remarkably, in their work it is the female body in and through which the grotesque takes shape as well—with this distinction that the parody or ridicule is aimed at the female self/selves instead of the other. Paula Cooey, for instance, draws attention to the grotesque quality in the construction of female characters in Toni Morrison's novels as well as in various of the self-portraits produced by Frida Kahlo. In the discussion of the Kahlo's painting *A Few Small Nips*, the notion of the *carcajada*, or burst of laughter, comes up, in this case a burst of 'biting laughter in the face of unrelieved pain'.[16] In my view, the *carcajada*, thus understood, is an important feature of many female grotesque writings. Here, the exaggerated, reversed or doubled female bodies or bodily parts point to a strategy to cope with pain, and more in particular with the suffering from the very female body, or from what this body culturally represents.

Tiptree's work offers various outstanding examples of such narrative and representational strategy, 'The Girl Who Was Plugged In', introduced in the previous chapter, being one of them. Philadelphia Burke is the enfleshment of grotesque femininity, first in her excessive ugliness and afterwards in her doubled cyborg body simultaneously living in under- and upperworld. Not only the representation of femaleness is grotesque but the narrative form as well, as the text is structured by an anonymous speaker evoking compassion for the wretched girl by snarling gross sarcasms at an implied masculine audience. ('Listen, zombie. Believe me. What I could tell you—you with your silly hands leaking sweat on your growth-stocks portfolio'.) P. Burke returns, as it seems, in the figure of

Carol Page (or 'Cold Pig') in 'With Delicate Mad Hands' (1981), whose otherwise sweet face is deformed by 'a huge, fleshly, obscenely pugged nose'.[17] Again the female grotesque both confirms and relieves women's pain, most convincingly in the 'cosmic joke' of CP's encounter with her alien double in outer space, an outcast from her/its community like she was on Earth. 'Oh God—aching half with laughter, half with pain, she recognized—the large folded, triangular earflaps of a pig! And the alien's muzzle was pugged, like hers.'

Striking though these elaborations of the female grotesque are, I think Tiptree has more than one string to her bow in the battle for survival. I want to argue that the *carcajada* is also guiding Tiptree's grotesque picturing of the male body such as in the monster-testicle-penis of 'A Momentary Taste of Being'. Harking back to the distinction introduced earlier between uncanny and vitalist grotesque, the image of the planet-testicle with its monstrous phallus seeking desperately for release appears to evoke the very *tension* between the two. It is obscene and horrific, yet one cannot help laughing about the picture of the imminent cosmic ejaculation. This ambiguous effect is reinforced by the displacement of the grotesque from a human body to a cosmic body. The uncertainty produced by such a linking of heterogenous elements is well illustrated in Sarah Lefanu's discussion of Aaron's dream. Lefanu rebukes the imaging of Earth as male genitals as 'masculinist', although she finds it 'undoubtedly original: earth as a 'planet-testicle' makes a change from earth as a womb, egg, source of all nurturance'.[18] So, along with surprise, the picturing of the traditionally feminine connoted Earth in rather blunt phallic colours evokes uncomfortable feelings as well. Probably it is especially distressing to find this image in the text of an author who is known for her feminist commitment. Connecting the image to the dramatic events in the story, Lefanu wonders if Tiptree is saying anything more in the story than 'that we exist only to mate and die'. Somewhat disappointed, she decides that 'A Momentary Taste of Being' is an 'overtly determinist tale'. However, I feel that the 'deeply pessimistic and … deterministic slant', which Lefanu rightly points out, meets resistance from an inclination to the grotesque in which mockery eases pessimism. This may be endorsed by Tiptree's story 'The Earth Doth Like a Snake Renew' (1973), in which a sardonic-comic tone dominates the entire narrative. Here too the Earth is designated male, by a female protagonist this time, and again linked to bizarre phallic imagery, albeit in a more derived way.

> Her father pointed; P. stared. Bursting from the moss in front of her nose were twenty startling pink naked dogs' pizzles. They were very
>
> lifelike; the smallest might belong to a Yorkshire, the largest to a

Dalmatian. Each rosy glans was capped with an ochre ooze, visibly succeeding in its aim of attracting bluebottles.

'They come up every year.' Her father shook his head. 'Aren't they awful? It's a mushroom. I never told your mother.'

P. was silent before this evocation from the ancient loam. From that day the Earth to her was explicitly HE.[19]

In this story, however, not just the male tool but also the female protagonist P. herself and her quest for an ecstatic union with HIM are the laughing-stock. In the cold apocalyptic conclusion of the story Earth turns out to be basically uninterested in human beings. Though in a far more gloomy mode, 'A Momentary Taste of Being' shares with it the terrifying prospect of the annihilation of humankind altogether. But while in 'The Earth Doth' it is, surprisingly, female heterosexual sexual desire that is the object of mockery, I want to argue that in 'A Momentary Taste of Being' it is principally, though not unambiguously, masculine sexuality, as it is on display in the icon of the gigantic testicle-phallus, that is under fire. And it is made to experience a complete burn out, as I shall explain below, by means of a grotesque blow-up of the human reproductive process.

Cosmic reproduction
In Aaron's perception of his dream the grotesque phallus does not seem to refer so much to sexual desire as to Earth's overpopulation. We see in the text a progressive comparison of human beings with a teeming mass of sperms hovering on the edge of extinction. Pressing himself not to ignore the individuality of every human being, 'each with a face, a name, a unique personality, and a meaningful fate', Aaron nevertheless catches himself thinking of Earth's inhabitants as 'teeming billions' (A75). With the force of a hallucination the phallic dream jumps back to his mind.

> [H]e sees again the monster penis groping toward the stars with *Centaur* at its tip. Pulsing with pressure, barely able to wait for the trigger that will release the human deluge (A75–6)

Aaron thus alludes to an understanding of his dream as an expression of deep solicitude about the horrific consequences of overpopulation—the one the *Centaur* fled from ten years ago—that tends to reduce people to just a 'deluge of sperms'. But the metaphor of human beings as sperms turns nightmarishly literal in the story: the crew members of the *Centaur* will be used as sperm in a cosmic process of reproduction which is as mysterious as it is banal. It is Bill Coby, Aaron's assistant, who proposes such outrageous hypotheses, just after the crew members have been in contact with the light the alien life-form is radiating.

'Post coitum tristum.' Coby's voice is very low. 'I am tristum.'

'What did it do to you, Bill, can you tell me?'

The silent, sad stare continues. Just as Aaron opens the hypo-kit Coby says clearly, 'I know a ripe corpus luteum when I see one.' He gives a faint, nasty chuckle.

… 'Did you, you didn't have some sort of intercourse with that thing, Bill?'

'In-ter-course?' Coby echoes in a whisper. 'No … not us, anyway. If somebody had … intercourse it was god, maybe … Or a planet … Not us … It had *us*.' …

Coby's face quivers, he stares up into Aaron's eyes, fighting to hang on to consciousness. 'Say we were carrying it … carrying a load of jizzum in our heads, I guess … And the jizzum meets … the queen couzy, the queen couzy of all time… and it jumps … jumps across. It makes some kind of holy … zygote, out there … see? Only we're left … empty … What happens to a sperm's tail … afterwards?' (A151)

An hypothesis that is as shocking to Aaron as it is plausible, as he ends up acknowledging. Hence his lament that human beings are:

Nothing but gametes. The dimorphic set—call it sperm. Two types, little boy sperms, little girl sperms—half of the germ-plasm of … something. Not complete beings at all. Half of the gametes of some creatures, some race … Maybe they aren't even intelligent. Say they use planets to breed on, like amphibians going to the water. And they sowed their primordial seed-stuff around here, their milt and roe among the stars. On suitable planets. And the stuff germinated. And after the usual interval—say three billion years, that's what it took us, didn't it?—the milt, the sperm evolved to *motility*, see? And we made it to the stars. To the roe-planet. To fertilize them. And that's all we are, the whole damn thing—the evolving, the achieving and fighting and hoping—all the pain and effort, just to get us there with the loads of jizzum in our heads. Nothing but sperm's tails. (A158–9)

This profound pessimism, however, not only applies to the crew of the *Centaur* and the small selection of people who will move out into space in response to the green signal mistakenly sent from the *Centaur*, but to all of humankind. For its insignificance is anticipated in Earth's twentieth-century's overpopulated megacities.

What happens to the people who don't go, the ones who stay on

Earth, all the rest of the race? Let us speculate, Dr. Kaye. What happens to unused sperm? Stuck in testes, die of overheating. Reabsorbed. Remind you of anything? Calcutta, say. Rio de Janeiro, Los Angeles ... Previews. Born too soon or too late—too bad. Rot away unused. Function fulfilled, organs atrophy ... End of it all, just rot away. *Not even knowing*—thinking they were people, thinking they had a chance ... (A162)

All the glories of human progress, including space travel, are unmasked as ultimately futile. Hardly without exception, the—sparse—references to 'A Momentary Taste of Being' in comments on Tiptree's work take Aaron's lament to be the meaning the story conveys to the reader: the fatalistic message that we exist, as Lefanu notes, 'only to mate and die'. However, the case may be more subtle, and at least more ambivalent than thus suggested. We need not simply identify Aaron's (understandably depressed) viewpoint with the text itself. As far as a cosmic perspective is concerned, I think that what Mark Siegel, in an article on transcendence and (im)mortality in Tiptree's work, notes as a major tendency applies to 'A Momentary Taste of Being' as well:

> Human life, in a cosmic perspective, is meaningless except as one of many examples of a bizarre, unpredictable, and ever-changing biological evolution. At the same time, however, she poignantly suggests the sublime passions of life as it is lived by real individuals, so that the reader cannot help sensing the melancholy nature of the joy of a physical existence balanced against cruel limitations, involving unavoidable suffering and pain, and ending in a pointless death. Human desire is pitted against an immense, often attractive, but always indifferent universe. While individuals may console themselves that their deaths sometimes are justified for the continuance of the race, the survival of humanity itself for any great length of time is often depicted as unlikely.[20]

We are reminded here of a famous line from the Dutch poet Lucebert suggesting that the human being is just a 'breadcrumb on the skirt of the universe'. Given the incomprehensible vastness of the universe as well as the short period of human history, rather than being the crowning glory of either divine creation or biological evolution, humankind is an insignificant moment in an immense process of continuing transformations. 'A Momentary Taste of Being' indeed contains a challengingly critical cosmological view.[21]

Yet we should not overlook that this cosmic perspective intersects with the language of human sexuality and reproduction. In a grotesque twist intelligent human beings are reduced to sperms. Anthropomorphization of sperms as actors in a drama is a narrative device that is not unique to 'A Momentary Taste of Being'. Think of Woody Allen's movie *Everything You Always Wanted to Know about Sex etc.* and John Barth's story 'Night Sea Journey'. In both examples human beings are equated with sperms. But the movement may be turned the other way round too: sperms are discussed as if they were human beings. In medical as well as popular texts it has become a widespread practice to describe the reproductive process in truly epic traits as a mythical journey, or even a battle, of the active male sperm-hero fighting his way through the dark corridors of the ovaria towards the passive female ovum.[22] What we see in Tiptree's story is a dramatic alteration of this conventional mythic account of the reproductive process. Here, the ova turn out to be the powerful force which strongly attracts the sperms which are completely overwhelmed and can do nothing but yield to it. I think we hear the sounds of the *carcajada* in the distance, accompanying the implosion of the spermatic logic.

> Oh hell, what does a sperm's tail die of? Acute loss of ability to live anymore. Acute post-functional irrelevance ... The symptoms start after brief contact with a certain life-form from the Alpha planet ... The gross symptoms are disorientation, apathy, some aphasia, ataxia, anorexia. All responses depressed; aprosexia, speech echolalic ... Symptoms cannot be interpreted as due to physical shock, electric or otherwise. Adrenergic systems most affected, cholinergic relatively less so. Adrenal insufficiency is not, repeat not, confirmed by hormonal bioassay. Oh hell—they've been drained, that's what it is. Drained of something ... something vital. Prognosis ... yes. The prognosis is death. (A159–60)

(Neg)entropy and dissipation

Admittedly, male and female members of *Centaur's* crew alike were drawn towards the alien and transformed into cosmic sperm ('little boy sperms, little girl sperms'). In this respect, women are granted no more innocence than men. Yet I do think that the grotesque male sexual imagery and its radical dethronement illustrate that the target of the *carcajada* is male sexual organization. That is, both in the sense of genital–spermatic sexuality and of the social-cultural organization according to male privileges and hierarchies, of patriarchy, in short. Women, indeed, may be either wilful or complying play-, work- and bedfellows in this 'world machine'. Patriarchy in its social aspect is pictured with sharp wit in 'A Momentary Taste of Being'. What we see is an apparently tightly organized social community suffering from increasing entropy until (sexual and cultural) exhaustion dooms both men and women. Having thus introduced the notion of *entropy* as an interpretive key, I shall first explain its contents and context.

Entropy is a concept commonly associated with thermodynamics and astrophysics. As reality is too complicated to be represented directly, physicists necessarily use metaphors and models to make sense of their perceptions of the physical world, some of which are adopted in science fiction. As Katherine Hayles points out, the emergence of or appeal to similar metaphors in divergent discourses need not be the result of direct influence, but rather indicates the existence of a common cultural matrix, and of shared everyday experiences that influence scientists and literary authors.[23] By definition, I would say, science fiction is an outstanding genre for exploring the impact of scientifically informed metaphors. Deeply embedded in the present scientific and technological era, science fiction's imaginary landscapes reflect the intellectual and emotional quests evoked by this era. Entropy has proved a pertinent metaphor in this respect. It was in particular adopted by New Wave writers, as demonstrated in famous examples like Thomas Pynchon's *Entropy* (1960) and Pamela Zoline's 'The Heat Death of the Universe' (1967).

The word entropy was brought into the language of physics in the middle of the nineteenth century by Rudolf Clausius, who coined it from the Greek *entrepein*, to turn, to transform. Entropy is a functional measure to determine the amount of heat that is lost for useful purposes. The important second law of thermodynamics says that in a closed system entropy always tends to increase to a maximum whereas the available energy tends to a minimum. In other words, no real heat transfer can be hundred per cent efficient. If the implications of the second law are fully considered, the running down of the most closed system, the *universe*, inevitably comes in sight. This is commonly referred to as the heat death of the universe and is 'a final state of equilibrium in which the temperature stabilizes near absolute zero (about −273°C) and there is no longer any heat differential to do work or to sustain life'.[24]

Hayles describes the second law as one of the most controversial results of thermodynamics. Owing to a paper by Clausius' contemporary James C. Maxwell, the implications of the second law were mitigated almost right from the beginning. Maxwell's 1859 paper supported the view that thermodynamic laws are statistical generalizations rather than laws in an absolute sense. Understanding entropy as a statistical measure of disorder rather than the absolute gauge of a law facilitates its use also for physical and cosmological systems entirely different from heat engines. Furthermore, the interpretation of entropy in probabilistic instead of deterministic terms makes the predicted fate of the universe's heat death less certain. The opening offered by this less deterministic view would in the late twentieth century be utilized by Ilya Prigogine to develop his own reinterpretation of the second law, to which I will return in due course in the light of 'A Momentary Taste of Being'.

First another moment in the development of the theory about entropy needs consideration, for it provides a direct link to James Tiptree's work. In order to explain this, I refer again at this point to Hayles, whose objective is to trace the transvaluation of entropy as it moves from classical thermodynamics to information theory in the 1950s. Of special interest in respect to my own study is her introduction of the thermodynamist Leon Brillouin. What is important in the first place, according to Hayles, is that Brillouin had an intuition that entropy and information are somehow connected. In his view, information and entropy are *opposites*, whence he coined 'negentropy', short for *negative entropy*, as a synonym for information.[25] And information was equated with order.[25] I do not know where Alice Sheldon 'encountered'[26] the concept of (neg)entropy, whether perhaps she became familiar with it during her training as an experimental psychologist. What is important, however, is the *moral* turn she has given to the concept. On several occasions she declared her affinity with it as a foundational value for her world view. In an interview with Charles Platt, she explained that:

> Life is a denial of entropy; it's a striking manifestation of *negative* entropy. So I believe it can be shown that things with a high degree of organization, meaning a low degree of entropy, seem good to us. For example, Nazism is a highly entropic form, and democracy is far more complex. An altruistic act is more complex than a selfish one; you can carry these concepts quite a ways, to show that most things we feel to be 'good' in the New Testament sense, and sensible, involve a more organized structure of action. To me, Lucifer is positive entropy, runaway breakdown of the system, the war of all against all, which I think will, unfortunately, recur.[27]

In another interview, she refers more directly to the inverse relation of entropy and information in the sense of complexity.

> [Negative entropy, that is] complexity, organization, high-bit information characterizes all I felt to be good, and it is at least in theory capable of objective proof that altruism is more complex, technically, than selfish greed; that the forward seat is more organized than bouncing on a horse's kidneys; that Yeats represents more information per bit than Edgar Guest; that consensus and democracy are more highly organized forms than tyranny and Nazism.[28]

Entropy is thus turned into a category of social, political and moral barbarism, expressed in all acts of tyranny and oversimplification. Negentropy, on the other hand, indicates democracy and complexity. Moreover, life itself is 'a striking manifestation' of negative entropy. In keeping with this, we can conclude that, consequently, death equals entropy.

Tiptree's reinterpretation of (neg)entropy proves to be an apt device to gain insight in the way patriarchy and its decline are envisioned in 'A Momentary Taste of Being'. Spaceship *Centaur* is truely an exemplary closed system according to the second law of thermodynamics in that it slowly but surely is sliding into disorder ending up in a terminal condition of maximum entropy and minimum energy. See Aaron's melancholy observation:

> A feeling of dumb weight comes over him. It is *Centaur*, the whole wonderful ship he had been so proud of, hanging over him mute and flaccid in the dark. The life-spark gone away. Voiceless, unfindable in the icy wastes ... (A155)

It is important to understand that the spaceship is Earth's *idealized* microcosm. On board every one of the sixty crew members is, as Aaron puts it, a 'token something' (A76) or, in Lory's phrase, 'sixty hand-picked indoctrinated specimens' (A121). Each of them has been carefully selected not only according to education and skills but also to sex, colour, nationality, outlook on life and sexual privilege. The command-structure of the ship is very lucid. The New Zealander Yellaston, Caucasian but an outsider in terms of global politics, leads the ship under the neutral colours of the United Nations. The two sub-commanders form a grotesque double, an American from Ohio and a Russian from Omsk, while the third sub-commander, who stayed behind on the paradisaical planet, is Chinese. The role of the chief of communications is performed by the prototype of black male dominance, Ray Bustamente. There are many skilled women aboard but none of them occupies a higher commanding position. Sexuality has never been a problem on the *Centaur*, the text says, because one of the selection criteria for the crew members had been 'low sex-drive', while the occasional needs, whether they are hetero- and homosexual, are supplied in a rational manner. No babies are born, moreover, and no marriages or divorces take place. Furthermore, the ship contains a self-sufficient system of food production.

I would qualify the *Centaur* as a rather ambivalent representation of civilization, suggesting a well-balanced, democratic and rational society, which, on second thoughts, may just as well be a superimposed social and political structure of suppression. What we see, then, is a literally and figuratively sterile closed social system with reminiscenses of the corporative state with its manifestations in Italian fascism and German Nazism. Except that the 'corporations' in this case are the world's factions that work together to maintain the artificial balance of the cold war détente.[29] It is a form of corporatism, moreover, which is accompanied by severe repression of sexuality. The spaceship thus may be designated as a representation of what Klaus Theweleit has called the 'mental armor' (*Pantzer*). In *Male Fantasies*, his famous investigation of the fantasies of *Freikorps* soldiers during German fascism, Theweleit described the mental armour as a defence strategy of the male psyche against the soft, the liquid and the slimy, elements associated with the female body, which is seen as the origin of feared libidinal energies that cannot be controlled.[30] The feminine, in other words, is all that recalls the erotic and the physical, and hence the vulnerability and mortality of being. The inclination to build an impermeable dam against the 'feminine' is manifested most extremely under Nazism, where the subject became part of a rationalized defence machine by the imposition of disciplinary and military technologies on the thus delibidinalized body. Theweleit nevertheless considers the formation of this defensive armour to be a structural element of the Western male psyche in modernity. It helps the male subject to attain invulnerability against the 'feminine flows' that threaten to overflow the rational ego and dissolve its boundaries.[31]

It turns out to be most helpful to look at spaceship *Centaur* in the light of Theweleit's notion of the mental armour. Although in terms of population policy opposing Nazist racism and xenophobia, the spacehip nevertheless strongly resembles a well-disciplined social defence machine. Its male-led command structure and all the rigid distinctions between the sixty unique individuals, who never really lose themselves in each other because of their low sex-drive, turn the spacehip into a canned collectivity of delibidinalized subjects. This makes it, in Tiptree's terminology, a place of entropy rather than negative entropy ('negentropy'), of death rather than life. After ten years of equilibrium, of which emotional and reproductive sterility have been the price, the little cracks in the system become more and more visible until it finally falls prey to 'the runaway breakdown of the system'. Or, in other words, the repressed, or canalized, libidinal energies burst out with a vengeance.

Significantly, the tendency towards maximum entropy aboard the spaceship manifests itself as a crisis of masculine authority. Captain Yellaston is described by Aaron not only as a 'very senior, idiosyncratic old primate', but also as 'a complicated fortress surviving by strange rituals' (A115). Yellaston is portrayed as a seemingly self-contained patriarch, in fact barricading himself against possible attacks on his autonomy. Attacks apparently associated with the feminine. In a conversation with Aaron taking place before the contact with the alien, the captain bursts out, without any direct reason in the eyes of the reader: 'We never should have had women on this mission' (A117). The text says that Aaron 'grins involuntarily', meanwhile thinking, however: '[T]here speaks the dead dick'. And:

> Thinking also of Soli, of Ahlstrom, of all the female competences on *Centaur*, of the debates of female command that had yielded finally to the policy of minimal innovation on a mission where so much else would be new. *But he knows exactly what Yellaston means.* (A117, italics added)

Since no further explanation follows at that point, the reader is invited to speculate on this point in the context of preceding interpretations. What Aaron and Yellaston are likely to share, then, is the fantasm that women, notwithstanding their social position and intellectual capacities, always embody a danger lurking in the dark: by their very physical existence they are a threat to the solidity and separateness of the male ego.

In fact, however, Yellaston's white patriarchal leadership is in the first place endangered by his fellow *men*. It is indirectly contested by Ray Bustamente's black power and directly by the insubordination of Tim Bron and Don Purcell. Aaron is very worried about the effects of this crisis. When Bill Coby too advocates 'a more realistic political organization', the former thinks:

> Elections, two years from nowhere? That'll mean the Russian faction, the U.S. faction, the Third and Fourth Worlders; scientists versus humanists versus techs versus ecologists versus theists versus Smithites—all the factions of Earth in one fragile ship. What shape will we be in when we reach the planet, if we live that long? (A129)

At first sight Aaron's fear of disorder on the *Centaur* seems perfectly rational: a multi-party system in a community of sixty really is ridiculous, and even dangerous. On further consideration, however, this view above all might express an anxiety about losing an already spurious cohesion, of either a socio-political or a subjective character, as we shall see below in the discussion of the second and third dream. Besides, his fear for disintegration is, no more than the pseudo-democratic aspirations of the other men, capable of averting the entropic tendency of whichever patriarchal sexual-political organization. The text plays a sardonic game on Aaron as well. In the course of the grotesque parody of human reproduction, ultimately *any* type of leadership and social organization is dissolved.

The posthuman

Entropy as a fading away of life. And yet, the story points to the reversed as well, Sheldon's view that life is a denial of entropy. After all, reproduction is not so much the 'waste' of sperm as the conception of a new creature. A while after the contact of crew members with alien life form through its radiance, Aaron starts to discern 'new things':

> They're more or less transparent, of course, even at the end. They float. I think they're partly out of the ship. It's hard to tell their size, like a projection or afterimage. They seem big, say six or eight meters in diameter, but once or twice I've thought they may be very small. They're alive, you can tell that. They don't respond or communicate. They're not … rational. Not at all. They change, too, they take on colors or something from your mind. Did I say that? I'm not sure they're really visible at all, maybe the mind senses them and constructs an appearance. But recognizable. You can see traces. I can identify most of them. Tim's was by ramp seven. It was partly Tim and partly something else, very alien. It seemed to swell up and float away out through the hull, as if it was getting closer and farther at the same time … They do *not* dissipate. It throbbed—no, that isn't quite right. It swelled and floated. Away. (A156)

Although for want of a better qualification Aaron at first calls these things 'ghosts', he hastens to stress that in fact they are not:

> What I think they are is blastomeres.[32]
>
> Holy zygotes, Coby said. I don't think they're holy. They're just there, growing. Definitely not spirits or ghosts or higher essences, they're not the *person* at all. They're a, a combined product. They develop. They stay at the site and then … move on out. (A156)

I propose to consider this from a cosmological point of view first. To that end let me add another dimension to the thermodynamically based concept of (neg)entropy, that is, the model of *dissipative structures*, presented by Ilya Prigogine with his co-author Isabelle Stengers in their book on irreversible thermodynamics *Order out of Chaos*.[33] Although it is unlikely that Alice Sheldon was familiar with Prigogine's theories, which were not popularized in the US before 1984, the model of dissipative structures is strikingly compatible with 'A Momentary Taste of Being''s narrative dynamic.[34] One of the basic assumptions of Prigogine and Stengers is that of 'a strong interaction of the issues proper to culture as a whole and the internal conceptual problems of science in particular'.[35] In this sense, their study could be seen as not just an intervention in the theory of science but also as a contribution to the philosophy of culture. As such it becomes relevant to a text like 'A Momentary Taste of Being', which I understand as a product of the interaction between science, culture and the powers of the imagination. I think Tiptree's story and the theory in *Order out of Chaos* share crucial intuitions about human life and the cosmos. Probably needless to say, my appeal to *Order out of Chaos* does not concern its scientific arguments as such but 'the visions that guide theory and research'.[36]

Pivotal to Prigogine and Stengers' project is its conception of *time*. Against the static Newtonian model of reversibility they oppose the *irreversibility*, the evolution of time. Classical science revolved around 'the basic conviction that at some level *the world is simple* and is governed by time-reversible fundamental laws'.[37] Without refuting that reversibility and determinism hold true in limited, simple cases, Prigogine and Stengers claim that irreversibility and randomness are the rule. Because there is only one single universe, their aim is to relate the various meanings of time involved in the divergent fields of knowledge: time as motion (classical mechanics), time related to irreversibility (thermodynamics) and time as history (biology and sociology). Philosophically speaking, this issue refers to the ontological question in Western thought about the relation between being and becoming. Prigogine and Stengers strongly advocate the recognition of both modalities as two different aspects of the same reality.

According to their theory, the universe has a pluralistic, temporal and complex character, its processes being marked by nonlinearity, instability and fluctuations. This implies that the mechanistic idea of matter as passive substance has been abandoned for a view of matter as capable of spontaneous activity. The research of Prigogine and Stengers concentrates on the appearance and evolution of new structures that originate spontaneously and which are called dissipative structures:

> In far-from-equilibrium conditions we may have transformation from disorder, from thermal chaos, into order. New dynamic states of matter may originate, states that reflect the interaction of a given system with its surroundings. We have called the new structures *dissipative structures* to emphasize the constructive role of dissipative processes in their formation.[38]

Thus this description both holds onto and escapes from the second law of thermodynamics, the law of increase of entropy and decrease of energy in a closed system. Contrary to systems governed by equilibrium, systems far from equilibrium can experience a local entropy *decrease*. They survive in an open exchange of energy/matter with the generally entropic universe in order to dissipate the products of their instabilities and evolve to higher complexities.

In my perception, it is illuminating to conceive of the cosmic reproduction in 'A Momentary Taste of Being' in terms of dissipative processes. The spaceship *Centaur* was slipping into a condition truely far-from-equilibrium. From Aaron's perspective we only see entropic disorder and dying people on board *Centaur*. In his eyes, the new creatures that have come into existence do not signify life but the death of humanity. When we change the point of view, then, it becomes possible to observe the culminative condition of chaos on board *Centaur* as prelude to an unexpected dissipative structure. Once the alien life-form has been brought aboard, the closed system of the spaceship becomes an open system. Through interaction with the alien matter/energy new dynamic states of matter spontaneously come into being. The products of the instability of the spacehip's system, *Centaur's* human cargo, are dissipated and evolve into higher complexities. Or, to put it bluntly, the dispersal of entropic energies which have pervaded twentieth-century culture—as projected on its miniature, the *Centaur*, with its masculine power structure—is a matter of 'waste-disposal': the sterile parts of the human are dispensed with, while the vital parts feed an alien being.

What takes place, literally and metaphorically, is a radical trans-formation of the human into the *post*human. It is important to note that Aaron conceives of the new creatures as *combined* products, which are partly human and 'partly something else, very alien' (A156). Siegel aptly describes the paradoxical 'negentropic' quality of the posthuman species in 'A Momentary Taste of Being'.

> In a biological sense, this fertilization is the completion of a biological function and is apparently neg-entropic as well. At the same time, Tiptree's code of morality is in paradoxical conjunction, because humans are becoming less rather than more human through this increase in neg-entropy.[39]

In her study *Alien to Femininity*, Marleen Barr affirms the feminist prospect of the posthuman, noting that in the world of Tiptree's fiction 'hope [for female equality] only becomes possible after biological differences have been eradicated, after humankind changes into something else'.[40]

In the concluding chapter of this book I shall return to the posthuman in 'A Momentary Taste of Being' as a specular figuration for posthumanistic thinking. At present I would like to elucidate 'A Momentary Taste of Being''s unsettling generation of the posthuman on the level of representation by pitting it against a contemporary cinematic repre-sentation of cosmic *regeneration*. It concerns Arthur C. Clarke/Stanley Kubrick's classic *2001: A Space Odyssey* (1968). The end of the third and last part of *2001*, titled 'Jupiter and Beyond Infinity', delineates the simultaneous death and rebirth of David Poole, the sole survivor of a space mission to Jupiter. After a mysterious force has propelled Poole through the barriers of infinity in an orgy/orgasm of fluid colours and forms (the famous 'trip'-sequence), the astronaut finds himself in a sort of rococo-styled room where he watches his own rapid ageing process. In the penultimate scene, we see the ancient gaunt spaceman on his deathbed raising his arm to point towards a black monolith. A flat black oblong which recalls computer chips and skyscrapers, but perhaps also the holy stone of the Kaaba in Mecca and, finally, the abyss of death. The next moment, however, we see Poole suffused with a glorious light and turned into a giant, almost full-term foetus within an amnion.

Scott Bukatman interprets this image of the foetus as 'a passage from the human to the-more-than-human', which is also a passage beyond the body as 'the 'Starchild' is more ethereal and celestial than physical'. And he adds that,

> [t]hus the fusion of sexuality is displaced into an ecstatic transcendence of the physical, just as the fact of death is elided through a cosmic, evolutionary perspective.[41]

In the previous chapter, I mentioned Bukatman's astute analysis of the death and the subsequent nostalgic reconsolidation of the *masculine* subject in cyberpunk texts like Gibson's *Neuromancer*. Yet it seems to have escaped his attention that the subject experiencing a rebirth into the 'more-than-human' in older science fiction products such as *2001* is also heavily male-coded. Kubrick's celestial foetus recalls Lennart Nillson's spectacular series of foetal photographs 'Drama of Life before Birth', published in *Life* in 1965. Since these first photos of 'life in the womb', the image of the foetus as a kind of spaceman floating in splendid isolation against a black or starry background, detached from the mother's body, has gained wide currency in Western culture.[42] Feminist theorists have pointed out that this type of visualization of the unborn not only tends to obscure women's subjectivity in the reproductive process but also titilates male fantasies of immaculate self-generation.[43] What Bukatman describes as the cosmic transcendence of corporeality in the final scene of *2001*, taking shape in the extraterrestrial foetus, seems to be a perfect expression of the myth of male parthenogenesis and a denial of maternal origins. And what's more, it is a 'triumphant rebirth' so that death is defeated.

A defeat which gets a really nasty glow in the light of an interpretation of the film as part of nuclear discourse. In a semiotic analysis, Zoë Sofia uncovers Kubrick/Clarke's cosmic foetus as an emblem of the converging forces of right-wing anti-abortion rhetoric, with its cult of foetal personhood, and the US military-industrial nuclear power to extinguish present as well as future generations. The pro-life foetus and the Starchild are similiar visualizations of fantasies emerging from twentieth-century technoculture. Both are a 'special effect' of a 'cultural dreamwork' in which attention is displaced from the tools and decision-makers of an actually possible extermination of humankind onto an imaginary signifier of extinction. Sofia concludes that:

> The extraterrestrial embryo is a perverse and misleading symbol whose engaging organic appearance invokes maternal fertility and belies its origin in the unholy union of man with celestial powers and the tools he's brought out of the excremental remains of his cannibalized mother, the planet Earth.[44]

From this viewpoint, I would like to add, the astral foetus not only signifies the resurrection of the self-sufficient masculine subject believed to have died, but also its rebirth into *innocence*. This would assume, consequently, that the metaphorical appropriation of female procreativity is not simply based on power fantasies but just as well on more opaque strategies of repression and projection of guilt.

If we compare all this with the transformative process from the human into the posthuman in 'A Momentary Taste of Being', the difference is telling. When death bears the sign of life in Tiptree's text, it is not to act out a fantasy of immortality and rebirth of the conventional subject but to create some prospect for new states of being beyond the entropic male-ruled dis/order. The representation of cosmic continuity does not serve to smooth over the fact of death, for humankind does die on board the *Centaur*, but to put the significance of the human in the right, modest perspective. The posthuman is not the same as the more-than-human: while the latter points to the triumphant celebration of the human as we know it, the former is a category of the future, in which something new may arise from the remnants of what has become inert and sterile. For this reason, the posthuman does not appear as a full-term human embryo but as a grotesque ghost-like zygote with still vaguely human traces. As I will elaborate in my discussions of the next dreams, the correspondence between zygotes and ghosts indicates that the past always casts its shadow on the future, whence the future might foster hope for renewal but never for innocence.

Aaron's second dream: the Lady of the Beasts

... Immensely tall, eternally noble, the woman paces through gray streaming clouds. In rituals of grief she moves, her heavy hair bound with dark jewels; she gestures to her head, her heart, a mourning queen pacing beside a leaden sea. Chained beasts move slowly at her heels, the tiger stepping with sad

majesty, the ape mimicking her despair. She plucks the bindings from her hair in agony, it streams on the icy wind. She bends to loose the tiger, urging it to freedom. But the beast-form wavers and swells, thins out; the tiger floats to ghostly life among the stars. The ape is crouching at her feet; she lays her long fingers on its head. It has turned to stone. The woman begins a death chant, breaking her bracelets one by one beside the sea ... (A83; italics in original)

In Aaron's first dream it was the grotesque imagery that offered an entry to the narrative dynamic of 'A Momentary Taste of Being', which I have interpreted so far as a cosmological fantasy of the exhaustion (or, its entropy and dissipation) of patriarchy in both its genital–sexual and social–political aspects. As yet I have not explicitly addressed the dimension of Aaron's subconscious as it gradually becomes manifest in the dreams. The second dream, then, I see as a transition from outer space to inner space. It does not yet thematize the contents of what Aaron has repressed but rather points to what may be called Aaron's 'anthropology', his contemplation of the nature of humankind. Here we will have to confront ourselves with the question of to what extent Aaron's views coincide with, or perhaps rather go against, the grain of the text, as elaborated in my interpretation proceeding from the first dream. For gaining access to the coded text of the second dream I shall turn to various implied intertextual references, which, in turn, are cross-references to other moments in the text.

The imagery of the dream calls up several associations with mythological woman figures. For instance, a desperate Queen Dido, in mortal grief and self-blame after Aeneas' fleet sailed away from the coasts of Carthage: 'a mourning queen pacing beside a leaden sea'. On the other hand, the relation between noble woman and animals seems crucial in this dream. In Chapter V, the connection of this dream with the battle of the woman and the dragon in chapter 12 of the Revelation of John will be investigated. In the context of the present chapter I will consider in the first instance the mythical Lady of the Beasts. This figure is not to be reduced to a particular goddess or mythical human being but rather should be taken as a traditional and recurrent topos of a goddess who presides over animal life. These goddesses are often imagined either together with animals or as animals themselves. In her book *Women as Mythmakers*, Estella Lauter has elaborated how the Lady of the Beasts serves as a source of inspiration for many contemporary female poets and visual artists (such as Remedios Varo, Léonor Fini, Margaret Atwood and many others). '[S]he symbolizes a purposive, active ordering of multiple drives.'[45] Taken as a modern image, she can function as an integrative model:

A Lady of the Beasts combining the interests of body, mind and spirit, she would be in tune with the ancient cycles of nature, familiar with the worlds revealed by modern science, and capable of the mystic's vision of wholeness. Fully conscious, she would be a reflective being as well as a sexual, procreative one.[46]

The Lady's image expresses aptly the permeability of boundaries between the self and other phenomena, which is, according to Lauter, experienced by many of the artists whose work she discusses. What happened to the Lady of the Beasts in Aaron's dream, however? Why is it that instead of joyful integration of forces we seem to witness their painful disintegration?

As I see it, here the Lady is a goddess in the sense of an idealized representation of humanity (*humanitas*): 'immensely tall, eternally noble'. We begin to grasp her fate when we involve the lines of poetry read by Lory to her brother at the end of the first part of the narrative. They are from a poem by Alfred Tennyson, the 'earnest Victorian' (A82), as Aaron calls him ironically. Aaron, absent-minded and not used to the 'convoluted' language of poetry, only catches the last two lines:

> ... *Grow upward, working out the beast, and let the ape and tiger die* ...
> (A82; italics in text)

These lines are derived from number CXIII from *In Memoriam A.H.H.* (1850), a long philosophical poem, composed of 131 short lyrics.[47] It contains an evolutionist account of the painful struggles of humankind to become a moral being. In the poem humanity is urged to get rid of its animality, that is its sexuality and aggression, symbolized by ape and tiger. The quotation marks a telling difference between Aaron and Lory's 'anthropology', conveyed to the reader partly through dialogues, partly mediated by Aaron's thoughts.

Aaron thinks of Lory as morally fanatic: 'A too-clear vision of good, a too-sure hatred of evil. No love lost, in between. Not much use for living people' (A82–3). He himself defends that there will 'always be some bad stuff as long as you have people', but 'people aren't all that rotten' (A121). Lory, however, objects that even on board of the spaceship she feels 'the savagery underneath, just waiting to break loose' (A121). And she opposes to it a radical morality: 'Human beings must change' (A121). In keeping with Tennyson, she places moral evolution in a direct line to biological evolution:

> Why do we use the word human for the animal part of us, Arn? Aggression—that's human. Cruelty, hatred, greed—that's human. That's just what *isn't* human, Arn. It's so sad. To be truly human we must leave all that behind. (A121)

In Aaron's view, on the other hand, the cure may be worse than the disease—'You'd liquidate ninety procent of the race to achieve your utopia', he flings in Lory's face. And later he thinks:

> [T]he life of this world is not gentle, Lory. It wasn't gentleness that got you out here. It was the drives of ungentle, desperate, glory-hunting human apes. The fallible humanity you somehow can't see ... (A124)

The transformation of the Lady of the Beasts that Aaron envisages in his dream anticipates his worst fears, as it seems. First the woman embodies, in Lauter's wording, the 'purposive, active ordering of multiple drives': notwithstanding her congenial relation with the ape and the tiger, symbols of human sexual and aggressive drives, the tall woman has the animals chained, that means under control. Yet her rituals of grief testify to her awareness that she is on the verge of a tragic if not fatal watershed. Some unknown urge, visibly going against her feelings, is making her loose not only the bindings from her hair but also the chains of the beasts. In Tennyson's words, she is 'working out the beast', attempting to establish a separation of human and animal. As we see, it even leads to the vanishing of the drives altogether. Does the death of the beast(s) bring about what Lory calls a humanity that is 'healed, made whole' (A142), and 'truly human at last' (A149)? On the contrary, the impending events on the *Centaur* apparently prove Aaron to be right: without their drives humans are 'drained of something vital' (A160) and therefore of their very humanity. The death chant of the woman in the dream is Aaron's own: 'Ah Christ, the poor old tiger, the poor ape, everything Lory hated—all gone now. Who cares about a sperm's personality?' (A161).

In the terms of cultural history, Aaron's opposition to Tennyson's device of 'working out the beast' could be marked as a modernist rejection of Victorian values.[48] His 'modernist' point of view implies a recognition of the indispensability of our animal aspects, the sexual and aggressive drives, as a factor in the vitality of humankind. As Aaron is no libertine, however, he certainly does not propose a celebration of the beast; rather his view involves a rational, we might say, 'negentropic' integration of seemingly dichotomous elements. Or, to put it in Lauter's terms, a purposive, active ordering of multiple drives. Only by dealing with our drives we will not get overruled by them, as, in this ironic twist of cosmic fate, happened to Lory and all the other crew members. Except Aaron.

Is the matter settled then? Should we perhaps even take Aaron's 'anthropology' as that of the text itself? Once again I find the case to be far more ambiguous. That is to say, Aaron himself is more ambiguous than his articulated views convey. Does he really stand apart from Lory and the other crew members? From Lory's utopic morality, yes. But what about the non-rational level, what about his own sexual desire and aggressive drives? Before moving over to the third dream, in which we will get as close to Aaron's subconscious as we can get, I still want to draw attention to a cluster of mythological images emerging from the text which underscore, in my opinion, Aaron's ambiguity.

First there is the image of the *Centaur*.[49] In Greek mythology the *Centauri* were rather rough creatures with a human body's upper part and a horse's rump. Originally they were demons of the inhospitable mountain woods and the animal drives. From the fourth century BC they can be found in the train of Dionysos, together with satyrs and bacchants. Considered in this light, the spaceship *Centaur* may be interpreted as a model of what Lory calls 'the savagery underneath, just waiting to break loose' (A121), or, in Alice Sheldon's words, 'the runaway breakdown of the system'. Or, in the mode of Theweleit, it is a mental armour against aggressive libidinal energies waiting to burst out with a vengeance. In addition, we find a kindred image implied when we recall Lory's quotation from Tennyson's. The whole stanza reads as follows:

> [...] Arise and fly
> The reeling Faun, the sensual feast;
> Move upward, working out the beast,
> And let the ape and tiger die.

Besides the ape and the tiger, the Faun also is urged to vanish. Faunus is the Roman transformation of Pan, the Arcadian pastoral god with goat's legs and horns. This Faunus/Pan, moreover, is evoked at the very beginning of 'A Momentary Taste of Being'. After his first dream,

> Aaron sits up still cold with meaningless bereavement. What the hell is it, what's tearing at him? 'Great Pan is dead,' he mutters stumbling to the narrow wash-stall. The lament that echoed round the world ... (A65/66)

This utterance about Pan is a reference to a legend told by the Greek writer Plutarch. It says that a voice instructed a group of sailors, on their way from Greece to Rome in the days of emperor Tiberius (AD 14–37), to announce while passing a certain island that *the Great Pan is dead*. In response the sailors heard a *deep lamentation*. In 'A Momentary Taste of Being' Aaron later will lament the death of humanity's vitality. But what other loss does he mourn first? What does 'the Great Pan' represent? Which 'reeling Faun, sensual feast' may be alluded to?

'What is tearing at me?' Aaron wonders—a different way of putting this is would be asking what is *haunting* him. Let me conjure up Aaron's 'ghosts' for a moment. The gigantic blastomeres he observes emerging from the dying crew members have a double identity: they are also ghosts. From this angle, 'A Momentary Taste of Being' is a science fiction descendant of the Gothic ghost stories, in which the ghost re-emerges in the guise of cosmic biology.

> They're not ... rational. Not at all. They change, too, they take on colors or something from your mind. Did I say that? I'm not sure they're really visible at all, maybe the mind senses them and constructs an appearance. But recognizable. You can see traces. (A156)

The posthuman is simultaneously human's double, its shadowy guarantee as well as negation. In a rereading of Freud's essay on the uncanny (*das Unheimliche*), Hélène Cixous identifies the ghost as the most direct expression of the uncanny.[50] The uncanny is a figure of deep uncertainty and ambivalence as it refers both to the familiar and to something strange and concealed, to what is visible and invisible, to what is real and imagined. Because they are the fiction of our relationship with death, ghosts reveal the highest degree of the uncanny. Unlike Freud, however, Cixous does not believe that the uncanny effect lies in the fact that the ghost announces or proves the existence of death as such. According to her, the ghost is intolerable because it

> erases the limit which exists between two states, neither alive nor dead; passing through, the dead man returns in the manner of the Repressed. It is his coming back which makes the ghost what he is, just as it is the return of the Repressed that inscribes the repression. In the end, death is never anything more than the disturbance of the limits. The impossible is to die. If all which has been lost returns, as Freud illustrated in the *Traumdeutung*, nothing is ever lost if everything is replaceable, nothing has ever disappeared and nothing is ever sufficiently dead ...[51]

Even though he did not want to credit them with any spiritual or psychic quality, Aaron did recognize the blastomeres as ghosts after all, *his* ghosts. His suggestion that 'maybe the mind senses them and constructs an appearance' points to awareness of ghosts as the (return of the) repressed. He sees creatures that are 'combined products', partly still human, and partly very alien, uniting in their 'form' the death of the old and the birth of something new. They are, as such, figures that 'erase the limit which exists between two states'. The zygotes transform into ghosts and vice versa; the past starts to haunt the future, while the future affirms the past. But what is this repressed which returns to inscribe the repression? Let us turn to Aaron's third dream, finally.

Aaron's third dream: the membrane

> Silence ... Bright, clinical emptiness, no clouds, no weeping. Horizon,
> infinity. Somewhere words rise, speaking silence: I AM THE SPOUSE.
> Cancel sound. Aaron, invisible and microbe-sized, sees on the floor
> of infinity a very beautifully veined silver membrane which he now
> recognizes as an adolescent's prepuce, the disjecta of his first
> operation ... (A128)

Aaron's third dream appears to the reader a very dense piece of text,
multidimensional and polysemic as dreams usually are. The atmosphere
in this dream is different from the previous ones—'no clouds, no weeping'.
Cosmic and psychic turmoil have calmed down and given way to silence,
bright, clinical emptiness and infinity. A vast space is evoked without any
hiding places; Aaron has to face what is 'tearing at him'. Reduced to the
size of a microbe, to the size of a sperm in other words, lost in the infinity
of outer space, he observes the remnants of his past. The universe looks
like an immense screen for the projection of silent movies. Explicative
words appear on this screen as a comment accompanying the images: I AM
THE SPOUSE. On the cosmic level the double-gendered word spouse may
refer to the unknown subject of the cosmic insemination, an alien from a
world in which the human sexes are irrelevant. 'Cancel sound', then, has
the function of a textual hinge. First, it suggests the registration of a fact:
there is a sound of cancellation: the differences between the sexes are
cancelled in the denotation of the word spouse. Next, it may also imply an
order or exhortation: cancel sound in order to let the images speak. To
speak of yet another kind of cancellation of differences. Therefore we have
to move over to the image of the membrane.

What precisely is this 'very beautifully veined silver membrane' Aaron
sees? He himself recognizes it as an adolescent's prepuce, his own as it
seems. Both the *clinical* emptiness and the notion of an operation suggest
a medical reason for Aaron's circumcision. On the other hand, circumcision
is, of course, a cultural and religious symbol for entering manhood (to
which I will come back in Chapter IV). Just *man*hood, though? Since in a
dream signs and meanings shift very quickly, I want to suggest that the
membrane might just as well refer to something else: to a girl's *hymen*. The
virginal membrane also is a traditional symbol of the demarcation between
childhood and adulthood, its removal hence the symbol (and the result)
of sexual initiation. From this point of view, the 'first operation' may have
been performed both *on* (circumcision) and *by* (sexual intiation) Aaron.

A third meaning of the membrane fits the description 'the disjecta of
his first operation' more literally than the other two. Earlier on in the story
the memory of 'his first psychosurgery patient a zillion years ago at Houston

Enclave' (A75) had crossed Aaron's mind. This first patient was a 'sad murderer' by the neutral name of Thomas Brown. The 'disjecta' of that operation, I deduce, were the parts of the brains that were supposed to cause Brown's uncontrollable and destructive drives. Later Aaron recalls the Thomas Brown of his medical practice on Earth when reflecting on the particular qualification Captain Yellaston has given to the alien encounter:

> He saw it as death, the whole thing. Intuition in his locked-up guts, the fear—Sex equals death. How right you are, old man. Funny, I used to treat patients for thinking that. Therapy—Of course it was a different, let's say order of sex. (A157–8)

Yet another, fourth interpretation would unite the triple meanings of the membrane—prepuce, hymen and cerebral membrane—and their various respective removals. When Aaron consents to the view that 'sex equals death' but that of course 'it was a different, let's say order of sex' (A158), he does not only refer to the human contact with the alien but also, and maybe primarily, to his own past.

The reader finds out about Aaron's past when Lory confronts her brother with it:

> I really brought it [the alien specimen] back for you, Arn. I wanted us to look at is together. Remember how we used to share our treasures, that summer on the island? (A92)

Aaron is deeply shocked by her unexpected and overt allusion.

> Aaron mumbles something, walks numbly back to his room. His eyes squeezed like a man kicked in the guts. Lory, little devil—how could you? (A92)

Yet the most shocking thing to himself is not the memory but the *actuality* of his desire for his sister.

> Her thirteen-year-old body shimmers in his mind, sends helpless heat into his penile arteries. He is imprinted forever, he fears; the rose-tipped nipples on her child's chest, the naked mons, the flushed-pearl labia. The incredible sweetness, lost forever. He had been fifteen, he had ended both their virginities on a spruce island in the Fort Ogilvy Officers' Recreational Reserve the year before their parents died. He groans, wondering if he has lost both their souls, too, though he doesn't believe in souls. Oh Lory … is it really his own lost youth he aches for?
>
> He groans again, his cortex knowing she is up to some damn thing while his medulla croons that he loves her only and forever, and she

him. Damn the selection board who had dismissed such incidents as insignificant, even *healthy*!' (A92–3)

He is very worried. 'Am I getting weird? Sex-fantasies about Sis, I haven't had that trouble for years. It's being locked up with her' (A103). He tries to mitigate his revived desire by taking refuge with his lover Solange whose impersonal receptivity and personal harmony are so comforting and normal—'Solace, Soul-ass …' (A103). 'Smart and beautiful, beautiful and smart. You're such a *healthy* person. What would I do without you?' (A108, italics added).

Linking the repressed memory of the incest back to the dream, then, first of all a rather different connotation of the phrase 'cancel sound' comes to mind: 'cross out the *adjective* meaning of sound = healthy'. Aaron and Lory did not experience a healthy, say normal, sexuality for they were each other's 'spouse'. The image of the membrane is the symbol of their shared sexual initiation. Aaron feals confused and guilt-ridden about this returned memory and desire, though he will later, after the alien contact, try to put the blame on Lory. When the latter destroys the ship's communication gear to prevent sending the red signal to Earth, her brother goes off into a fit of rage: '*She* broke it!' he yells, and a 'preadolescent fury floods him' (A147). This strongly suggests that he is not only referring to the communication equipment but to earlier 'broken' things as well …

In a 1981 postscript to her short novel *Anna, Soror …*, originally written in the 1930s, Marguerite Yourcenar mentions two predominant themes in literary presentations of brother–sister incest.[52] The first is the perfect accordance (of souls) between two people of the same blood, who are isolated because of this very relationship. Secondly, there is the dizzy spell of transgression experienced by both spirit and senses.[53] Unlike cross-generation incest, between father and daughter or mother and son, the transgression of brother and sister is usually represented as a *voluntary* act of incest. In the light of Yourcenar's findings, can 'A Momentary Taste of Being' be called a typical brother–sister incest story (apart from the science fiction dimension of course)? To a certain extent this may be the case, provided that the reader, as I have done so far, adopts Aaron's viewpoint. Aaron's actualized memories attest to a special, passionate bond between himself and his sister, which, indeed, was consummated on an isolated island. Presently the bond is causing in him a mixture of melancholy, fear and, irrefutably, desire. Until the very end he will be torn apart by his desire, or 'the pull' as it is called in the story. During the crew members' frantic race towards the alien light after the opening of the module, at a certain moment Aaron too is overtaken by the alien spell.

[He] lets himself start across the ship, going with the pull. Joy opens in him, it is like a delicious sliding, like letting go sexually in his head ... Am I acting rationally? (A152)

In no comment on 'A Momentary Taste of Being' with which I am acquainted is there mention of the incestuous relation between Aaron and Lory. Without this dimension, however, the story makes sense only in a superficial way. In my interpretation, its significance is derived from the very analogy between humanity's desire for the alien and Aaron's desire for Lory: both are forms of 'alien' sexuality. In a general sense, the connection between macrocosmic and subjective level is acknowledged by Siegel:

> We are ... constantly aware of Aaron's sexual impulses, which Tiptree ironically juxtaposes to the broader, metagenetic or biological 'meaning' of reproduction when the humans fertilize the alien eggs.[54]

However, the emphasis on reproduction obscures the typical role of sexuality in the narrative, in either 'micro' or 'macro' perspective. The story may indeed be seen as a statement about the insignificance of humankind in cosmic perspective, 'except as one of many examples of a bizarre, unpredictable, and ever-changing biological evolution'.[55] Yet no less pertinent is the negative outlook on sexuality, which is represented as an entropic drive of a closed system, that is, as anti-cultural disorder, a fatal dissolution of boundaries. This concerns, respectively, the closed systems of the blood-bond of Aaron and Lory Kaye and the overrationalized bond of the *Centaur*'s population. We see, then, the drive for incestuous transgression surging from beneath Aaron's well-balanced medical and sexual identity, as well as the outburst of sexual drives from beneath the constrained organization structure of the spaceship.

Notwithstanding the vehemence of the entropic pull, however, Aaron does not yield to it this time. As such he apparently represents a 'negentropic' morality. He is 'the sperm who said no', as he ironically calls himself, although he does not consider it a heroic resistence at all: 'Why didn't I go, too? Who knows. Statistical phenomenon. Defective tail. My foot got caught ...' (A161). Besides, can the desire ever be really stopped again? Will the ghosts ever stop haunting him? Or in the *pen*ultimate words with which Aaron, on the edge of delirious dissolution, signs off:

> Little sister, you were a good sperm, you swam hard. You made the connection. She wasn't crazy, you know. Ever really. She knew something was wrong with us ... Healed, made whole? All those months ... a wall away from heaven, the golden breasts of god. The

end of pain, the queen couzy ... fighting it all the way ... Oh, Lory
stay with me, don't die—*Christ, the pull, the terrible sweet pull*—
(A162–3, italics in text)[56]

Signing off?

The *ultimate* thing Aaron imparts to the reader is: '[Maybe my condition is
of deep scientific interest ...] I don't dream any more.' I have step by step
provided the images of the dreams with possible significations by connecting the images, on the one hand, to the events in the story, and, to
other textual signs, on the other. What we see expressed in Aaron's
conclusion is his awareness of the repressed that has become manifest to
him: he has performed his *Traumarbeit*, while I as a reader followed in his
tracks, or, in my turn, guided the interpretation. Now Aaron faces the
ghosts of his past which, ironically, are the germs of the future as well. He
is the witness of an ineluctable process in which humankind dissolves into
a posthuman future.

We look with him at/in the distorting mirror of the cosmos, in which
humankind appears as a swarm of sperms swimming into annihilation. It
seems a terrifying solution, the product of a ruthless imagination. Perhaps
it is. But we simultaneously hear the echoes of the *carcajada*, the sardonic
laughter in the face of unrelieved pain. By launching the grotesque phallus,
'A Momentary Taste of Being' right at the start identifies as well as ridicules
the icon of patriarchal power, in both its sexual and social-symbolic
dimensions. By the end of the story it droops in the face of powers beyond-
the-human. In a grotesque reversal, the spermatic logic (the *logos spermatikos*,
the seminal reason of the phallus) is emasculated by means of the cosmic
fertilization in which human beings are 'nothing but gametes' (A157).

At this very point we heard Captain Yellaston mumble that 'sex equals
death', while Aaron consented to this view. What I want to suggest is that
'A Momentary Taste of Being' at the same time repeats and subverts this
view. The use of the grotesque implies an indictment against it as well as
its endorsement. On the one hand, therefore, we have to grant Lilian
Heldreth's observation that many of Tiptree's stories show great affinity
with George Bataille's philosophical views on the close relation between
eroticism, violence, and death.[57] In reference to Yellaston/Aaron, Heldreth
summarizes:

> Sex equals death. Life equals death. In Bataille's words, 'In the long
> or short run, reproduction demands the death of the parents who
> produced their young only to give fuller rein to the forces of
> annihilation'.[58]

Bukatman also finds common ground between Bataille's language and science fiction in a more general sense, in that both of them 'eschew the perspective of the individual for an evolutionary, anthropological, and even cosmological discourse of the nature of the human existence'.[59] In both discourses, transcendence and dissolution of individual subjectivity is the central point, but 'rare is the science fiction text that produces "death" through an explicitly physical (or textual) violence'.[60] 'A Momentary Taste of Being' obviously is one of these exceptional texts. Many other texts use what Bukatman considers to be strategies of denial, fantasies of resurrection of the (male) subject, like the rebirth in *2001: A Space Odyssey* discussed above. As we have concluded, the dissolution of humankind into the posthuman species in Tiptree's is entirely at odds with this model.

And yet, I believe this 'Bataillean' interpretation of Yellaston's sex/death equation covers only part of the story, for it ignores the fact that sex in 'A Momentary Taste of Being', as in Tiptree's other work, in the first place refers to *masculine* sexuality, or rather, to a particular model of sexuality that haunts the Western mind and body. It is the fantasy of what Elizabeth Grosz calls a 'hydraulic sexuality, a biologically regulated need or instinct, a compulsion, urge, or mode of physical release'.[61] Yellaston repeats the *intrinsic* linkage between sex and death assumed in Freudian psychoanalytic theory, in which Eros and Thanatos, pleasure principle and death drive, presuppose and reinforce each other.[62] In fact, it is a thermodynamically informed model, in which the death drive imitates the 'heat death' of the universe in its inclination towards maximum entropy and minimum energy. To an extent, 'A Momentary Taste of Being' as such seems to repeat the Freudian 'hydraulic' model of sexuality.

> Not only is the sexual act *grosso modo* linked to death and through it, to the reproduction of the species, but more significantly, the eroticism of orgasm—at least of male orgasm ...—is modelled by Freud on the build-up of excitation, the swelling of the sexual organ, the accumulation of energies and fluids, their release, and then the organ's detumescence and state of contentment.[63]

But once again, the representation of this model in 'A Momentary Taste of Being' implicates its very exhaustion. Furthermore, in displacing sexuality to the cosmological level, Tiptree, I propose, deploys her own strategies of denial. Highlighting cosmic chance and mystery mitigates an unfashionably pessimistic view of, and even repugnance to the masculine. Aaron Kaye reflects this process of veiling: the fact that we are made to observe and suffer with him, share his memories, desire and worst fears, obfuscates that he finds himself stuck in the middle of a grim ridicule of masculine, 'hydraulic' sexuality. The grotesque, we can summarize now, is a means to keep the either feared or experienced horror of aggressive and violent outbursts of this type of sexuality at bay. Aaron is an ambivalent if not tragic figure, apparently embodying the tendency of Tiptree's text in its entirety. Being the 'sperm who said no', he resists the entropic inclination of the other crew members, that is, the urges of the death drive. Facing a meaningless life in utter solitude, his fate nonetheless is even more cruel than that of the others. The aporia of the text is that the negativity of masculine sexual and symbolic organization weighs heavy upon protagonist and reader, while, on the other hand, there is *no other model of sexuality available*.

In conclusion, Aaron doesn't dream any more. In terms of a subjective history, there is no future for him. Neither hope nor illusions are left. Only the pull of entropy, the transgressive desire for his sister, is still acting on him. *But what about this sister?* Many questions on different levels might be addressed to her, were it only possible. How did she experience the incest with her brother? Why did Tennyson's device matter so much to her? What was her relation with the alien? Throughout the narrative the reader was guided by Aaron's perception not only of the macrocosmic events and his own erotic relation with Lory, but also of Lory herself. Methodologically speaking, so far I both acknowledged and in turn observed and criticized his focalization in my interpretations of the text. Now let me go a step further and ask whether it is also possible to obtain a different view from within the narrative? Lory is no focalizing agency. Nevertheless, I think it is possible to shed light on Lory's point of view by drawing attention to elements of the text that until now have been neglected or underexposed. For instance, at the prime moment of crisis, in the midst of the flood of crew members fighting their way to the Light, the following thought jumps to Aaron's mind: 'Lory! She's in league with that thing, he knows it, this is her crazy plot' (A140).

That 'thing', of course, is the alien life-form, producing the hypnotizing light. And indeed, being the only eyewitness Lory has a special connection to the planet from where she took the specimen as a 'treasure to share with Aaron'. In the next chapter I will examine in what ways and to what extent focusing on the alien may disclose what Aaron grasped as Lory's 'crazy plot'.

III. Father in Crisis, Mother Rises?
1. The *Choric* Fantasy

An alien mother/daughter plot

If Lory is indeed 'in league' with the alien, and if the dissipation of hu/man entropic energy and the cosmic reproduction are part of her 'crazy plot', the question arises what the nature of her alliance with the alien could be. What alternative plot besides the one derived from Aaron's focalization emerges when we highlight Lory's relationship with the alien?

I want to suggest that another possible plot in 'A Momentary Taste of Being' is what Marianne Hirsch indicates as a 'mother/daughter plot'. In her book *The Mother/Daughter Plot*, Hirsch examines the intersection of familial structures and structures of plotting in Western women's writings of the nineteenth and twentieth century. At the centre of her attention is the relation between mothers and daughters, who are 'the female figures neglected by psychoanalytic theories and submerged in traditional plot structures'.[1] Freud's notion of the family romance (*Familienroman*) functions as a controlling figure for her interpretations of nineteenth-century, modernist and postmodern novels by women writers. The Freudian family romance comes down to an imaginary interrogation of the subject's origins, by which story and the familial experience get linked together.

> Through fantasy, the developing individual liberates himself from the constraints of family by imagining himself to be an orphan or a bastard and his 'real' parents to be more noble than the 'foster' family in which he is growing up. The essence of the Freudian family romance is the imaginative act of replacing the parent (for boys clearly the father) with another, superior figure.[2]

Hirsch investigates the divergent versions of the family romance that surface in female-authored novels. The development of the female revision of the Freudian pattern she summarizes as follows. In conventional nineteenth-century plots the female family romance is guided by the heroine's desire for self-determination, and hence a disidentification with the fate of other women, in particular of her mother. This implies that mothers tend to be absent or silent in these novels, while maternal attachments are often displaced by fraternal bonds. In modernist plots, the heroine's desire for independence is supplemented by artistic ambitions, while she displays an oscillation between maternal/female and paternal/male affiliations. The feminist family romance pattern of postmodern writings from the 1970s onwards allows still more varieties of relational identities to arise, which are all 'based on the heroines' refusal of conventional heterosexual romance and marriage plots, and, furthermore, on their disidentification from conventional constructions of femininity'.[3] These writings, fictional texts as well as psychoanalytic revisions of Freudian paradigms, feature mothers prominently and explore fantasies and models of mother–daughter bonding. According to Hirsch, however, the story of motherhood remains the unspeakable plot of Western culture. Even in the last-mentioned texts the daughterly perspective is dominant. Nevertheless she observes the emergence of maternal discourse at various places in feminist discourse, ranging from the psychoanalytic theory of Julia Kristeva to the complex and multiple featuring of the maternal subject in the tradition of black American authors such as Toni Morrison and Alice Walker from the 1960s onwards.[4]

To read 'A Momentary Taste of Being' as a mother/daughter plot and a female revision of the family romance at first glance seems anything but an obvious option. A recognizable mother is nowhere near to be seen in Tiptree's story, and the female 'heroine' of the story, Lory Kaye, is not portrayed as a daughter but as a sister that is enveloped in her brother's perspective. I want to argue, however, that in science fiction mother/daughter plots may be expressed in rather unusual and sometimes—such as in the case of 'A Momentary Taste of Being'—opaque terms.

There are not many human mothers in science fiction, especially not in the traditional male-written type. *Aliens* with maternal connotations, on the other hand, could be encountered more frequently, especially in and even more so on of the covers of the American pulp-magazines of the 1940s and 1950s, where they appear as monstrous, demonic, gigantic and mostly malignant. These pulp representations of female aliens were largely anthropomorphic, reminiscences mostly of mythological figures like amazons, giantesses, Medusa-like figures and witches. Robin Roberts may have a case when she suggests that feminist writers, many of whom were introduced to the science fiction genre through reading the pulps, have transformed the negative qualifiers of these monstrous images of women into features of feminine strength. I do have problems, however, with her conclusion that feminist science fiction thus 'tames the figure of the archaic mother',[5] which I consider a simplification for various reasons. Firstly, not all monstrous or gigantic maternally connoted aliens in science fiction can be attributed feminist potential since many of them do not resemble human women at all. Think of the cinematic *Alien* trilogy, in which the alien clearly has maternal connotations but is too monstrous to allow for any feminist identification. Furthermore, as we shall see in the next chapter, the Kristevan archaic mother (to which Roberts refers here) is a much more ambivalent figure, both life-threatening and life-giving, than usually suggested in the plot aimed at 'taming' her. Especially in feminist science fiction, contrary to classical male-authored science fiction, the female/ maternal alien need not represent unambiguously a horrific mother but might also be an object—and who knows, even a subject—of desire.

As regards the alien in 'A Momentary Taste of Being', it is anything but an anthropomorphic (let alone gynemorphic) figure which is encountered face to face by the human protagonists. The actual alien remains an unseen mystery in the story. Instead, there is a strange substance, which looks like a bunch of big colourful grapes endowed with hypnotic power. According to Aaron Kaye, the alien could be anything: 'some creatures or some race' (A158), or according to his assistent Bill Coby's speculations: 'it was god, maybe ... Or a planet ...' (A151). Nevertheless Aaron and Bill recognize the 'grapes' as a form of cosmic female reproductive material, as the 'ova' coming together with the human 'sperms'. The alien's palpable sign is interpreted as female procreative matter. In other words, what surfaces in Tiptree's text is, no matter how odd it seems at first sight considering the dominant spermatic logic of the text, a manifestation of maternal discourse.

I want to go on and argue that the story's invisible alien in outer space points to the repressed powers of maternity in Western culture. We can achieve a closer understanding of its re-emergence in 'A Momentary Taste of Being''s posthuman setting by turning to the structure of the female family romance Hirsch detected in the novels of nineteenth-century authors like the Brontës, George Sand or George Eliot. Remarkably, Tiptree's narrative shows many correspondences with respect to the familial organization in these texts. The mother is conspicuously absent; not only did none of the crew members of the *Centaur* leave any close ties behind, but neither is there any explicit memory of a mama Kaye in the old days. There is only mention of Aaron and Lory's *parents* having been killed in an accident the year after the incestuous incident on the spruce island, and that their *father* had been Lieutenant-General Kaye. In addition, incestuous fraternal bonds have replaced maternal attachments as a primary site of affection.

Unlike in the nineteenth-century realistic novels, however, the repressed maternal returns with a vengeance in Tiptree's twentieth-century science fiction text. It does so not as a female human character, not even as a distinct extraterrestrial being, but as an undefinable posthuman force. I shall argue that this unrepresentable maternal alien should be interpreted in terms of an unfulfillable desire for a return to an imaginary oneness with the mother. Further examination of the text will disclose that it is pervaded by symptoms of such maternal desire. Let me first spot these symptoms to continue my argument from there.

Traces of a desire for the mother
The first points I would like to draw attention to are the moments of Aaron's awakening from the three dreams discussed in the previous chapter. After he wakes up from his first dream about the planet–testicle pushing the monster penis towards the stars, Aaron's 'throat is sobbing reflexively, his eyes are weeping', he experiences an 'icy grief', and he is feeling 'cold with meaningless bereavement' (A65). In the previous chapter, I have discussed his then muttered sentences about the death of Great Pan, and 'the lament that echoed round the world' (A66), as an intertextual reference to various (Victorian) shapes of the classical god of the fields. But Pan can also be taken more literally as the Greek neuter word *pan*, traditionally indicating the all-embracing unity of either the philosophical Universe or the nourishing great Mother. Not surprisingly, therefore, in the next sentence Aaron wishes for Solange, his emphatical, *motherly* lover.

Then, waking up from his second dream, Aaron again feels his eyes 'streaming with grief', his pillow is even soaked. He hears his own throat gasping, 'a sound he hasn't made since—*since his parents died*, he remembers sharply' (A83, my italics). This time the next sentence says that 'he is acutely aware of a direction underfoot, an invisible line leading down through the hull to the sealed-up scouter, to the alien inside. Lory's alien in there' (A83–4).

Finally, after his last dream, he finds himself awake in 'foetal position' (A128), which directly points to Aaron's two other dreams that were not introduced until now. These dreams circle around the figure of the homosexual Lieutenant Tighe, nickname Tiger, who, at first sight, has the looks of a 'prototype Beautiful Boy who lives forever with his white aviator's silk blowing in the wind of morning' (A79). Nevertheless, Tighe 'stands for disaster' (A78) because, as the result of an accident with a loose oxygen tank three years ago, he has 'an obscene dent where his left parietal arch should be' (A79). And indeed, Tighe was the first to be transformed into a 'blastomere-ghost' and whose dead body was found by Aaron. The latter dreams about Tiger twice. In the first of these dreams,

> ... *Tighe drifts in through the walls, curled in a foetal clasp, his genital sac enormous. But it's a different Tighe. He's green, for one thing, Aaron sees.*

And vastly puffy, like a huge cauliflower or a cumulus cloud. Not frightening. Not anything, really; Aaron watches neutrally as cumulus-cloud-green Tighe swells, thins out, floats to ghostly life among the stars. One bulbous baby hand waves slowly, Ta-ta ...' (A85; italics in original).

The metaphorical tiger from Tennyson's poem, which we saw popping up in Aaron's second dream in the previous chapter, now slips into Tiger Tighe. As Aaron sees him floating to 'ghostly life among the stars', green, moreover, like the signal that will be sent to Earth, the dream apparently has a predicting value. On the other hand, we are dealing with Aaron's dream, and therefore with his fears and projections, his memories and desire, no matter how 'neutrally' he watches them. The Tighe in this dream, then, is most likely to represent Aaron's desire to be like a baby. It is a rather ambiguous image, however. While curled in a foetal clasp, Tighe's genital sac has enormous proportions, mirroring those of the testicle–Earth from the first dream. It is a fact that the testicles of new-born baby boys are often relatively large, so maybe the image can be taken in the first place as a downright physical description of a baby. On the other hand, it very much suggests a mockery of men's desire to return to the imaginary safety and innocence of the womb, a desire we already encountered in the final sequence of *2001: A Space Odyssey*. The image of the Italian bambino (a sweet Baby Jesus figure) into which Tighe is transformed in Aaron's next dream may be read as another expression of ridicule. Here the metamorphosis of Tighe/Aaron into a grotesque baby is completed:

> Tighe's face big as the wall, garlanded with fruits and flowers like an Italian bambino plaque. The pink and green flowers tinkle, chime elfland horns. *Tan tara!* Centripetal melodies. *Tan tata! Tara! TARA!'* (A125)

This dream is described in the text as a 'neutral, almost comic hypnagogic vision' (A125) and, unlike the other four dreams, it has no italics. It comes up when Aaron drifts peacefully asleep after making love with motherly Solange. The tiger has turned into a merry and harmless baby who is back in the maternal womb. The fact that Aaron hears *centripetal* melodies also points to such maternal origin. And in their sounds, 'Tara! T A R A !' we are reminded of Scarlett O'Hara in Margaret Mitchell's all-American epic *Gone with the Wind*, going back to her place of origins: the plantation Tara and her black 'mammy', 'the last link with the old days', as is stated on the novel's concluding page. Perhaps we could say that the allusion to the context of North American slavery and obsolete racist familial relations underlines in a roundabout way the profound ambivalence of the return to the maternal origin which, as I shall contend, characterizes Tiptree's text

at large. Although the desire for the mother obviously cannot be
suppressed, the reference to Tara at the same time exposes this desire as
regressive and nostalgic, not only in an individual but in a socio-cultural
sense as well.

Lieutenant Tighe himself had already hinted at Mitchell's text, or at
least what it points to, before Aaron incorporated it in his dream. Because
Tighe was mentally injured after his unauthorized approach of the alien
life-form, he is held in sleep-therapy. During a checkup, Aaron observes
the following:

> Tighe's mouth is working, trying to say something in his sleep. 'Hoo,
> huh.' The speech circuits hunt across the wastelands of the ruined
> lobe. 'Huhhh ... Huh-home'. His lashes lift, the sky-blue eyes find
> Aaron. (A79)

Later, after the opening of the alien's module, Tighe's relationship
with/desire for the maternal becomes still more explicit. During the turmoil
of people all running towards the alien light, Aaron suddenly spots Tighe
near the port of the module. He asks him, 'What's in that boat, Tiger? The
alien, did you see it? What is it?' (A144). And then, Tighe's face wavers,
crumples. "Mu ... muh," his mouth jerks. "Mother"' (A144). Aaron,
however, uncomprehendingly concludes that Tighe does not talk sense,
'No help here' (A144), and hurries on to get away from the lure of the
alien.

Psychomachia: the story as mother/daughter plot
So far it seems as if in 'A Momentary Taste of Being' we are dealing with
the representation of a classical Oedipal desire for the mother by the son.
To what extent does it make sense to speak of a mother/daughter plot with
respect to the story? My response would be that it does not so much concern
an alternative plot *in* the story, but that the story *as such* can be read as a
mother/daughter plot. Let me explain.

Tiptree's stories from the 1970s especially contain many examples of
complex mother/child dyads. Seldom, however, they do appear as
unconcealed mother/daughter plots. In 'Mother In the Sky With
Diamonds' (1971), for instance, a male space insurance inspector is trying
to protect his very old mother, who lives in an ancient spaceship called
Ragnarok, from the influence of drug-runners; 'Painwise' (1972) is a
stylistically experimental narrative overflowing with veiled signs of
maternal discourse; 'Love is the Plan, the Plan is Death' (1973) is a horrific
tale featuring furry aliens involved in a deadly mother/child intimacy. 'A
Momentary Taste of Being' can be located among this type of displaced
mother/child stories. Unlike in the previous stories, here an actual daughter

is put on the scene, even if mediated by her brother's eyes and/or voice. As such 'A Momentary Taste of Being' presents a paradigmatic example of what Nancy Steffen-Fluhr calls Tiptree's *psychomachias*.[6]

Psychomachical configurations are dialogues between various parts of the self, or, as I prefer to say, the multiple selves of a subject in change. In many of Tiptree's writings, these dialogues rather appear as dramas of a subject at *war* (from the Greek *machè*) with itself/its selves, that is to say as projections of inner conflicts on cosmic conflicts. Outer space becomes a metaphor for inner psychic space. In 'A Momentary Taste of Being' we find a 'psychomachical doubling across ostensible gender lines'.[7] In this story, the classical mother/son relation makes place for a brother/sister relation to the mother. Aaron and Lory Kaye, in other words, are two conflicting sides—or aspects—of one and the same child. Let me emphasize, however, that the focalizing brother/son figure nevertheless still embodies the dominant aspect of the narrative. The story of *daughterhood* is not altogether unspeakable but expressed in a still muffled voice.

When the daughter's story begins to surface in 'A Momentary Taste of Being', moreover, it shows a profound ambiguity, communicated through the *doppelgänger* Aaron/Lory. One might say that Aaron's desire for the mother reflects Lory's, while simultaneously contradicting it: whereas the latter is directly allied ('in league') to the alien/the mother, Aaron desires her but resists her as well ('the sperm who said no'). His own desire is displaced onto Tighe, who is a homosexual, someone who in his sexual practices crosses the gender lines, in other words. In this manner, Tighe functions as an emblem of the (re)union of Aaron and Lory, of the male/son and female/daughter part of the same subject.

With respect to the psychomachical configuration of Aaron/Lory, it is illuminating to draw attention to some striking parallels with another novella by Tiptree, 'Houston, Houston, Do You Read?', published only one year after 'A Momentary Taste of Being'.[8] In this story three male astronauts are propelled by accident 300 years into the future and come into contact with the future dwellers of Earth, an all-women community as it turns out, who reproduce themselves by cloning from a gene pool of 11,000 types. Two of the astronauts, Bud and Dave, are classic macho stereotypes, 'split projections of primitive, entropic forces within patriarchal society—and within the human personality—which threaten its dissolution'.[9] The third man, 'Doc' Orren Lorimer, is a different type, physically weaker, emphatic and sensitive, belonging neither to the men's nor to the women's world. His ambivalent position is conveyed convincingly to the reader because Doc is the focalizing agency of the narrative: 'Doc is a stranger in two lands, a psychosexually displaced person'.[10] At the end of the story, the women decide to kill Bud and Dave, 'in order to weed out the uncontrollable forces of aggression the men embody'.[11] The women also kill Lorimer, 'for his own good', because, according to them, he has incurable emotional problems.

I see a structural analogy between 'Doc' in this story and 'A Momentary Taste of Being''s psychomachia. In Doc both Aaron and Lory Kaye are incorporated. Aaron most obviously is a doctor, but Lory is a doctor too, though not a medical one (when Frank Foy, during the interrogation after returning from the planet, calls her 'Miss Kaye' (A67), she insists on being addressed as 'Dr. Kaye'). 'Orren' sounds very much like 'Aaron', while 'Lorimer' not only includes the root 'Lory' but also the French phonemes *mer* (the sea) and *mère* (the mother). These textual elements strike me as strong indications of Doc's intimate complicity with the Aaron/Lory figure. It seems that, whereas in 'A Momentary Taste of Being', as we shall see, the male and female protagonist, the brother and the sister, are divided in their relationship to the maternal, in the later story they are merged into one. That the two novellas can be seen as mirroring each other is finally confirmed when the single male that Doc Lorimer spots amongst the women of the future world turns out to be a hormonally engineered androgyne. His/her name is Andy Kay.

Steffen-Fluhr has related the psychomachias in Tiptree's work to elements of Alice Sheldon's remarkable biography, most notably to her extraordinary childhood in the interior of Africa and Asia, and to her complicated relationship with her mother, Mary Hastings Bradley. Although her interpretations are performed with scrutiny, and have stimulated me to be more observant with regard to anomalies and ambivalences in Tiptree's texts, I will not follow the biographical road in my further discussion of 'A Momentary Taste of Being'. My interpretative framework does not focus so much on the psychomachia's possible origin in the author's life as on its textual *effect*. My attention, therefore, will be directed towards unravelling the kind of mother/daughter plot that is conveyed by the narrative double Aaron–Lory in its relation to the alien.

Kristeva's *choric* fantasy

In the remaining part of this chapter and in the next chapter, I will provide two different intertextual readings of 'A Momentary Taste of Being', both presented from the viewpoint of the mother/daughter relationship. What these readings have in common is that they are connected to a particular aspect of Julia Kristeva's theory of the signifying process and the meaning of the maternal. Kristeva's psychoanalytic and cultural philosophical work has offered a rich elaboration of the issue of the structures of subjectivity, especially in relation to the paternal and maternal linguistic modes and models of authority. Her views on the maternal subject as split subject, as both present and absent, omnipotent and powerless, that is to say as locus of the semiotic, are a pertinent contribution to both literary and feminist discourses. Of particular importance is Kristeva's recognition, often neglected elsewhere in feminist discourse, of the significance of the death drive and of negativity in the process of constructing the subject.[12]

Furthermore, I want to emphasize the value of Kristeva's sensitivity to the cultural and psychological meaning of religion, as well as her original reading of the actual writings and practices of Judaic–Christian and other religious traditions.

Nevertheless Kristeva's work, precisely because of its richness and complexity, does not escape critical discussion and even controversy. My aim is to highlight certain aspects of Kristeva's work that I consider relevant to the interpretation of Tiptree's text. The critical discussion of Kristeva's theory will play an important role in this interpretation. I want to deploy Kristeva's theory to come to new understandings of 'A Momentary Taste of Being'. My method is to create a dialogical situation, in which Kristeva's theory and Tiptree's narrative text shed light on each other's imaginative and conceptual limits and possibilities. As explained in the introductory chapter, in my view there is no rigid, hierarchical distinction between theory and literature, according to which theory is used as an objective tool to extract the correct meaning from the literary text. Instead, both are forms of discourse that reflect and produce different insights and styles of thinking, which are able to illuminate as well as criticize each other. On the one hand, the multifaceted character of Tiptree's text justifies an intense deployment of theoretical tools, while, on the other, the interpretation of the narrative text may point to the omissions and contradictions, as well as the unthought potential of a particular theory.

While in the next chapter the interconnection of 'A Momentary Taste of Being' and Kristeva's views of the Judaic–Christian tradition will be explored more fully, this chapter will be devoted to the exploration of Tiptree's story as a *choric* fantasy.[13] The notion of the *choric* fantasy is borrowed from Kaja Silverman, who introduced it to indicate a specific product of the intersection of feminism with alternative cinema, film theory and Kristeva's psychoanalytic theory. It concerns

> not only a fantasy about pre-Oedipal existence, the entry into language, and the inauguration of subjectivity; it is also a fantasy about biological 'beginnings', intra-uterine life, and what she [Kristeva] calls the 'homosexual-maternal facet'.[14]

Silverman sees the *chora* not only theorized in Kristeva's writings of the mid-1970s but also visualized in contemporaneous 'cinematic texts' (such as Robert Altman's *Three Women* from 1977, and Laura Mulvey and Peter Wollen's *Riddles of the Sphinx* from 1976). Silverman explains this concurrence by situating these texts in what she calls the same 'fantasmatic space'. Although there are no indications (but certainly no counter-indications either) of a *direct* influence of either feminist psychoanalytic or film theory on Alice Sheldon's writing, I want to argue that 'A Momentary Taste of Being' also inhabits this same fantasmatic space. More explicitly, it shares with the other texts the context of the Western European and North American feminist movement and feminist theory, in which traditional definitions of motherhood and feminity are challenged. In the introduction I have already mentioned Tiptree's participation in the *Khatru* panel, in which she defended the concept of mothering, or rather the maternal *pattern*, for Tiptree rejects essentialist notions of the sexes:

> Yes, I think we have two sexes. But I do not—repeat, *not*—think that they are men and women. I see them as *patterns*, which may or may not be present singly or together in a given individual at a given time.[15]

Her understanding of the maternal pattern is obviously influenced by her mother's study of gorillas as well as her own education as a experimental psychologist.

> My try at defining the maternal pattern is deeply influenced by the picture of the female primate endlessly, tirelessly lugging her infant, monitoring its activities at every moment, teaching, training, leading it to the best of her animal abilities. Not for a day or a week, but throughout its whole infancy and into self-sufficiency. The bond created can be very lasting; it is now speculated that the permanent alliance of mothers and daughters and granddaughters may be the true origin of society.
>
> Look at what Motherhood involves. Leadership without aggression. Empathy of a high order—can it be the true root of speech?[16]

Although these opinions surely affect Tiptree's narrative work, they need not be simply reflected in her stories. It is more likely that they are interwoven with fantasies pointing also at less obvious desires and anxieties with respect to the maternal. I want to demonstrate that this at least is the case for 'A Momentary Taste of Being'. However, I do not treat these fantasies as outcome of Alice Sheldon's highly personal struggles but as a particular expression of a shared psychic-cultural preoccupation—both manifest and subliminal—with maternal discourse in which the *choric* fantasy plays an important role.

Before being able to examine further the ways in which Tiptree's 'A Momentary Taste of Being' can be read as a *choric* fantasy, however, we need to take a closer look at Kristeva's concept of the *chora*, and the way it functions in her theory of the constitution of the subject and its acquisition of language. This theory has found not merely approval but also criticism from feminist theorists. At the heart of the debate is, as I will explain shortly, the ambivalent positioning of the maternal figure in respect to the symbolic order, that is, the order of language and social and symbolic relations. In particular Silverman's discussion of the *choric* fantasy in Kristeva's writings is of interest as it puts the desire of the daughter for the mother at the centre of critical attention. Her critique of Kristeva's *chora*, therefore, will prove specially pertinent to the interpretation of 'A Momentary Taste of Being''s mother/daughter plot.

Kristeva has borrowed the term *chora* from Plato's *Timaeus*, where it refers to:

> an archaic, mobile, unstable receptacle, prior to the One, to the father, and even to the syllable, metaphorically referring to something nourishing and maternal.[17]

denoting:

> a non-expressive totality formed by the drives and their stases in a motility that is as full of movement as it is regulated.[18]

The *chora* (the Greek *choora* = space, area, place of residence) is a more topological name for what Kristeva calls the semiotic (i.e. the drives and their articulations) modality of the process of subjective becoming, which is inseparable from and engaged in a dialogical relation with the symbolic modality of the same process. Kristeva understands the symbolic, in keeping with Lacan, as the realm of language and culture, in which the Law of the Father rules: the either symbolical or physical male figure of power who is the third party outside the mother–child dyad.

The semiotic, on the other hand, is a pre-Oedipal, that is pre-symbolic modality, the 'realm' of the body, the drives—which are energy charges as well as psychical marks—and the unconscious. In it, an imaginary unity between mother and child reigns—a 'semiotic continuum'—although at the same time the first verbalizations of the child inevitably signify its distinction as a subject from the mother and its entry in the socio-linguistic order.

Represented in a spatial manner, the semiotic drives can be said to articulate a *chora*. Kristeva stresses that, although its theoretical description is itself necessarily part of the discourse of representation, the *chora* can never be definitely posited, it lacks 'evidence, verisimilitude, spatiality and temporality'. 'Neither model nor copy, the *chora* precedes and underlies figuration and specularization, and is analogous only to vocal or kinetic rhythm'.[19] Notwithstanding its non-definability, the *chora* is subject to some process of ordering, which is different from that of symbolic law but nevertheless effectuates every time new temporary articulations. This regulated aspect of the *chora*, its vocal and gestural organization, is subject to an objective ordering which stems from physical or socio-historical constraints such as the differences between the sexes and family structures. In that way, the social organization, which is always already symbolic, acts on the semiotic in a *mediated* form by which the *chora* is not organized according to a law (like the symbolic) but by an ordering (*ordonnancement*).

This mediating function is, according to Kristeva, performed by the *mother's body*, towards which the child's oral and anal drives are oriented. She emphasizes the fundamentally ambiguous character of the drives, which are at the same time assimilating and destructive, both life drives and death drives, and which turn the semiotized body into a place of permanent fission.

> The mother's body is therefore what mediates the symbolic law organizing social relations and becomes the ordering principle of the semiotic *chora*, which is on the path of destruction, aggressivity and death. For although drives have been described as disunited or contradictory structures, simultaneously 'positive' and 'negative', this doubling is said to generate a dominant 'destructive wave' that is drive's most characteristic trait: Freud notes that the most instinctual drive is the death drive.[20]

A different way of describing this profound ambiguity is that the semiotic *chora* is the 'site' where the subject is both generated and negated, where its unity gives way to the process of the drives' charges and the stases that produce it. This process Kristeva calls a *negativity*, to be distinguished from negation, which is considered to be the act performed by a judging subject.

Hardly any aspect of Kristeva's rich and complex work has received more attention than the relation between the symbolic and the semiotic, of which the *chora* is a main element. Marilyn Edelstein even thinks that one 'can almost divide Kristeva's critics into those who excoriate her for privileging the semiotic and those who do [so] for privileging the symbolic'.[21] Nevertheless several commentators emphasize the relation between both modalities as 'dynamic', 'dialogical' or 'dialectic'—'a confrontation between contradictory forces which enables change to occur'.[22] Kristeva herself emphasizes, especially in *Révolution du langage poétique* (1974), that *both* modalities are always operative in the subject, which is, therefore, never finished but always a subject-in-process. Thus no signifying system is ever exclusively symbolic or semiotic. Furthermore, her subsequent work of the 1970s and 1980s by no means offers a univocal and definite picture with respect to this matter. Therefore Kelly Oliver's suggestion is interesting, that Kristeva's work is not only *about* the relation of the symbolic and the semiotic but that her writings *themselves* demonstrate a permanent oscillation between the semiotic and the symbolic.[23] In a similar way, Silverman understands Kristeva's work as a theoretical analogue for the two different desires—for the father and for the mother—surfacing in it. It is from this perspective that she discusses the meaning of the *choric* fantasy in Kristeva's writings.

One of the issues considered most problematic by the critical reception of Kristeva's theory of the semiotic/symbolic is, as already mentioned above, the position of the mother. To what extent does the relegation of the mother to the semiotic realm, where she is an almighty figure for the child, necessarily imply her disempowerment in the symbolic order? Whereas Oliver thinks that reading Kristeva's texts about motherhood 'against the grain' shows that the mother is not sacrificed for the father, others rebuke Kristeva for denying the mother a voice in the symbolic, due to the fact that the symbolic is identified with the paternal law.[24] Hirsch illustrates this oppositional stance by quoting Kristeva, who states in 'Motherhood According to Giovanni Bellini':

> As long as there is language-symbolism-paternity, there will never be any other way to represent, to objectify, and to explain this unsettling of the symbolic stratum, this nature/culture threshold, this instilling the subjectless biological program into the very body of the symbolizing subject, this event called motherhood.[25]

Silverman, then, tackles the problem of the positioning of the mother *vis-à-vis* the semiotic *chora* in Kristeva's texts from a topographical point of view: where is the mother 'situated' in relation to the *chora*? She argues that Kristeva's concept of the *chora*, notwithstanding its expansiveness, in each text again suffers from a peculiar conflation: 'the mother is either fused or confused with her infant, and in the process comes both to be and to inhabit the *chora*'.[26] The contradictory character of the semiotic is connected to this conflation: on the one hand it seems to be an enclosure, while on the other it has an interruptive dimension with respect to the symbolic. Even though it forms a fundamental challenge to the symbolic order of the paternal law, that is, to representation and signification, the semiotic displays a highly problematic tendency to lock up the mother in the semiotic 'womb'. This specifically happens through the suggestion of the child's linguistic accomplishments being a first 'victory' over the mother. Silverman locates the enclosure of the mother in the implicit subtext of the *chora*: the 'auto-erotic circle of pregnancy', in which the mother is simultaneously the receptacle and its inhabitant. '[E]nclosure within that circle is synonymous with non-differentiation, objectless libido, and meaninglessness, just as it is within the *chora*'.[27]

What could be, Silverman wonders, the desire guiding Kristeva's inclination to displace the mother inside the womb? She comes to the remarkable conclusion that Kristeva's *choric* fantasy is a homosexual–maternal scene. By placing the son on the side of the paternal law (giving him a 'phallic investiture' Silverman says), he is also excluded from the *chora*. With the ejecting of the son, the mother herself is placed inside, and in that way the *chora* becomes a privileged site of a (re)union between a mother, her own mother and her daughter. Here we see the fantasy of a female *enceinte*.

The problem remains, however, that, by relegating the mother to the interior of the 'womb', Kristeva excludes both her and the daughter from language. No matter how appealing the image of a joyous all-women undifferentiation might be, it is a regressive fantasy. Therefore the assumption of a pre-Oedipal mother, of a primordial unity of mother and child, either as an 'area for resistance to the symbolic' or as 'an erotic refuge' is rejected by Silverman.

> [T]o impute the daughter's erotic investment in the mother to the pre-Oedipal phase is to suggest that female sexuality precedes language and symbolic structuration—to give it, in other words, an essential content.[28]

Her alternative for maintaining the potential of the *choric* fantasy without conceiving the maternal challenge in deterministic and biologistic terms, is to place the semiotic, unconscious mother *back into* the symbolic order. Instead of the pre-Oedipal phase, she defends the concept of a 'negative Oedipus complex'.

Whereas the classic, heterosexual positive Oedipus complex posits the child's ambivalent and hostile attitude towards the parent of the same sex and its affectionate object-choice toward the parent of the same sex, the negative version organizes subjectivity along homosexual lines. For the girl this implies, in other words, that her first love-object is the mother and that the experience of separation and loss she feels when entering the symbolical order relates in the first place to the mother. The desire for the mother generated by this sense of loss (or 'symbolic castration') is normally repressed in our culture but never totally absent. Silverman's conclusion is that by situating the daughter's desire for the mother within the Oedipus complex, one allows for it not only as an effect of language and loss, but also as the emergence of a genuinely oppositional desire *inside* the symbolical order.

Kristeva's own approach does not lightly facilitate such an oppositional desire. Silverman points for instance at the problem that Kristeva seems to disavow the erotic nature of the mother–daughter union; 'homosexual' cannot mean 'homo*sexual*' in Kristeva's view. This same issue has been elaborated extensively by Judith Butler. Her conclusion is that Kristeva's 'reification of the paternal law not only repudiates female homosexuality, but denies the varied meanings and possibilities of motherhood as a cultural practice'.[29]. With Silverman, however, I would rather stress the *tensions* in Kristeva's conception of the *chora*. Silverman justly recalls the latter's own ambiguity about the *choric* fantasy, brought up, for instance, in her famous essay on feminism, 'Women's Time', written in 1979. Kristeva both acknowledges and warns against the seductive power of radical subversion entailed in the image of primordial maternal plenitude, which is described here in terms of an 'archaic mother' (to which I shall return in Chapter IV). In particular, she warns against the political dangers inherent in this image.

> If the archetype of the belief in a good and pure substance, that of utopias, is the belief in the omnipotence of an archaic, full, total englobing mother with no frustration, no separation, with no break-producing symbolism (with no castration, in other words), then it becomes evident that we will never be able to defuse the violences mobilized through the counter-investment necessary to carrying out this fantasm, unless one challenges precisely this myth of the archaic mother.[30]

As in the aforementioned, more linguistically framed, description of the *chora*, this 'anti-totalitarian' warning is founded on an understanding of motherhood less as an emblem of unity and plenitude than of *division*. The semiotic *chora* organized around the maternal body is the 'place' of the painful splitting of the subject, of its simultaneous generation and annihilation. According to Silverman, the negativity inscribed by Kristeva in this process is the negativity of the negative Oedipus complex, not the trace of a more primordial (pre-Oedipal) union of mother and child. It is the negativity of 'a desire which challenges dominance *from within* representation and meaning'.[31] It thus implies a non-regressive rejection of the law of the Father and the phallus as prime signifier of the symbolic.

At this very point I want to return to 'A Momentary Taste of Being'. In retrospect, Aaron Kaye's confrontation with the death of humankind effected by an alien force with female reproductive connotations might be interpreted as the narrative's emphasis on the annihilative moment of the mother–child dyad, on the priority of the death drive over the life drive. The question that has to be investigated now is whether a reading of the story from a mother–daughter perspective would produce a different vision of negativity. In keeping with Silverman, that might be a vision in which the phallus is rejected, while the daughter's desire for the mother implies an oppositional desire *inside* the symbolic. What kind of *choric* fantasy does 'A Momentary Taste of Being' contain and how subversive is it? What hope could 'A Momentary Taste of Being' offer us?

The spaceship and its men: configurations of symbolic and semiotic

In order to understand to what extent and in what way 'A Momentary Taste of Being' can be called a *choric* fantasy we first have to bear in mind that it is bound to present itself by means of the language of science fiction. It takes shape not so much in the representation of human relations but first and foremost in graphic metaphors of which human beings are themselves elements. The images around which the *choric* fantasy is built are generic conventions from space travel stories: the voyage away from Earth, the spaceship, the distant alien planet, extraterrestrial life. Together these elements constitute a configuration of what may be called a dialogical relation of the symbolic and the semiotic. While Earth and the alien planet represent these two respective modalities of the signifying process, the spaceship is the actual place of dialogue. There, in its core, is where the fusion of human 'sperms' and alien 'ova' takes place.

In this section I explore the ways in which the symbolic and the semiotic interact in Tiptree's text, not only in the representation of the spaceship, but also in the positioning of the male crew members, especially of the actual leader, Yellaston, and the virtual leader, Bustamente. In the next section, I shall focus on the psychomachic figure of the Aaron/Lory double in its relation to the maternally connoted alien (the 'mother/daughter' plot).

The spaceship *Centaur* is described, at a number of points in the story, in terms of a maternal womb, a nourishing container. The thought that 'Earth's sanest children are in this frail bubble of air and warmth twenty-six million million miles away' (A75) produces 'an odd, oceanic awareness' (A137) with Aaron. At other points, however, Aaron refers to the spaceship as 'a tin can' (A72) in which the sixty people are stuffed together, while the normally constrained computer chief Ahlstrom 'suddenly stands up as if gazing into a cold wind and says bleakly, 'I could wish to go home. I am tired of this machine''' (A77). When Aaron thinks of the 'ten years of cramped living with death lying a skin of metal away' (A78), we are even reminded of Theweleit's image of the armour, the defence machine *against* the feminine, as explained in the previous chapter. The *Centaur* thus proves an ambivalent place: one could say that the symbolic has been superimposed on the semiotic *chora*, or even that the latter is inhabited by the symbolic. A symbolic order, moreover, that seems inevitably paternal/patriarchal. Captain Yellaston embodies the paternal law, while security officer Frank Foy is the law's more than loyal guardian and Aaron Kaye an ironic though consenting prop.

If we adopt, for a moment, a mythological frame of reference, the male protagonists in the story can be seen as representing a particular version of Freud's parable of the primeval horde and the birth of society in *Totem and Taboo*.[32] The disobedient commanders Don Purcell and Tim Bron, but also Kuh from the *China Flower*, who did not even return to the mothership, perform the roles of the rebellious sons. After 'killing' the archaic father and leader of the horde, this 'last of the dinosaurs' (A73) Yellaston ('old Yellowstone', according to the tender nickname given to him by Aaron), they nevertheless end up restoring his paternal authority. At least, for the time being.[33] Freud, however, was by no means able to imagine the ultimate collapse of the father, as it inevitably comes about on the *Centaur* when Yellaston's vital energies are exhausted. Nor did Freud, who suffered from cultural colour-blindness, reckon with the possibility of a *counter* father-founder as embodied by Ray Bustamente, the Afro-American spaceship's communications officer.[34]

> The real living original of which Yellaston is only the abstraction. Not a team-leader like Don or Tim. The archaic model, the Boss, Jefe, Honcho, whatever—the alpha human male who outfights you, kills your enemies, begets his bastards on your woman, cares for you as his property, tells you what to do—and you do it. The primordial Big Man who organized the race and for whom the race has so little more use. (A111)

This sardonic though envious perception of Bustamente by Aaron fits completely with the former's self-image:

> To quote the words of an ancient heavyweight boxing champion, George Foreman, *'Many a million has fall and stumble when he meet Big George in that ol'black jungle ...'* (A113)[35]

Bustamente's jungle is displaced to the 'virgin' planet. Aaron finds out in amazement that Bustamente has already started to select his prospective family, amongst whom is Aaron's lover Solange. He is getting ready to be the founder of a new humanity, a black Adam surrounded by competent Eves of all colours. I want to go a bit deeper into this figure of Bustamente and his future ambitions because he appears to be a highly ambivalent figure in this revision of *Totem and Taboo*.

Ray Bustamente

Roz Kavaney points at a type of science fiction writings, starting with Robert Heinlein's *Farnham's Freehold*, that can be called survivalist. In these—male-authored—works:

> [i]t is assumed that the moment atomic war breaks out, or a comet brushes the earth, or your spaceship crashes, you—the assumed you of such stories is of course always male—start reverting to a pioneer mentality, start carving a domain in the wilderness, and get your women breeding.[36]

Isn't this stock convention of the primitive male colonizer reproduced in Tiptree's story? And what is more, does the suggestion of a black breeder in a virgin jungle not corroborate the worst racist stereotypes? How are we to understand the appearance of Bustamente in 'A Momentary Taste of Being' in this respect?

I want to bring forward one of bell hooks' provocative insights from her studies on the complicated relations between sex, race and class in popular and theoretical culture. According to hooks in her book *Yearning*, white male oppressors and black oppressed men *share* the patriarchal belief that political dominance and revolutionary struggle actually are about the 'erect phallus'.[37] In 'A Momentary Taste of Being', Yellaston is ironically referred to by Aaron as 'dead dick': the end of white political dominance expressed in sexualized terms. Correspondingly, Ray Bustamente's preparations for his kingdom on the 'virgin' planet fit in with 'the sexualization of black liberation in ways that support and perpetuate sexism, phallocentrism, and male domination'.[38] In my view, one of Tiptree's most salient narrative strategies throughout her work is operative here as well: the grotesque mimicking of all traditional sexist representations of masculinity in order to cause them to implode. 'A Momentary Taste of Being''s dynamic of entropy and dissipation ensures that even in their erection, white as well as black supremacy, basking in the sign of the phallus, are drained of their vitality.

If we return from the Freudian myth of the primeval horde to the psychoanalytic–linguistic scope, what is Bustamente's position with regard to the symbolic? He turns out to embody a transitory position: as a man he is a representative of the phallic law, while as a black he is an 'alien', representing otherness, culture's 'dark side' that for a long time was not allowed an official voice. He is furthermore a figure wandering on the borderline between the symbolic and the semiotic: he is, after all, the spaceship's *communications* chief. But he also has the features of the (male) artist that Kristeva endowes with the faculty of speaking for the mute mother in the interior of the semiotic 'womb'. Besides his official communications task, Bustamente is engaged in designing music-and-light shows in the seclusion of his quarters.

> The door slides open. Aaron goes warily into a maze of low music and shifting light-forms in which six or seven big black men in various perspectives are watching him. (A111)

This passage may serve as a comment on the profound ambiguity inherent in Kristeva's assessment of the artist's position in the signifying process. Notwithstanding its semiotic connotations—the vibrations, sounds and colours reminiscent of the drives structured around the mother's body— Bustamente's 'light-show jungle' (A113) is also a mirror hall of endless masculine self-reflection. In other words, the male artist communicates with the semiotic without putting his position in the symbolic in jeopardy. Analogous to the maze of light- and sound effects in Bustamente's space, the entire spaceship is 'a warren of corridors' (A106) in which he has installed the electronic *surveillance* network. 'Ray really has been weaving in *Centaur*'s wall' (A113). In this way the semiotic and the symbolic are literally interwoven; however, since the semiotic, on the *Centaur*, seems absorbed or occupied by the symbolic, the dialogical process is eventually male-controlled.

After the contact with the alien life-form, however, Ray Bustamente puts his position in the symbolic radically at stake. His own artistic lightshow must appear to him as just a faint shadow of the alien light by then, and hence he takes off for the alien planet. He moves deeper and deeper into the semiotic, in other words, until his voice is no longer heard. Ray too, like Lory, is 'in league' with the semiotic/maternally connoted alien now. Aaron still begs him to come out of the *China Flower*, glowing with the alien radiance, to help him restore the damage caused by Lory's destruction of the symbolic's symbol: the gyroscopes '—the great pure beings who have spun there faultlessly for a decade holding their lifeline to Earth are in mortal agony' (A146). But Ray has lost interest in restoring the symbolic: 'I'm going to ... that planet ... boy' (A154). Finally the *China Flower* takes off and with it 'the last *ray* vanishes' (A155, my italics).

It is of interest, then, to observe Aaron watching the *China Flower* vanish into the universe:

> He stands there, a foolish man holding a rope, knowing that all sweetness is fading. Life itself is falling out to the dark beneath him, going away forever. Come back, he whispers. (A155)

What did Ray Bustamente represent to Aaron, a ray of *what* he was? In my view, the figure of Bustamente signified to Aaron the possibility of communication with semiotic drives and energies *within* the paternal symbolic. Thus, he reflected Aaron's own hope for the affirmation of his transgressive desire for (incestuous) non-differentiation without him having to give up his attachment to Yellaston, that is, to the symbolic and the paternal law.

What is left, however, to the lonely survivor on the spaceship is neither a paternal order nor a nourishing maternal container but a *void* of meaning, and a terrifying silence in which no voice will be audible any more but his own:

> A feeling of dumb weight comes over him. It is *Centaur*, the whole wonderful ship he had been so proud of, hanging over him mute and flaccid in the dark. The life-spark gone away. Voiceless, unfindable in the icy wastes ... (A155)

Earth and its dwindling Sun

Let us then have a closer look at the position of Captain Yellaston in the symbolic/semiotic configuration of Tiptree's text. In the following passage, Aaron's thoughts provide a telling perspective on this matter:

> Dear god—*what if we have to go back to Earth*? The thought is horrible. He remembers their first year when there was another viewscreen showing the view astern: yellow Sol, shrinking, dwindling. That had been a rotten idea, soon abolished. What if the planet is somehow no good, is toxic or whatever—what if they have to turn around and spend ten years watching Sol expand again? Unbearable. (A98, italics in text)

Among the many images of the erosion of Yellaston's paternal/phallic power this one struck me in particular, in view of Kelly Oliver's article 'Kristeva's Imaginary Father and the Crisis in the Paternal Function'. Oliver discusses the divergent evaluations by Freud and Lacan, on the one side, and Kristeva on the other, of the Father and his phallus, pointing out the following:

> Although both Freud and Lacan acknowledge that the primary dyad is made up of mother and child, they emphasize the function of the Father and his phallus. The Oedipal situation revolves around him and the big stick with which he enforces the Law. He initiates the speaking being into language. In this scenario, especially Lacan's version of it, the third term (the father), or, more precisely, the fourth term (the Symbolic), is not merely a satellite that circles the primary

dyad. Rather, it is their sun, which while burning through the Milky Way that connects mother and child provides life and light to the speaking being. If this sun is eclipsed, the speaking being gives way to something subhuman, even animal.

Kristeva [however] takes us back to the Milky Way of the primary dyad.[39]

Thanks to its parallel planetary imagery, this passage indeed sheds light on 'A Momentary Taste of Being'. In Tiptree's story, the sun of the paternal symbolic—yellow Sol/Yellaston/'Old Yellowstone' (A72), according to Aaron's tender nickname for him—was 'shrinking, dwindling' (A98) more and more, until it was dulled completely. Literally speaking, it was the distance to Earth and its solar system that made Sol invisible. Earth's yellow Sol is, in Oliver's term, 'eclipsed' by the alien planet through the absorbing light of its life-form in the *China Flower*. Transferred to the metaphors of psychoanalysis, it seems apt to say that the paternal symbolic, which is embodied by Yellaston, becomes extinguished by the force of a maternally connoted semiotic. The phallus of the father has been turned into a 'dead dick' by the interruptive power of the semiotic. Aaron observes this 'usurpation' of power by the semiotic at the expense of the patriarchal symbolical in terms of 'that marvelous light' that 'will be in fact behind the command console where Yellaston was' (A152).

Must the conclusion follow that 'A Momentary Taste of Being' is a dramatized corroboration of the Lacanian version of the paternal symbolic? A version, moreover, that is to some extent reproduced by Kristeva who is sometimes considered a too 'dutiful Lacanian daughter'.[40] Judith Butler reproaches Kristeva with tending towards 'reification of the paternal law', that is an equation of the symbolic with the paternal law.

Kristeva does not seriously challenge the structuralist assumption that the prohibitive paternal law is foundational to culture itself. Hence, the subversion of paternally sanctioned culture can not come from another version of culture, but only from within the repressed interior of culture itself, from the heterogeneity of drives that constitutes culture's concealed foundation.[41]

The overall tendency of Tiptree's story points to a similar conflation of the symbolic order with the paternal law. The desperate message the text seems to convey to us is that there is no culture beyond the Father and his phallus, no matter how violent and death-ridden his order may be. The collapse of Yellaston's power (the eclipse of the sun/yellow Sol by an alien light coming from an alien planet) indeed implied that, to use Oliver's phrase, the speaking being gave way to something 'subhuman'. That is to say, the crew members turned into a bunch of aphasic zombies after indulging in the alien light in the spaceship's core, which may be understood as a particular image of the semiotic *chora*.

So Lory's desire for the alien did not represent any real opposition to the paternal symbolic but rather the emergence from within the repressed interior of culture of a force that was as lethal as it was joyous. Or to put it differently, Lory's desire entailed the complete rupture of the symbolic by the semiotic. This collapse of culture affirms Aaron's fear that the daughter's desire for the mother, as expressed in the Lory/alien connection in 'A Momentary Taste of Being', is a 'crazy plot', for it annihilates the speaking subject. Helplessly, Aaron sees his sister gliding into a dimension beyond communication: 'The warm light enwraps her, she has turned, is walking into it, gone—' (A154). The story takes us, in Oliver's imagery, back to the Milky Way of the primary dyad of mother and child, but by doing so also posits the concomitant end of human culture. There is no room for Silverman's idea of the negative Oedipus complex which asserts the mother's position, and hence the daughter's, inside a different, non-phallic version of the symbolic. Instead, the alien/Lory 'league' appears to represent a *choric* closure, symbolized in the eventual muteness and flaccidity of the *Centaur*.

And yet I want to suggest a further alternative reading. This reading does not undo the previous view on the Lory/alien 'league' which implies that the realm of the Father or a *choric* enclosure with the Mother *neither* are places where new forms of the symbolic will thrive. I have to concede, however, that once again Aaron's perspective has crept in too easily in this interpretation of the mother/daughter dynamic. While granting the validity of the conclusion derived from this perspective, I nevertheless think that approaching 'A Momentary Taste of Being''s 'crazy' mother/daughter plot from a different angle generates a more complex view. It means making a swerve from Aaron's observation of Lory's 'league' with the alien to our own consideration of the Aaron/Lory double itself.

The composite daughter and the lure of the semiotic
It is tempting to simply make Aaron and Lory into the protagonists of an allegory of the two modalities of the signifying system, applying a gendered division that identifies Aaron with the paternal symbolic and Lory with the maternal semiotic. This, however, would be a misleading exercise in simplicity, for it fails to see that Aaron and Lory are not opposite figures but reversed sides of one female psychomachical configuration struggling with the desire for the mother, as I argued previously. With regard to this, Steffen-Fluhr's remark is noteworthy that Tiptree 'often uses her protagonists to express her sense of herself as a female Oedipus who, try

as she might get out of town, always ends up back in her mother's bed'.[42] As explained earlier, in my opinion it is less relevant whether Tiptree/Sheldon expresses herself in her texts than that the texts themselves, approached as texts of a female author, provoke the reader to discuss the question of female subjectivity. From this viewpoint, Aaron/Lory can be certainly conceived as a 'female Oedipus'. The question is just how powerful and subversive her desire for the mother is.

I have to come to the conclusion that both Lory and Aaron refer to the mother, inasmuch as she is metonymically represented by the alien, in procreative, semiotic and pre-Oedipal terms. No matter its odd science fiction guise, I think Lory's connection to the alien planet recalls a *choric* fantasy, in which the daughter's desire for the mother brings about a return to the presumed unity of the primary dyad. She has seen wholeness and bliss on this 'virgin' planet, which can be understood as an imaginary place where the subject is untouched by processes of splitting and separation. Since wholeness is achieved by making contact with the planet's life-form, the site of union is displaced from the planet to the *Centaur* once it lodges a specimen of this life-form. When Aaron, during the run towards the alien light, presses her to explain to him what happened to the Chinese crew who stayed behind on the planet, she anwers in an ecstatical manner: '"Changed," she is panting. Her face is incredibly beautiful. "Merged, healed. Made whole"' (A142).

Later Aaron asks her if the crew of the *China Flower* were involved in some kind of fight when they went to explore the beautifully coloured life-forms on the planet.

> 'Oh, no!' Her eyes widen at him. 'No! Oh, I made that up to protect it. No hurting any more, never. They came back so gentle, so happy. They were all changed, they shed all that. It's waiting for us, Arn, see? It wants to deliver us. We'll be truly human at last.' (A149)

I suggest that 'deliver' is to be read here not just in the sense of salvation but also as a grammatical displacement from 'being delivered of' to 'deliver', implying a birth-giving faculty of the alien.

In Aaron's case, there is occasional allusion to maternal presence *in* the symbolic. His maternal lover, Solange, is a subject within the patriarchal symbolic; she is motherly and emphatic but competent and active as well, and faithfully serving the cultural order—she is 'Soli', in her name and attitude reflecting 'yellow Sol' (A98). Furthermore, Aaron was greeted with 'a surprisingly warm, almost maternal smile on the worn Caucasian face' (A114) of Captain Yellaston.[43] Once the alien light—'the shining glory' (A141)—has been released from behind the port of the *China Flower*, however, Aaron is also overflown by the desire for a *choric* primordial union with the mother. But whereas Lory—and following in her wake all the other human beings—finally succumbs irreversibly to the semiotic force of the alien, Aaron is struggling against its pull to the very end: 'It has called us and we have come—*I must go*. But he frowns, blinks; a part of him has doubts about the pull, the sweet longing' (A142).

The siren call

Aaron's struggle is expressed by dint of the classic(al) mythological image of Odysseus (Ulysses) and the sirens. To protect his companions against the sirens, the winged women who lure sailors into destruction by their singing, Odysseus (Ulysses) has their ears plugged with wax. He himself wants to hear the song without paying for it with its life, so he has himself tied securely to the mast of the ship. This is how he succeeds, albeit with great difficulty, to pass the dangerous charm of the sirens. Like Odysseus, Aaron attempts to resist an alien lure by the protection of a rope. By accident his leg gets trapped in a web of cables, and he feels that:

> He is going to be very ashamed, he thinks vaguely, tied here like Ulysses against the siren call, huddling under an analyzer bench while the others—What? (A142)

Lory frees his leg from the cables, so he can move on to *China Flower*'s radiance with her, 'the sweet pull grabs him again' (A143). Then he discovers that he is still holding a thick cable, which is a computer lead, running towards the inboard lock. He decides to follow the lead, away from the alien, planning to shut off all the ports to the corridor where the *China Flower* is, in order to save his mates.

> He clasps it, starts to shuffle on his knees, dragging Lory. The thing down there is pulling at the atoms of his soul, his head is filled with urgent radiance calling to him to drop the foolish cable and run to join his mates. 'I'm a *doctor*,' he mumbles; it requires all his strength to slide his gloved hand along his lifeline, he is turning away from bliss beyond his dreams. (A143–4)

Finally, with great difficulty, he reaches the command-room, where he ties one end of the cable to a wall-hold and knots the other end around his waist: 'Multiple knottings, must not be able to untie these in a hurry' (A153). Even so he manages to untie them again in the end, urged to it by the sight of *China Flower*'s imminent departure. The spaceship with the alien (and Bustamente and Solange) inside takes off after all. Aaron 'lets fall the idiotic rope', wondering: 'What have I saved, what have I lost?' (A155). And he feels that 'it is forever now, nothing will ever be right again' (A155).

Of the various speculations over the nature of the singing of the sirens, some seem particularly relevant to an understanding of what was tearing at Aaron.[44] Max Horkheimer and Theodor Adorno, in their *Dialectic of Enlightenment*, understand the song of the sirens as the allurement of losing oneself (one's 'self', in their terms: the identical, purposeful, masculine character of the human being, achieved with great pain and difficulty) in what is past, in the pre-historic mythical era.[45] With their irresistible promise of lust and pre-rational knowledge, echoing in the sounds of the song, the sirens threaten the patriarchal order. The measures taken by Odysseus on the ship to resist the sirens can be seen, according to Horkheimer and Adorno, as the allegorical prefiguration of the dialectic of enlightenment, that is, the loss of freedom and unity that is concomitant to the progress of civilization. Odysseus acknowledges the overwhelming power of the archaic song by having himself chained (or, 'enlightened on the point of technic', as Horkheimer and Adorno put it), but being under its spell does not lead to his death. He is a victor.

Maurice Blanchot, on the other hand, puts such a view in question.[46] Although he agrees in understanding the singing of the sirens as a dangerous song from an unordered world which precedes the symbolic order, Blanchot doubts whether Odysseus is a true victor. Did Odysseus really hear this interruptive singing, or is that a privilege of those who do not seek to safeguard themselves against it beforehand?[47] On the other hand, it cannot be denied that the song of the sirens keeps pulling at him; after all, it haunts the pages of Homer's *Odyssey*. Just like it haunts the pages of 'A Momentary Taste of Being'; Aaron is no true victor either.

In Tiptree's narrative, Ulysses–Aaron resists the strong call coming from the pre-patriarchal, pre-symbolic twilight zone of the semiotic *chora*. He clings to the means of technological reason (the computer cable). The overwhelming beauty of the alien matter does not prevent him from being aware of its terrible ambiguity, as the maternal semiotic is co-directed by both life and death drives and therefore 'on the path of destruction, aggression and death'.[48]

> The great flare of warm light is about twenty meters ahead. He must go back, go back and close the port. He stops himself at the command console and looks up at the videoscreen, still focussed on *China Flower*'s fiery heart. It *is* like jewels in there, he sees, awestruck— great softly glowing globes, dazzling, changing color as he looks ... some are dark, like a heap of fiery embers burning out. *Dying?* Grief wells up in him, he puts his hand up to hide it, looks away. (A153)

But unlike Odysseus, who had the ears of his mates plugged with wax, Aaron is not able to shut off the senses of the crew of the spaceship *Centaur* for the lure of the alien light. And what is more, he does not succeed in blocking its way to Lory, his other side. For this reason, he is not a victor but a bare survivor, yearning forever for an imaginary pre-symbolic realm of bliss and nondifferentiation: 'Oh, Lory, stay with me, don't die—*Christ, the pull, the terrible sweet pull*—' (A163). Once the patriarchal–phallic order can no longer be taken for granted, the symbolic and the semiotic both turn out to be shaky and ambivalent places. As Aaron says after the 'last ray' of the alien life has disappeared, 'nothing will ever be right again' (A155). Does this imply, however, that once there was a time when everything was right? Either a secure patriarchal time or a time of primordial bliss and unity, a time (or place) without negativity? On the contrary, for eventually Aaron admits that Lory 'wasn't crazy, you know. Ever, really. She knew something was wrong with us ...' (A162).

Conclusion: a non-regressive chora?
I understand this desperate lament of Aaron as an expression of the painful sense of the subject's split being in general, and of the unstable position of the *female* subject in the symbolic in particular. Let me explain this with reference once more to the parallel with Homer's *Odyssey*. In order to escape from the cyclop Polyphemus, Odysseus cunningly says that his name is No-one, *oudeis*, a pun on the word *Odysseus*, so that the monster will call for help from his fellow-cyclops to slay 'no one'. Horkheimer and Adorno understand the subject's disavowal of his own identity in terms of self-preservation by means of self-negation. They explain the fact that Odysseus, after escaping, reveals his true name after all as his fear of actually becoming No-one again, a fear of regression into the pre-rational world of myth and magic, from which the subject has only just dissociated himself. It is interesting to notice that this explanation is supported by Catherine Keller, who gives a positive assessment of the fact that Odysseus' fear of losing his masculine, identical and rational identity comes to light in this name-play. According to her, it opens up the possibility of different notions of self and subjectivity.

> Perhaps Odysseus told the truth when he meant to dissemble. For if such a [masculine heroic] subjectivity ultimately loses itself in its own bid for fame, name and immortality, then here it inadvertently names its repressed anxiety: 'No-one is my name.' I am not important. Not real. Not one. Not *one*. Not a self-possessed monad.[49]

In a similar manner, Aaron Kaye comes to face up to the fact that he is no(t) one, not *one* self-identical and solid subject but a split subject holding a difference within, a subject-in-process, that is always on the verge of both annihilation and generation. He is and is not both Aaron and Lory, who are different sides of one daughter in a mother/daughter plot.

In this psychomachia, Aaron represents the daughter's efforts to *maintain* subjectivity, hovering on the boundary of the symbolic and the semiotic. It is a kind of subjectivity, however, that is embedded in a phallic symbolic, he/she is a daughter loyal to the father's laws. Lory, on the other hand, is involved in a very paradoxical move, as she seeks to *achieve* a different kind of (female) subjectivity by going beyond the human, that is to say, by giving up her position in the symbolic altogether. The terrifying aporia displayed in 'A Momentary Taste of Being' is that moving beyond the phallic symbolic implies giving up cultural symbolic existence as such. The only alternative that is offered to the daughter, whose desire for the mother has to be repressed in the realm of the father, is a speechless indulgence in a fusion with the mother in an imaginary *choric* enceinte outside the symbolic.

This dramatized aporia in 'A Momentary Taste of Being' mirrors Kristeva's theoretical model to the extent that both seem to suffer, as Butler and others have suggested, from structuralist either/or assumptions: either a paternally connoted symbolic or a maternal semiotic, as if the symbolic and the maternal were mutually exclusive. Both discourses nevertheless point to ways out of this impasse as well. First, although Kristeva tends to lock up mother and daughter in a *choric* enceinte, as Silverman rightly asserts, her writings, on the other hand, emphasize also the fundamentally dialogical character of the symbolic and the semiotic, and hence of the semiotic as the 'place' of radical fission, in which the subject is both annihilated and generated. Secondly, in 'A Momentary Taste of Being', the impasse is tentatively breached in an alien and heterotopic way typical of science fiction, which, however, recalls the same process of splitting. While the narrative does not offer affirmative visions of female subjectivities, it does sketch the space in which such visions could come into existence.

We get an outlook on such space by means of Aaron's record—Aaron, who is the part of the daughter that still has some voice in the symbolic. He is the sole survivor of the obsolete phallic–patriarchal symbolical order, of which, however, he was not a die-hard defender but rather an acute, though powerless observer. He has experienced the collapse of the phallic realm of the Father as well as the consumption/consummation of its offspring by an unknown, though in any case, maternally connoted alien. Now he is the only human being left who can report on the appearance of what look to him like uncanny ghosts, shadows of what was repressed in the past and may be transformed in the future. I would describe these combined products—partly human, partly very alien—as metaphors of the simultaneous annihilation of phallocentric views of the subject and the generation of posthuman views. While the crew members of the *Centaur* and the alien 'egg-things' are dying, their zygotes leave the spaceship to nestle in the uterine of outer space and start their growth. They are the germs of different subjectivities that one day will thrive in a non-phallic cultural order. While Aaron fearfully wonders whether they are 'brutes or angels' (A160), I suspect that they are neither but rather combined or hybrid beings. At the same time, I can only hope—utopian as it may seem— that these beings, these shadowy visions of a different future will also enable new voices for *female* subjects.

For now, it is still by reading *beyond* the narrative's visible horizon, which is dominated by Aaron's tragic view of the end of human culture, that, in my view, it becomes possible to imagine a non-regressive *chora*. I find an adequate representation of it in the image of the vast cosmic space in which these unknown posthuman beings are starting to evolve. The cosmos is the most radically open and non-enclosed space the female imagination could wish for, large enough to accommodate the ghosts of the past and the embryonic hopes of the future, and unknown enough to comprise both the familiar and the alien. In this open space there could come into being a mother–daughter *chora* that is rather different from the deadly bliss Lory and the crew experienced in the choking container of the *Centaur*. What I have in mind here is the affirmative utopian project of a cosmos of female feminist writing and reading practices, like Tiptree's, in which subjects-in-process inscribe themselves, contributing thus to—sometimes fearful but never definite—negotiations of new forms of the symbolic.

IV. Father in Crisis, Mother Rises?
2. (Extra)biblical Scenarios

Hey, energy sucker, I am a goddess, not your mother.
Luscious Jackson[1]

Introduction

Aaron Kaye sensed that his sister and the alien were in some way 'in league' with each other. 'This is her crazy plot' (A148): a mother/daughter subplot in science fiction guise, as I have explained in the previous chapter. 'A Momentary Taste of Being''s posthuman setting accommodated a *choric* fantasy, an ambivalent fantasy of a union with the mother that is both desirable and terrifying. The intention of the present chapter is to provide a complementary perspective on the collapse of the patriarchal–phallic order and the emergence of the maternally connoted alien in 'A Momentary Taste of Being'. We shall see, then, that another dimension of the mother/daughter plot comes to light, in addition to the *choric* fantasy. I want to show that it is possible to observe a dimension of religious desire in the 'league' between Lory and the alien. From that viewpoint, the alien does not point only to the maternal but also to the divine.

For this reading of Tiptree's text, I shall move on to a quite different 'fantasmatic space': the *Wirkungsgeschichte* of biblical mythology. Even the uninitiated can recognize in the story a set of basic narrative themes from the Hebrew Bible. At a closer scrutiny, however, far from being smoothly matching analogies, these images appear to be distortions carved on the palimpsest. What is the meaning of these biblical distortions, and how do they refer to the maternal? I will find my answer as a set of readings between three interacting partners. To begin with, the biblical text and 'A Momentary Taste of Being' mutually highlight each other but as a third party Julia Kristeva plays an important role again.

In Kristeva's studies, the Hebrew and Christian Bible, as well as other Christian writings, are a regular focus of attention, which she motivates as follows:

> Let us reread the Bible, once again. In order to interpret it, certainly, but also to allow it to make our own fantasms, our interpretive delusions, give themselves away and stand out clearly.[2]

While Kristeva rereads the Bible to trace the roots of certain obsessions and fantasies that persist in Western secular culture, I turn to the Bible as well as to Kristeva's reflections to gain insight in particular fantasies that appear in 'A Momentary Taste of Being'. I want to suggest that especially Kristeva's views on the so-called *archaic mother* in *Powers of Horror*, in which psychoanalysis, cultural philosophy and religious studies intersect, will prove pertinent to a further understanding of the alien in Tiptree's mother/daughter plot. The archaic mother is, according to Kristeva, a primeval maternal force which can be approached as an element in the process of constructing the subject, as well as in terms of general cultural–religious developments. As such this concept/image is of interest not only for the interpretation of 'A Momentary Taste of Being' but also for feminist theological reflection insofar as it attempts to reassess feminine aspects of the divine.

The biblical parallels in 'A Momentary Taste of Being' that immediately catch the eye are from the Pentateuch or Torah ('law'), the first five books of the (Hebrew) Bible, starting with the creation of the world and ending with the death of Moses: the Fall and the expulsion from Paradise, Noah's Ark, the Exodus and the quest of the Israelites through the desert. In Tiptree's narrative these themes, however, are not (chrono)logically ordered but appear in conflated and entangled forms. All of them are quite common tropes in science fiction, where they mostly appear as either timeworn images, tawdry metaphors or parodic devices. Although the parodic touch is not absent from the biblical tropes in Tiptree's story, more salient is the deconstructive dynamic with which they are invested. The various transformations of biblical stories seem to lead irreversibly to the preclusion of fulfillment in any type of gendered God, either paternal or maternal. As we shall see, the story contains traces of the images of both a patriarchal God and a primordial Mother-Goddess, but neither of them generates an affirmative spiritual vision for the female subject, as represented in the 'daughter' Aaron/Lory. Thus, 'daughterhood' remains symbolically unhinged.

But what, one wonders, in that case is the meaning of Tiptree's story for feminist theological reflection? Would it not be much simpler to resort to more affirmative stories? Feminist science fiction after all contains many examples of myth-making in which goddesses arise and female spiritual powers come into bloom.[3] I will argue that the significance of a 'A Momentary Taste of Being' is that, by moving beyond any gendered visions of the divine, and hence beyond mirror-images of/for female subjectivity, it brings about the condition for a more radical understanding of the divine.

From a theological point of view, the postmodern loss of certain foundations, of transcendent sources of the divine, does not imply a concomitant vanishing of a desire for the divine altogether—a desire which I consider to be a crucial aspect of the narrative dynamic of 'A Momentary Taste of Being'. Neither does the decline of metaphysical certainty imply that any kind of experience that could be interpreted in terms of divinity has become permanently impossible. It does entail, however, a movement beyond the modern aporia of the presence (theism) or absence (atheism) of God. It demands that naming and imagining of the divine be dissociated from any understanding of the divine as a substance. In connection to the imagery of 'A Momentary Taste of Being', such a non-substantialist view could become visible in the alienness of the alien, that is, in what eludes the meanings and names that are actually attributed to the alien by the crew members, including its maternal connotations.[4]

The steps that I take to develop my argument are as follow. First I will describe how the biblical themes mentioned are recycled mostly in distorted ways in 'A Momentary Taste of Being'. This includes a discussion of the references to the figure of the ancient mother-goddess which can be found in Tiptree's text. Subsequently, the results of this interpretation will be assessed in the light of Kristeva's theory of abjection and the archaic mother, in particular as it refers to the repression of the maternal body in the biblical texts and contexts.

While in the first section the main issue is the deconstructive force of 'A Momentary Taste of Being' with regard to gendered and familial visions of the divine, in the last section the focus of attention will change considerably. I will move away from the biblical analogy to another analogy suggested in Tiptree's narrative, the one between Lory Kaye and Jeanne d'Arc. By doing so, my perspective follows the transition from Judaic to Christian forms of abjection that Kristeva makes in her explorations of the repression of the maternal body in Judeo-Christian history. This discussion of the Lory–Joan connection provides, I claim, an important element for feminist postmodern discourse.

Biblical distortions

The most obvious biblical parallel in 'A Momentary Taste of Being' is the quest in the book of Exodus. Like the Israelites in the slave house of Egypt, the people of the *Centaur* fled an unbearable place in search of a promised land, which they would not reach except after lengthy wanderings through 'the wastes', under the guidance of a 'Moses' figure. Still, Aaron's 'good-wise-father projection' (A94) of Yellaston may also point to an even more ancient patriarch of biblical history, Noah.

We are indeed reminded of Noah, surrounded by his kin in the safe isolation of his Ark. God, in the biblical scenario, disappointed with his own creation which had produced nothing but vice and violence, decided to swallow every living being in a terrible Flood (Gen. 6:5–9:7). Noah, the only human being who found mercy in the eyes of God, was advised by God to build an ark for himself and his family and to take one pair of every living being with him on the Ark. When God sent the eradicating rains to the earth, the Ark floated on the waters and Noah and his kin, and all the animals, survived. Like Noah's ark, the *Centaur* escaped the threat of earth's destruction by the flood. However, in 'A Momentary Taste of Being' the deluge is formed by human beings themselves: the 'teeming billions' of Earth's overpopulated surface. A deeply ironic twist has thus been added to God's blessing of Noah in Gen. 9:1 (in which God's original blessing of humankind in Gen. 1:28 is regained): 'God blessed Noah and his sons, he said to them, "Be fruitful and increase in number, and fill the earth".'

But humankind on Earth has reproduced so well that it ends up consuming itself. Thus the judgement on history is not executed by the wrath of God, but by humankind itself. Also the population of the space ark has experienced a great shift in comparison with its biblical predecessor. Contrary to the variety of animals brought aboard *in pairs*, here we see a wide range of *unique* human animal types: 'sixty hand-picked indoctrinated specimens'. The only people who did go aboard as a kind of couple were Aaron and Lory. As brother and sister, however, they were assumed to be governed by the incest taboo and thus to have a sterile relationship.

Noah's ark safeguarded the reproduction of earthly life in a second chance offered by God after the deluge. Since an almighty God, however, has become an obsolete concept in the technoscientific space age, the people on Yellaston's ship did not receive any guarantee nor promise of a new chance. They could just *hope* for the possiblity of new life far away from the home planet. But the strangest of things happened. In place of raising their offspring on a second Earth, situated on the new planet, as in Bustamente's imaginative preparations, the crew members of the *Centaur* themselves were turned into reproductive material for the creation of an extraterrestrial life form. They were brought on board not in pairs but as solitary people because they are 'nothing but gametes ... Two types, little boy sperms, little girl sperms—half of the germ-plasm of something ...' (A158). And Noah–Yellaston turned out to be just one of these insignificant germs; there was no God to enter into a covenant with him that would support the continuity of humanity as a chosen species in the history of the world and the cosmos.

Let us pass on to Exodus again. Aaron Kaye does not carry his name without reason. Like his namesake from the Hebrew Bible, Aaron the brother of Moses, sons of Amram and Jochebed (Ex.6:19), he is on confidential terms with the leader of the exodus. The biblical Aaron was appointed to be the spokesman for Moses, who was not a good speaker. The science fictional Aaron too is supposed to help the big man control his weakness, which, however, takes a different and sardonic form: in all secrecy he has to bring the captain 'four ounces' of alcohol every night. In his identity as a medical doctor, moreover, resonances sound of the ancient figure of the priest-shaman, which also recall biblical Aaron's designation as the first priest of the Israelites. Priests mediate between humans and gods.

In Aaron's pet name for Yellaston, Old Yellowstone, a variety of connotations echo besides the ancient rocky park, and besides the 'yellow Sol'. The 'yellow' refers also to the yellow signal, instead of the green, that Yellaston should have sent to Earth after the subordination of Tim Bron. But he was too fuddled and yellow, that is, a coward: 'I should have sent code yellow and announced I had sent the green … I failed to think it through in time' (A134). As for the 'stone', in the present context of biblical leadership, it recalls the 'stone' which was the material of the two tables Moses received on Mount Sinai (Ex.31:18; 34:1), the tables of the covenant God entered into with the Israelites. As Moses represents the divine Law, so does Yellaston represent the human—or in fact, paternal–phallic—law.

After the euphoria-rousing display of beautiful blow-ups of the paradisaical planet, Yellaston speaks sensible words of warning against rashness in colonizing the planet, drawing on parallels with 'the history of human exploration and migration on our own planet' (A98).

> He was looking directly at them now, his fine light greenish eyes moving unhurriedly from face to face. '… It is the first totally alien living world that man has touched. We may have no more concept of its true nature and conditions than the British migrants had of an American winter'. (A100)

In other words, paradises may be deceptive. Frank Foy, the security officer, is terribly impressed by Yellaston's homily, as Aaron observes ironically: 'Frank has received the Word. Captain Yellaston (who art in Heaven) has explained' (A102). Aaron, however, feels faced with the fact that Yellaston's patriarchal and quasi-divine power is eroding more and more. We are reminded again of Tiptree's story 'Houston, Houston', the parallels of which with 'A Momentary Taste of Being' I have discussed earlier, where the spaceship's captain is 'gradually revealed as a ranting Old Testament patriarch deluding that he is god-almighty'.[5] In 'A Momentary Taste of Being', however, the captain himself is by no means self-delusive but it is rather the guardian of the phallic law, Frank Foy, who ascribes divine qualities to the patriarch. On the sly, Yellaston himself is as insecure about his own qualities as Moses was. But then, what a difference it makes when one is backed up by divine authority. How different is the inspiration of the respective leaders of the expedition! It is written about Moses when he came down from Mount Sinai with the tables in his hand that 'the skin of his face shone because he had been talking to the Lord' (Ex. 34:29). So strong was this light that Aaron and the other Israelites shrank away from him. Moses then covered his face with a cloth, hiding the light of God inside, to only unveil his face when he was speaking to God in 'the Tent of meeting'. Yellaston, on the other hand, does not cherish the light of God but, instead, a very dark force. Behind his public veil of patriarchal leadership he is tormented by a 'demon', '[s]omething inherent in life itself, time or evil maybe, for which he has no cure' (A115) but which he tries to exorcize by alcohol. Yellaston's 'Tent of meeting' is the privacy of his commandor's room where he meets his doctor–bootlegger to discuss the situation on board. I will come back to Yellaston's demon in the next section.

Moses and Aaron had a sister too, Miriam, famous for her Song of Miriam (Ex.15:20–21). She was a prophet, who according to some traditions had the same position as Moses and Aaron in the exodus (Micah 6:4). In Numbers 12:1–16, this tradition is in conflict with another in which the superior position of Moses was emphasized. Miriam protests against God's favouring of Moses over Aaron and herself ('And they complained, "Is Moses the only one by whom the Lord has spoken? Has he not spoken by us as well?"' Num. 12:2), for which she is struck by leprosy, whereupon Aaron begs God not to punish her so harshly:

> My Lord, do not make us pay the penalty of sin, foolish and wicked though we have been. Let her [Miriam] not be like something stillborn, whose flesh is half eaten away when it comes from the womb. (Numbers 12:11–12)

Inspired by the Lord, Moses decides to put Miriam in quarantine outside the encampment for seven days before she is allowed to enter the community again. Apart from the material rationality, the danger of infection, it would seem that Lory after her return from the alien planet was held in quarantine for very different reasons. Still, the parallels between Miriam and Lory are bigger than expected when considered from the angle of the 'sin' they committed. It is not unlikely that Moses would have anticipated Yellaston in thinking incidentally 'God damn it … We never should have had women on this mission' (A117). In Tiptree's echo of the Exodus story, Lory has picked up the marginal tradition of female leadership in a patriarchal society, challenging the supremacy of the sacrosanct male leader.

But does Aaron Kaye also take sides with his sister, as the first Aaron did with Miriam by suggesting a jointly committed felony? He turns out to be much more hesitant in unconditionally backing Lory up. During the interrogations by Frank Foy he feels uncomfortable by both Foy's methods *and* what he perceives as Lory's evasive anwers, while he 'grins unvoluntarily' at Yellaston's anti-female outburst. Furthermore, notwithstanding his guilt-ridden feelings, he tends to make Lory responsible for the sin they actually joined in together, the incest in their youth. He constantly wavers between his affinities for the sister and for the patriarchal leader.

However, let us not turn the Bible into a model of male–female bonding against patriarchy. Both Aarons are characterized by ambiguities. Closely tied up with the patriarchal social and religious constellation, they nevertheless tend to violate its law, unlocking in that manner the dark recesses of what is alien to its rule. The biblical Aaron encouraged the grumbling Israelites to cast the idol of the golden calf and dance around it when they thought Moses was lingering too long with God on Mount Sinai (Ex.32). His science fiction descendant is involved in a different type of transgression. He has perverted (or 'profaned') the circumcision, the sign of the covenant between God and male human being, by turning it into the sign of incest between brother and sister. While Aaron and Miriam transgressed by contesting the patriarch's unique relation with God, Aaron and Lory violated the cultural law against incest.

Let us also remember that the biblical tradition of female leadership was rather precarious. It may be significant that Miriam was the first of the three leaders of the exodus to die, indeed in the middle of the desert (Num. 20:1). In the biblical text her death immediately precedes the account of the most serious punishment God inflicted on Moses and Aaron. Neither Moses nor Aaron was allowed to actually enter the promised land of Canaan, for they neglected to hallow God in the desert when God made water appear from a rock (Num. 20:2–13). Aaron died along the way, near the border of Edom close to the Dead Sea, still far away from Canaan (see Num. 20:22–9). Moses himself continued the guidance of his people through the desert until they reached Mount Nebo in the land of Moab, opposite Jericho. God then allowed him to climb to the top of the mountain to see the entire land of Canaan but did not give him permission to enter. And Moses died in the land of Moab, in accordance with God's word (Deut. 34:1–12).

Although Moses died before he could enter the promised land, he 'was a hundred and twenty years old when he died, his sight undimmed, his vigour unimpaired' (Deut. 34:7). Yellaston is a tough old guy too, who remains the most intact person after the encounter with the alien, although the painful irony is that it is not so much a case of strength, but probably a consequence of 'a lifetime practice in carrying on with half of his cortex shot' (A157). Nevertheless, he himself and the patriarchal order which he represents are inevitably dying. Whereas in the biblical story the death of Moses preceded numerous generations of patriarchs and other brave men of the chosen people, the decline of Yellaston and his crew marks the beginning of an alien existence beyond the familiar patriarchal order.

In these events Lory Kaye performs a crucial role. She is the only one who actually visited the Promised Land, the alien planet, and returns to bring its deceptive milk and honey home to the mothership. The people on board trust her knowledge of the promised land too much; they follow her blindfold to the alien light, a highly ambivalent force. Merging with this light simultaneously signifies completion of the decline of patriarchal religion as well as the emergence of a devouring yet procreative cosmic power. None of the crew members of the *Centaur*, Lory not excluded, will enter the promised land, they are all pining away in the wastes, in the deserts of outer space. Lory turns out to be an ambiguous prophet (or a wandering star). She promises the salvation of humankind by the alien power:

> No hurting anymore, never. They [Kuh and his people] came back so gentle, so happy. They were all changed, they shed all that ... It wants to deliver us. We'll be truly human at last. (A149)

In reality, however, she leads her people not just beyond the confines of patriarchy but also into the uncertainty of posthuman existence.

Lory's dream of deliverance and wholeness directs our attention to a third possible thematic parallel. The similarities between the biblical Garden of Eden and the spruce island of Fort Ogilvy Officer's Recreational Reserve brings the Genesis myth of Paradise and Fall into sight. Both places of pleasure and joy were guarded by the watchful eye of God or the guardian of the secular paternal law, respectively. Whereas Adam and Eve were not aware of the boundaries of their paradise until they got expelled from it, Aaron Kaye must have realized that he and his sister were transgressing. After all, the spruce island was located on *army* property, formally placed under surveillance of the paternal law in other words. Aaron knows the taste of the fruits of the tree of knowledge of good and evil (see Gen. 3:1–24). But who is to deny the sweetness of sin? It seems to me that this very paradox is tormenting Aaron throughout the story, and through him the narrative text, without it ever being neutralized. To Aaron it is very clear that Paradise is a 'noplace' (A155); there is no human existence before the Fall.

Lory, on the contrary, is obsessed with the eradication of evil, she is a 'lost child of paradise striving ever to return' (A121). Her error is that she mistakes the alien planet for paradise—by which the archetypical Paradise from Genesis and the historical–mythical Promised Land from Exodus are conflated. To Lory, the specimen of the life-form which she brought back with her, and which in the beginning is referred to in terms of fruits or vegetables (A84, A95), represents the possibility of returning to innocence and wholeness. This, of course, is an awkward reversal of the fruit scene in the biblical story, where the fruit was the symbol of *losing* innocence and gaining the knowledge of good and evil. To Aaron, therefore, Lory is an Eve who seeks to seduce him into innocence instead of transgression. I will come back in detail to Lory's desire for innocence below in this chapter.

Ultimately, for Lory the goal of a return to innocence is attained. After Ray Bustamente has vanished into the vastness of the universe with the *China Flower*, Aaron sees that 'Her face is clear, empty. Very young. All gone now, the load in her head' (A155). But in Aaron's eyes, Lory's returned 'pureness' does not signify a beautiful salvation but a horrific lethargy. Lory's paradise of sexual innocence or 'wholeness', which means an imaginary state before or beyond the dynamics of desire, is horrific because it results to be tantamount to cultural indolence. The 'little sister as she had been long ago', the sister before the incest, equals a zombie, the 'life-spark gone away. Voiceless, unfindable in the icy wastes ...' (A155). Utopia does not exist. Paradise and the Promised Land are equally imaginary places: 'Gently he helps Lory up and starts walking with her to noplace, she trustful to his hands; little sister as she had been long ago' (A155).

The archaic mother

In the reading of 'A Momentary Taste of Being' as a distortion of biblical motives we saw once again that Lory's being 'in league' with the alien does not provide her with a lasting position in the symbolic. While the destructive/generative force of the alien signifies the exhaustion of the phallic–patriarchal cultural and religious order, it does not imply an alternative religious voice for the daughter. In terms of the psychomachic configuration, the Lory-part is absorbed in divine bliss to such an extent that she is struck with permanent muteness and a fading sense of subjectivity. In contrast, the Aaron-part resists the lure of bliss and wholeness in the divine and remains a speaking yet deeply wounded subject that never stops yearning.

> ... Healed, made whole? All those months ... a wall away from heaven, the golden breasts of god. The end of pain, the queen couzy

> ... fighting it all the way ... Oh, Lory stay with me, don't die—*Christ, the pull, the terrible sweet pull*— (A162–3, italics in text)

The question now is how the maternal is to be understood in the light of 'A Momentary Taste of Being''s awkward incorporation of biblical imagery. What does it mean to attribute a religious dimension to the maternally connoted alien? In what context does Aaron's confused cry about the 'golden breasts of god' in the quotation above make any sense?

In the following I intend to deal with the alien as a reference to the *archaic mother*, a figure with both psychoanalytical and mythological-religious connotations. The concept of the archaic mother is derived from Kristeva's essay *Powers of Horror*, where it is situated in her theory about abjection. An important part of this theory is devoted to the particular forms of abjection in the Bible, that is, of the repression of the maternal body as a code behind Judeo-Christian monotheism. I want to relate Kristeva's reflections to 'A Momentary Taste of Being', insofar as they may further illuminate the alien as reference to both the maternal and the divine. Tiptree's story is not a confessional story nor a kind of Midrash. At issue here is its digestion of the fundamental cultural dynamic of Judeo-Christian history that, as Kristeva rightly says, has a lasting effect on the structure not only of the Western frame of mind but of its unconscious desire as well. Let me first explain in brief Kristeva's view of abjection and its elaboration in the context of biblical Judaism as a preliminary to Tiptree's text.

Abjection and biblical abomination
The abject signifies, according to Kristeva, an uncertain, transitory state between the subject and the object, appearing to consciousness as both fascinating and repulsive, a state of insecurity with respect to the identity of self and other. The abject must be radically excluded from conscious identity boundaries for it threatens the boundary between self and not-self, it disturbs identity, system, and order: abjection is caused by the in-between, the ambiguous, the composite. It thus signifies a hovering on the edge of the symbolic and the 'space' where the drives hold sway in all their ambiguity, the semiotic *chora*, which is so closely related to the mother's body. It is the place where meaning collapses, where the subject is in perpetual danger.

> The ego of primary narcissism is thus uncertain, fragile, threatened, subjected ... to spatial ambivalence (inside/outside uncertainty) and to ambiguity of perception (pleasure/pain).[6]

Abjection ultimately refers to the individual's real or fantasmatic dependency on the mother, and its fear of annihilation, of its existence as separate subject sinking back into the maternal body. As Rosi Braidotti puts it:

> We are all of woman born, and the mother's body as the threshold of existence is both sacred and soiled, holy and hellish; it is attractive and repulsive, all-powerful and therefore impossible to live with.[7]

Abjection is experienced in various ways, of which food loathing may be the most elementary and most archaic form. Kristeva gives as an example her own disgust of the skin on the surface of milk. Food becomes abject when it signifies a border between two distinct entities or territories. In a similar way all kinds of corporeal waste (excrement, pus, vomit, blood, in particular menstrual blood[8]) are experienced as horrific, as they signify 'the other side of the border, the place where I am not and which permits me to be'.[9] The 'most sickening of wastes', however, is the corpse, for it is an absolute border. 'It is no longer I who expel, "I" is expelled'.[10]

Kristeva argues that, historically, one of the important facets of religion has been the task of warding off the danger of the both fascinating and repulsive 'abject'. Religious rites and prohibitions aim at a *catharsis*, the purifying of the abject. To dam up the abject, or, in other words, to realize the prohibition placed on the maternal body, a whole social and symbolic economy of separation and exclusion is mobilized. The execution of this exclusion, the sacrifice, is the very erection of the sacred. In Kristeva's view, in the history of religion Judaic monotheism marks an extraordinary development with respect to abjection. In a sense Judaism announces the *exit* of religion and the unfolding of morals; a logic of abominations takes over from a religion of sacrifice. Pagan rites of defilement and pollution that persist as exclusion or taboo (dietary or sexual) in Judaism drift over to more secondary forms as *transgression of the sacred Law*, a profanation of the divine Name, for nothing is sacred outside the One.

> Biblical impurity is ... a *logicizing* of what departs from the symbolic, and for that very reason it prevents it from being actualized as demonic evil. Such a logicizing inscribes the demonic in a more abstract and also more moral register as a potential for guilt and sin.[11]

Another way of saying this is that Judaism as a religion of abomination tempers the fascination of murder: the Law with its system of taboos restrains the desire to kill. The 'feminine', that is to say, that which recalls the maternal body and one's biological origin, is a threat to be contained, not destroyed.

In Kristeva's view, the biblical text offers, through its profound elaboration of the limits of abjection, 'truly an archeology' not only of the history of religion but also of the construction of the subject's identity.

With Kristeva, I am interested in this 'intra- or infra-subjective dynamique of the sacred text'.[12] However, I am also particularly interested in the possible embodiment of this dynamic in a science fiction story such as Tiptree's 'A Momentary Taste of Being' that bears all the signs of a desire for the sacred but lacks faith in a transcendent and omniscient God to fulfil it. Back to the text therefore. Back to Yellaston's demon, to be more specific.

Yellaston's demon

We have already seen that Captain Yellaston is an alcoholic.

> Why? He [Aaron] has wondered that many times. He knows all the conventional names for the demons the old man must poison nightly. Hidden ragings and cravings and panics, all to be exorcised thusly. His business is those names—but the fact is that Aaron suspects the true name of Yellaston's demon is something different. Something inherent in life itself, time or evil maybe, for which he has no cure. He sees Yellaston as a complicated fortress surviving by strange rituals. (A115)

This 'demon' of Yellaston I conceive to be a key figure to the present interpretation of 'A Momentary Taste of Being' as a narrative informed by biblical reminiscences. We might obtain an indication of its meaning by placing it in the context of the following passage in *Powers of Horror*:

> What is the demoniacal—[but] an inescapable, repulsive, and yet nurtured abomination? The fantasy of an archaic force, on the near side of separation, unconscious, tempting us to the point of losing our differences, our speech, our life; to the point of aphasia, decay, opprobium, and death?[13]

In this passage, Kristeva describes the particular interpretation given by the biblical prophets, like Ezekiel and Isaiah, of the dynamic of abjection. Thus, in the framework of Kristeva's views on biblical abomination, Yellaston's demon can be understood as a literary reference to abjection as it was transformed in Judaic religion. This enables us to further specify the demoniacal that haunts Yellaston, modelled on the biblical patriarchs. While Aaron Kaye assumes that Yellaston's demons point at a general existential plague—'time or evil maybe'—I suggest we understand them as references to the abject maternal body. As such, the text gives shape to the fantasy of the archaic mother.

The concept of the archaic mother, as I indicated previously, can be understood from both the angle of the structure of the subject and of the history of religion. At first sight, the archaic mother may be identified with the mother of the semiotic *chora*, the pre-Oedipal mother, or, following

Silverman's revision discussed in Chapter III, the mother of the negative Oedipus complex. In her psychoanalytical study of horror films, *The Monstrous-Feminine*, Barbara Creed, however, suggests that the figure of the archaic mother should be distinguished, though not separated, from the semiotic mother. The latter is a figure that is imagined in connection to the family and the symbolic order, 'as a figure about to "take up a place" in the symbolic'.[14] In the history of human imagination, however, the archaic mother also appears as a parthenogenetic and generative mother, who exists prior to knowledge of the symbolic and the paternal law. In the mythological narratives of all human cultures, this aspect of the maternal is projected on the figure of the mother-goddess who alone created heaven and earth. A guise of the archaic mother that will be examined in the next section.

Creed develops her argument on the basis of her analysis of Ridley Scott's science fiction horror film *Alien* (1979). What characterizes the horror film is the unconcealed display of the abject, and in films like *Alien* the abject is construed directly in relation to the female body and its reproductive functions; the maternal body is reconstructed as the 'monstrous-feminine'. Although the archaic mother is not visible in the film herself, many images point to her existence (images of birth, rows of hatching eggs, the body of the mothership, long winding tunnels leading to inner chambers, the birth of the alien, and so on), of which the monstrous alien itself is the ultimate sign.

Despite the difference in medium, there are many striking similarities between *Alien*'s cinematographic and 'A Momentary Taste of Being''s literary environments. In the previous chapter, the spaceship *Centaur* was situated in the dialogical relation between the symbolic and the semiotic. As a result, the spaceship appeared invested with both maternal and paternal connotations. Focusing on the spatial aspects of the *Centaur*, however, highlights references to an archaic maternal figure as well. As in *Alien*, the archaic mother does not appear as a visible figure in 'A Momentary Taste of Being', but is nevertheless omnipresent.[15] What we see are such images as the *Centaur* as the mothership to which the *China Flower* returns and from which it leaves again: a 'warren of corridors' (A106), corridors as 'long tubes' (A119), later explicitly called 'oviduct' (A162), the alien 'ova', the zygotes leaving the 'womb', and so on. A remarkable difference between Scott's film and Tiptree's story, however, is the actual significance of the alien in both narratives. Whereas the alien in *Alien* is a hideous cannibalistic creature bursting out of the hatching eggs, in 'A Momentary Taste of Being' the alien itself is a mysterious and unfathomable power. The latter ultimately escapes identification with its palpable signs such as the ova from the planet, the wonderful light, the power of procreation, the posthuman zygotes. To put it differently, while the alien is legitimately associated with the maternal, it eventually transcends the maternal as well. I will return to this at the end of the next section.

In the case of *Alien*, the proliferation of violence and death caused by the alien creature reconstructs the archaic mother as a *negative* force.

> It is the notion of the fecund mother-as-abyss that is central to *Alien*; it is the abyss, the cannibalizing black hole from which all life comes and to which all life returns that is represented in the film as a source of deepest terror.[16]

It almost seems an inescapable condition in patriarchal signifying practices that the mythological figure of woman as the source of all life is constructed as a negative and destructive figure. Creed nevertheless stresses the importance of positing a more archaic dimension of the mother, for in any case it starts off a way of thinking about the maternal figure, and consequently of the feminine, *outside* the patriarchal family constellation and independent of the masculine. '[T]he womb signifies "fullness" or "emptiness" but always it is its *own point of reference*.'[17]

It is this same ambivalence about the negative and positive meaning of the archaic mother that can be found to propel 'A Momentary Taste of Being'. From the perspective of Yellaston's dread/desire, she appears as a demoniacal force, what Creed calls 'the blackness of extinction—death',[18] the threat/promise of return to original oneness with the mother. Aaron (before the alien encounter) thinks of Yellaston as 'a complicated fortress surviving by strange rituals', and wonders if perhaps 'the demon is dead now, the fort empty' (A115).[19] Aaron has never dared to risk inquiring, the text says, but my answer would be that the demon is still there, that it/she cannot ever be completely exorcized. The (threat of the) abject may be made more abstract and, in keeping with Kristeva's views about abomination in relation to the Judaic law, inscribed in a moral register, but it is never definitely banned. Overtly it appears, for example, in the language of abjection used by Yellaston and Aaron when they refer to the spaceships that will leave Earth for the deceptively paradisaical planet:

> And then the emigration ships will start coming in, the—what was it Yellaston called it—the pipeline. Typical anal imagery. The pipeline spewing Earth's crap across the light-years ...—whole industries and nations all whirling down that pipeline onto the virgin world. Covering it, spreading out. (A120)

It is significant that in this instance the imagery of spermatic (that is, non-abject) waste that is used to refer to humankind throughout the narrative is taken over by abject imagery like faeces. Here, the phallic–patriarchal discourse that Yellaston represents suppresses the 'maternal' discourse of alien procreativity and posthuman existence. For Yellaston, the demoniacal is what recalls the fantasmatic absorption in the maternal body (the submergence in the alien light) and, by extension, what refers to the feminine ('we never should have had women on this ship'). His demon was staring him right in the face, and he called it/her Death. And to a certain extent Yellaston's demon is Aaron's as well, as he sadly agrees with his leader: 'He saw it as death, the whole thing. Intuition in his locked-up guts, the fear—Sex equals death. How right you are, old man' (A157–8).

And how would we disagree with Aaron, who, after all, witnesses the horror of his fellow humans being reduced to zombie-like figures! Does his survival not affirm the imperative need to resist the lure of the 'archaic force ... tempting us to the point of losing our differences, our speech, our life; to the point of aphasia, decay, opprobium, and death' (Kristeva)? Yet again, the figure of Aaron represents in fact a very heterogeneous desire. He is torn between Yellaston and his Lory-part, as the biblical Aaron was between Moses and Miriam, wavering between the patriarchal law, which attempts to control the archaic mother signifying death, and a full rehabilitation of the maternal as autonomous force signifying life. Most clearly, Aaron's ambiguous position is expressed in the transgression of the incest taboo. Let me turn to Kristeva again to clarify this.

In designating the mother of the primary dyad or the archaic mother as the object of (sublimated) murder, Kristeva offers an inversion of Freud's classic thesis of the murder of the archaic father and the substituting sacrifice or totem animal in *Totem and Taboo*, and later in connection with Judaic religion in *Moses and Monotheism*. Crucial to her argument is the prohibition of incest, which she considers the first taboo that founds religion, preceding even the murder taboo. Her understanding of the incest taboo is farther-reaching beyond that of Claude Lévi-Strauss' structuralist approach, in which the incest taboo is posited as the fundamental law establishing social and family relationships and the signifying function. Kristeva understands the incest prohibition as a protection against abjection, as a safeguard against nondifferentiation and the loss of identity.

> Incest prohibition throws a veil over primary narcissism and the always ambivalent threats with which it menaces subjective identity. It cuts short the temptation to return, with abjection and jouissance, to that passivity status within the symbolic function, where the subject, fluctuating between inside and outside, pleasure and pain, word and deed, would find death, along with nirvana.[20]

Also the biblical logic of differences derived from the pure/impure distinction is based on the prohibition of incest, the taboo of the love of the son for the mother: it is its 'originating mytheme'.[21] Most poignantly, this taboo finds expression in the circumcision. The woman who gives birth is unclean (for seven days if the child is male, two weeks if it is a girl) and needs purification. On the eighth day the son's 'flesh of his foreskin shall be circumcised' (Lev. 12:3). Thus the boy is ritually separated from maternal impurity and defilement and symbolically allied to the One God.

What circumcision, in its repetition of the natural scar of the umbilical cord, 'carves out on his very sex' is the other sex.[22] The identity of the speaking being with his God is based on the separation of the son from the mother, and on the masculine from the feminine. The symbolic identity of the male, in other words, presupposes the violent difference of the sexes.[23] The impurity of incest, therefore, threatens the strong division between the sexes and hence allows the ambiguous maternal/female body to permeate the symbolic order. I want to recall, in this connection, Aaron's last dream containing allusions to a blasphemous entanglement of circumcision and incestuous—that is, led by the desire for undifferentiation—sexual initiation. Aaron transgressed the law of the symbolic realm of the father (incest) at the very moment he entered it (circumcision).

In this dream, moreover, some invisible being broke through the silence with the bisexual uttering 'I AM THE SPOUSE' (A128). It appears that not only is sexual difference erased in it ('cancel sound' A128) but also that in its/her act of *speaking* this re-emerging archaic force shakes the very foundation of the divinely sanctified order: the unifying transcendent Word of the Father God. Whereas Kristeva states that biblical abomination '*points* to but does not *signify* an autonomous force that *can* be threatening for divine agency', Tiptree's post-biblical fiction has indeed realized this threat: in the end no one speaks in the Name of the holy Father any more. But should we conclude, then, that someone speaks in the name of a sacred Mother in 'A Momentary Taste of Being'?

The mother-goddess

Until now I have discussed the archaic mother in the context of 'A Momentary Taste of Being''s biblical resonances mostly from the viewpoint of the psychic structures of the subject. Several times also the mythological aspect of the archaic mother as autonomous life-giving force has been mentioned. In this section, I will continue discussing these echoes of the mother-goddess in 'A Momentary Taste of Being'. First, however, such an approach needs to be contextualized.

With respect to the *choric* fantasy I stated earlier on that Tiptree's story can be understood to inhabit the same fantasmatic space as the feminist films and theoretical writings from the mid-1970s discussed by Silverman.

By analogy the story can be said to move around in another fantasmatic space, in which feminist science fiction intersects with (mostly though not exclusively North American) feminist deconstruction of the patriarchal character of the Bible and the Judeo-Christian tradition is paired to the spirituality of the Goddess. In the second half of the 1970s the image of the Goddess emerged from a mixture of historical information, mythological memories, and creative mythmaking as an empowering symbol rather than as a hypostatized deity.[24] By no means do I intend to suggest that Tiptree, who called herself an atheist, was actually involved in any of these spiritual practices, but rather that the narrative text she wrote reflects, consciously or unconsciously, particular elements of this discourse and thus, in turn, contributes to it.

'A Momentary Taste of Being' contains all kinds of reference to a divine dimension of the maternally connoted alien. Bill Coby imagines a god or a planet having had intercourse (A151), while the most evocative reference emanates eventually from Aaron in a delirious cry for 'the golden breasts of god' (A162). This expression recalls both biblical Aaron's subversive casting of the golden calf (Ex.32) and the fantasmatic power wielded by the fertility goddesses from the contemporaneous polytheistic nations surrounding Israel. Finally, Aaron Kaye claims that the American subcommander, Don Purcell, stated about the 'egg-things' that 'it was god' (A161). It is Don's naming of the alien that bears particular relevance to an assessment of the subliminal narrative of the archaic mother-goddess in 'A Momentary Taste of Being'.

Aaron's conclusion is prompted by the following passage. During the maelstrom after the exposure of the crew members to the alien light, Aaron bumps into Don Purcell. The hard-boiled commander from Ohio has turned into a sluggish and meek creature with a 'poleaxed steer'. And: '"The power," Don says in the voice he uses at the chapel. "The hand of the Almighty on the deep ..."' (A148)

While Lory concludes—smiling 'tremulously', though—that 'He's changed. He's gentle' (A148), Aaron ignores Don Purcell's words and is just worried about his strange condition. I suggest that Purcell's phrase is to be read as reference to an ancient image of the divine surfacing from under the patriarchal dust. It is very likely that at the chapel this prototypical American hero worshipped the white male Protestant middle-class god of civil religion.[25] His present utterance, however, evokes a different vision; it recalls the biblical cosmology of Genesis 1, as well as the echoes of an even older cosmogony.

Tehom and Tiamat

In Gen. 1:1–2 we encounter the *deep*, the sea: the primeval waters, pre-creational chaos and undifferentiation:

> In the beginning God created the heavens and the earth. The earth
> was a vaste waste (*tōhu va bohu*), darkness covered the *deep* (*tehom*),
> and the spirit of God hovered over the surface of the water.

Tohu is related to the Hebrew loan word *tehom*, which is interpreted as the
Hebrew rendering of *Tiamat*, the mother-goddess from the Babylonian
creation epic, the *Enuma Elish*. Of course the monotheist and patriarchal
biblical scriptures brook no conscious remembrance of any other deity,
but, as Catherine Keller explains,

> the fact that nowhere in the Hebrew Bible is the grammatically
> feminine *Tehom* preceded, like normal Hebrew nouns, by an article
> seems secretly to commemorate its status as a proper noun: the name
> of the First Mother.[26]

The oldest versions of the *Enuma Elish* date back to the first half of the
second millenium BC, perhaps even earlier. The biblical book of Genesis
knows two creation accounts, of which the second one of Gen. 2:4–14
in fact *pre*dates the first of Genesis 1. The oldest versions of Genesis 1
probably go back to the period between 1200 and 900 BC. Opportunities
for influence of the *Enuma Elish* on the different editings of Genesis
(between 1000 and 400 BC) extend from the period of the biblical patriarchs
(from 1900 BC on) through that of the Babylonian exile of the Israelites
(sixth century BC).

Many parallels exist between the cosmogony, the passage from chaos
to cosmos, of Genesis 1 and the *Enuma Elish*. The classic tabulation of
structural relations, framed by A. Heidel, is as follows.[27]

Enuma Elish	*Genesis*
1. Divine spirit and cosmic matter are coexistent and coeternal.	1. Divine spirit creates cosmic matter and exists independently of it.
2. Primeval chaos; Tiamat enveloped in darkness.	2. The earth a desolate waste, with darkness covering the deep (*tehom*).
3. Light emanating from the gods.	3. Light created.
4. The creation of the firmament.	4. The creation of the firmament.
5. The creation of dry land.	5. The creation of dry land.
6. The creation of luminaries.	6. The creation of luminaries.
7. The creation of humans.	7. The creation of humans.
8. The gods rest and celebrate.	8. God rests and sanctifies the seventh day.

Tiamat is the female force of the salt waters, who has intercourse with Apsu, the male force of the fresh waters. Together they are primeval chaos and undifferentiation. Then a discord breaks out among the young (male) gods in the belly of Tiamat. The young gods arise to fight the old ones. Tiamat takes revenge by giving birth to monster-like creatures. However, the final result of the battle is the slaughter of Tiamat, manifestly sea-monstrous by then, by the Babylonian warrior-god Marduk. Marduk splits Tiamat's body in two and creates the upper and lower parts of the cosmos from her carcass.

In *The Great Code*, Northrop Frye also understands *tohu* and *tehom* of Gen. 1:1–2 as less personified transformations of the Babylonian Tiamat. One of the assumptions of Frye's typology of biblical motives is that every apocalyptic image, interpreted as a positive and idealistic image, has a demoniacal counterpart.[28] Frye locates Tiamat, and hence the *tehom*, on the side of the demoniacal and the negative: they bear the sign of the primordial 'chaos or abyss'. In this appreciation we are reminded of Captain Yellaston's 'demon', intimation of the fantasy of the fearful archaic mother, the fecund mother-as-abyss, who needs to be conquered in order to enable, or guarantee, symbolic creation (as opposed to feminine procreation). Moreover, it recalls a negative conception of chaos recently contested by theories such as Prigogine and Stenger's *Order out of Chaos* (see Chapter II). In their view, chaos is not an absence of order (no order) nor order's antagonist, but rather a creative force that makes possible more complex states of being. With respect to the generation of the posthuman in 'A Momentary Taste of Being' we explored the premiss that: 'Life arises not in spite of but because of dissipative processes that are rich in entropy production'.[29] It is noteworthy, then, that Katherine Hayles, the provider of this quotation, reminds us of the traditional guise of chaos as a mythopoetic concept, a concept, moreover, with feminine connotations, as is reflected in her own description, 'Chaos is the *womb* of life, not its *tomb*'.[30]

In Keller's rendering of the Tiamat mythology one can observe a similar positive assessment of chaos, opposed to views like Frye's (and Yellaston's for that matter). Keller qualifies Tiamat's defeat not as the conquering of chaos but as the sanctification of matriphobia and matricide. In her view, a cosmogony in which creation (by the male hero) means the victory over 'an enemy older than the creator' suffers from a 'bizarre paranoia'. 'Who could constitute such a preexistent threat but a Mother, indeed the "First Mother"?', who, once conquered, functions as 'the facelessly inhuman, the *prima materia*, the defaced stuff, upon which his [the male hero, the warrior-god's] transcendent andromorphism enacts his new creation'.[31] For Keller, on the other hand, chaos is a creative force in itself: the seeds of form and differentiation are present in the unformed and unordered. Consequently, she eventually interprets the murder of Tiamat as the dismissal of creative chaos as regressive disorder, while depth is turned into an atmosphere of death. Paraphrasing Hayles: chaos is now conceived of as the tomb of life, not as its womb.

According to Keller, the *Enuma Elish* and Genesis share the same defamation of the feminine depicted forces of chaos. Such outstanding elements as the primeval intercourse and Oedipal rivalry, combats, sea-monsters and crushed she-carcasses are absent from the biblical book of origins. In the biblical monotheistic mode, of course, there is no place for divine origins apart from God, the divine One, the Almighty. Structurally, however, the two myths show great similarities, as explained in Heidel's tabulation. And beneath the surface of the biblical account the sounds of Tiamat and the slaughter of the First Mother are still echoing. In the *tehom*, Tiamat has turned into a Deep rendered completely abstract, while Marduk's warrior attributes are sublimated to a more dignified father image in the biblical God. Nevertheless:

> Somewhere in the back of the minds of the writers of Genesis is the Tiamat world of dark and storm, and the story of the masculine warrior-god who creates the cosmos from out of chaos, splitting the dragon-mother's corpse as the initial act of creation. The transparent image of Marduk is thus superimposed upon Jahweh.[32]

A divine beyond gender

Returning to 'A Momentary Taste of Being', and to the question whether someone speaks in the name of a sacred Mother, I propose that it is this transformation of the Babylonian Tiamat into the biblical Deep that is alluded to in Don Purcell's utterance, 'The power … The hand of the Almighty on the deep …' The precise purport of this allusion is not beyond doubt, however. Is it to be read as a call for aid to the almighty patriarchal god to lay his hands on the deep, to get the abject maternal power under control once and for all? Or is it just the opposite: are Purcell's words to be understood as an acknowledgement of the primordial power of the Deep and hence a celebration of its return? In other words, does Don Purcell speak in the name of a holy Mother?

My answer would be—in keeping with previous assertions during previous chapters and the present—that, whereas Don Purcell may hallow either paternal or maternal deity, Tiptree's text eventually deconstructs both options. For, as it turns out, neither the demise of the patriarchal religious order by means of the unknown alien force nor the suggestion of an almighty and all-encompassing mother-goddess allows for the daughter's position in the symbolic *on her own terms*. The Aaron-part remains tragically subjected to the paternal law and its monolithic God, though ceaselessly tending toward transgression, even when the alleged heavens of older days have turned into 'icy wastes' (A155). The Lory-part, on the other hand, which is 'in league' with the alien, disappears as a speaking subject as soon as she submerges in the fantasmatic depths of primordial maternal bliss. And as such Lory is emblematic for Don Purcell and for all the others on board. Eventually no one speaks in the name of either Mother or Father. Silence rules, like in Aaron's last dream:

> Silence … Bright, clinical emptiness, no clouds, no weeping. Horizon, infinity. Somewhere words rise, speaking silence: I AM THE SPOUSE. Cancel sound. (A128)

In my view, Tiptree's story does not move only beyond gendered and familial visions of the divine, but beyond theist models altogether. The alien is more alien than the archaic mother, whether she be perceived as the mother of the primary dyad or as the Goddess. The alien is divine in its ultimate ineffability and unfathomability. *Emptiness. Silence.* Yet it would be an error to ignore the value of certain features of the archaic mother-goddess, as manifested in the alien subjective and cosmic processes imagined in 'A Momentary Taste of Being'. The cosmic procreation is not just the description of a horrific fusion of alien and human life-forms, but it also imagines a profound transformation of humanity and human subjectivity, even though it is highly uncertain what this transformation will lead to. It is in this ambivalent process that the Deep as an allusion to the divine plays its part. With a view to a feminist discourse of the divine, it would be significant to move beyond the Deep's theist, gendered identity as mother-goddess, while at the same time emphasizing the qualities of creative chaos, chance, and change. It would contribute to visions of the divine that transcend the classic gender dichotomies allotted to the human subject in the history of Western culture. This would imply images of divinity in which ('feminine') procreativity and ('masculine') creativity are no longer mutually exclusive, no more than the forces of life and death, of generation and annihilation. Images also of a divine that is as material as the alien 'egg-things', while being, at the same time, as decentred and unfathomable as the alien itself.

The sin of innocence

Finally, I move back from the figure of the mother-goddess to the intra-psychic realm to add still another viewpoint to the discussion of the abject in the context of 'A Momentary Taste of Being'. Lory was, as Aaron put it, 'in league' with the alien. I have interpreted this in Kristevan terms as an indication that, through Lory, the child's fantasmatic oneness with the maternal body is revived and relived in Tiptree's text. However, such striving towards a pre-symbolic fusion brings the Lory-part of the daughter psychomachia in tension with her counterpart Aaron, who in desperation seeks to maintain her/his subjective identity in respect to the maternal. It is a tension which calls the attention to a particular representation of abjection in the text, namely the Christian modification of biblical abomination in the notion of sin. Of special interest, moreover, is the psychic defence strategy against this form of abjection embodied by Lory: that what can be called a *fantasy of innocence*. I expect to derive from these investigations an important prerequisite for feminist theological discourse.

First I would like to call to mind the revision of the Paradise myth in 'A Momentary Taste of Being' discussed earlier. Lory's reaching out to the alien light as the gateway to the lost Paradise before the Fall, to wholeness and innocence, aroused both pity and resistance in Aaron.

> He knows the secret lightning in Lory's bones. Not sex, would that it were. Her implacable innocence—what was the old phrase, *a fanatic heart*. A too-clear vision of good, a too-sure hatred of evil. No love lost in between. Not much use for living people. Aaron sighs again, hearing the frightening condemnation in her unguarded voice. (A82–3)

And not much later he thinks of her in the following terms:

> Lory, lost child of paradise striving ever to return. That look in her eye, you could cast her as the young Jeanne, reminding the Dauphin of the Holy Cause (A121),

to which is significantly added that 'Aaron has always had a guilty sympathy for the Dauphin' (A121). Before going into this comparison of Lory with Joan of Arc, I will situate Lory in the general framework of Kristeva's views on the transformation of abjection in the Christian notion of sin. From there, I will arrive at the peculiar twist the figure of Lory appears to have given to the reality this notion refers to.

In the writings and practices of Christian tradition, the Judaic logic of abomination received a remarkable modification. Kristeva recalls Freud's observation in *Moses and Monotheism* that Christian religion is a compromise between paganism and Judaic monotheism. In her view, Christianity has interiorized Judaic abomination through the notion of *sin*. From the New Testament (or Christian Bible) onwards, evil is displaced into the subject, and is hence no longer a polluting substance but 'the ineradicable repulsion of his henceforth divided and contradictory being'. One could say that by this interiorization of the Law in the category of sin, the abject is swallowed up, reabsorbed. Now the impure is inside. By that token Christian defilement is 'a revenge of paganism, a reconciliation with the maternal principle'. This should not be misunderstood, however, as a revalorization and rehabilitation of the maternal principle, for 'of its nourishing as much as threatening heterogeneity' the Christian texts will primarily keep 'the idea of sinning flesh'.[33]

By interiorizing and spiritualizing the abject, that is by symbolizing it, Christians are no longer beings of abjection but divided subjects. Sin is subjectified abjection. The distinction between pure and impure has been displaced to the subjective space. The subject is now seen as *internally* divided between flesh and spirit, corporeality and speech. Flesh, that is, according to Kristeva, 'what might be called, by anticipation, the overwhelming release of drives, unrestrained by the symbolic'.[34] Moreover, Christians are lapsing subjects, for the ideal of Christ constitutes a permanent reminder of human incompletion. Christ alone is a body without sin. In the catharsis of the Eucharist, 'purifying, redeeming all sins, it punctually and temporarily gives back innocence by means of communion'.[35] Rendered in the terms of Kristeva's unbiased reinterpretation of the Christian frame of reference, it effectuates a momentary reconcilation of the semiotic and the symbolic.

Kristeva's revision of the concept of sin differs from that of the Christian church fathers from Paul and Augustine to Aquinas, and onwards to Kierkegaard, to the extent that the divided subject is not so much a moral failing as in the first place a tragic subject. For Kristeva, Christian sin is 'both the memory and the repression of the violent struggle we have undergone within the semiotic and in our attempts to move beyond it'.[36] Therefore, sin is not just a transgression of the law of God/the father (see e.g. I John 3:4), but '*the refusal to recognize* the divided, heterogeneous, composite nature of the human mode of being'.[37] To acknowledge this condition, which in traditional Christian terms is the spoken confession of sin, means, according to Kristeva, not neutralizing sin but overcoming the repression it entails, the fusion with the maternal body.[38]

Making a turn of 180 degrees with respect to Lory's wish for innocence, I propose to name the refusal to recognize the meaning of sinfulness, the fact that the human subject is irreparably divided: the *sin of innocence*. It is an expression I gratefully borrow from Toni Morrison's novel *Tar Baby*, where it refers to being wilfully blind to the signs of evil in order to keep up one's own imaginary construction of the world and humankind.[39] I have come to the conclusion that Tiptree's narrative has projected on the Lory figure a deep sufferance from the 'sin of innocence'. Let me further explain this by highlighting the suggested analogy between Lory and Joan of Arc.

Joan of Arc

In Aaron's view, Lory is a Joan of Arc fighting for the Holy Cause, and more particularly she is cast/casting herself as the young Jeanne d'Arc, or *Jehanne la Pucelle*, Jeanne the Virgin, as the latter would call herself. Lory is identified, at this point, with the peasant girl from Lorraine, who at the age of thirteen heard divine voices and, at about seventeen, in 1429, introduced herself to the Dauphin Charles of France as his God-given saviour in the battle against the English. What are the possible implications of this identification? Let us not forget after all that Lory, unlike Joan of Arc, was not a virgin any more. At the age of thirteen, she did not hear divine voices but the call of sexual desire. It is no coincidence that the new-found planet is called a 'virgin planet', the reversal of the spruce island in Fort Ogilvy.

In her compelling study of Joan of Arc as object of cultural mythmaking, Marina Warner points out how Joan of Arc is at the same time a historical figure and a protagonist in a myth that is subject to constant creation and reinterpretation. Nevertheless the shared leitmotivs of these divergent interpretations are the characteristics of virginity and virtue: the abrogation of carnal womanhood and the celebration of masculine heroism paradoxically coupled in a female body. Joan's transvestism is the sign of this 'ideal androgyne', which, however, always remains an ambiguous state for a woman, because it unsexes and dehumanizes her yet does not confer manhood upon her. In the context of the Christian tradition, the state of nondifferentiation achieved by a transvestite girl was even considered holy. 'Sexlessness is virginity's achievement and a metaphor for martyrdom, as hagiography bears out.' For the martyrs of this kind, their self-obliteration was 'a rebirth into an exaltated state of original wholeness, where sex did not obtain'.[40]

Warner compares this exaltated state with death in the Freudian sense, the state of *nirvana* or the state of the reduction and neutralization of inner tensions, 'because in seeking to cancel sexual difference, it seeks to arrest time and to deny the mutability to which all flesh is heir'.[41] Of great interest, then, is the linkage Warner suggests between the stasis implied by supposed sexlessness and, on the other hand, *moral* stasis. Such relation becomes manifest in the fact that Joan of Arc has functioned in later centuries as the figurehead for many moral causes 'that proclaim the absoluteness of their way, their impregnability to moral relativism, which means their sovereignty over time'.[42] In my view, it is this version of Joan of Arc as the sexless and morally pure girl that resonates in Lory modelled on the young

Jeanne. What Aaron sees in Lory, at this point, is the suggestion of 'implacable innocence', a fanatic desire to rule out time, which is physical, and hence flawed, existence. In the terms of Kristeva's vocabulary used above, Lory refuses to except the irreparably split condition of human existence.

In her moral 'crusade', Lory is, I would say, infected with the inquisitorial virus inside the Christian conception of sin. Since sin is intrinsically related to conflicts of the conscience and (self)judgement, it holds 'the keys that open the doors to Morality and Knowledge, and at the same time those of the Inquisition'.[43] In the first place, the inquisition is imposed on her own body; she has abjected her female, potentially maternal body—the 'sinning flesh'—not so much by exterior transvestism, like Joan of Arc, but by trying to neutralize sexual difference in the body itself. She has a 'slim, almost breastless body', and 'with that pleasant, snub-nosed face she could pass for a boy' (A68). Her body 'strikes most men as sexless', according to Aaron, 'an impression confirmed by her task-oriented manner' (A68). And 'as far as Lory herself was concerned she would have been happy in a nunnery' (A68).

As Joan of Arc wore her cuirass to convert her into a virtuous knight for God and nation—into a man with a body-as-armour, so to speak[44]—so did Lory make her body itself into a cuirass to battle for the moral perfection of humankind. Inspired by 'alien' voices, both women wage war against violence and injustice. Lory insists on the necessity of human beings to change, that is to eliminate their animal part: aggression, cruelty, hatred, greed, sexual drives. 'To be truly human we must leave all that behind' (A121) is her belief. Her fanaticism provokes Aaron to object that she would, paradoxically, 'liquidate ninety percent of the race to achieve [her] utopia' (A123)—an acute prophesy, in retrospect! Notwithstanding Lory's shocked facial expression, Aaron says to himself that 'Torquemada was trying to help people, too' (A123). (Tomás de Torquemada, or Tomas de Turrecremata, 1420–1498, was a Spanish Dominican priest and grand inquisitor who authorized over 2,000 autos-da-fe.)

Lory, however, concludes this discussion by giving, with any lack of political irony, a line 'from some ancient work', which 'the martyr Robert Kennedy' had quoted before he was killed: '"To tame the savage heart of man, to make gentle the life of this world"...' (A124). Ill at ease Aaron turns away, mumbling his reality-principle:

> the life of this world is not gentle, Lory. It wasn't gentleness that got you out here. It was the drives of ungentle, desperate, glory-hunting human apes. The fallible humanity you somehow can't see ... (A124)

With these words, Aaron can be said to declare his sister guilty of the sin of innocence, thus reversing her desire to return to the paradise (the paradisaical planet) of wholeness or, to put it differently, her desire to be personally and collectively *innocent of sin*. In her search for moral purity, Lory refuses to recognize the split and composite nature of the human mode of being, symbolized in the text by the figures of Pan, Centaur and, in particular, the Lady of the Beasts. More specifically, she does not acknowledge the aggressive and destructive tendencies inherent in the death drive.

Fantasies of innocence
With the notion of the fantasy of innocence, Grietje Dresen offers, in her study of the same name, *Onschuldfantasieën* (Fantasies of Innocence), an apt model for describing such a striving for moral purity by women. A fantasy of innocence is:

> a seemingly plain image of satisfying harmony, the effect of which (namely satisfying) is based on a complex of feelings and images; especially on more or less conscious guilt feelings. These guilt feelings are relieved by staging practices of penance, in fantasy or reality. The real or fancied penance lightens the sense of discomfort for a while, bringing about satisfaction (in the twofold acceptation of the word satisfaction: reparation as well as contentment). The image of satisfying harmony thus reflects a longing for *innocence*—for a situation in which guilt doesn't exist anymore, or doesn't exist yet.[45]

In this psychic scenario of the fantasy of innocence, Dresen sees reflected the mythical tripartite of paradise, guilt (sin) and penance, and salvation. The sense of a loss of paradise plays an important role in the fantasy of innocence, whether it concerns a fantasy of a religious or secular kind. This corresponds with my own interpretation of the representation of Lory's desire in Tiptree's narrative, as well as the identification of the lost paradise with the child's earliest symbiotic relation with the mother of the primary dyad. Besides drawing on thoughts derived from Kristeva's theory about the semiotic/archaic mother, comparable to the ones playing such an important role in the previous and the present chapters of my own study, Dresen draws on psychoanalyst Jeanne Lampl-de Groot's interpretation of moral masochism for discussing the psychic dynamic involved in the fantasy of innocence.

Freud's concept of moral masochism indicates a more or less conscious striving for suffering meant as a punishment (*Strafbedürfnis*), to get rid of feelings of guilt and imperfection. Lampl-de Groot introduces the fantasy of omnipotence as a specific form of masochistic fantasy. In this case, the satisfaction derived from suffering is coupled with regressive feelings of omnipotence. It is a counterforce against what, biblically speaking, is the loss of innocence: the discovery of sexual difference.

> It is no exaggeration to assume that sexual difference is one of the major attacks on the child's earlier fantasies of omnipotence, in particular on the sexually neutral idea of being 'all'.[46]

Fantasies of omnipotence, in the sense of moral innocence and elevated sacrifice, are not reserved to the female subject. Nevertheless women may be, according to Dresen, more susceptible to this imaginative solution to barely conscious feelings of guilt and malaise. In the first place, the girl's identification with the mother of the primary dyad is relatively more unbroken than the boy's because she is of the same sex. Because the maternal figure represents omnipotence, fantasies of omnipotence may haunt the female mind. Moreover, Dresen suggests, this dynamic is likely to be enforced by traditional family life and educational practices in Western society, in which girls until recently were not encouraged to develop their own cultural project in life. Furthermore, she remarks that:

> The narcissistic wound which is the recognition of one's powerlessness can be averted by transforming the powerlessness itself into heroism: into heroic martyrdom.[47]

However, although fantasies of innocence are forms of fantasies of omnipotence, they need not be fantasies of martyrdom. Both fantasies aim at the elaboration and dissolution of aggression and feelings of guilt but in the fantasy of innocence the aggression is much better concealed. In Lory, as modelled on Joan of Arc, the fantasies of innocence and martyrdom appear to converge. With true heroism and sacrifice she has brought back with her the presumed salvific alien life-form, in order to regain through it paradisaical innocence and wholeness for Aaron and herself: 'I had to tie myself, even in the suit. I *had* to bring it back to you. And I did, didn't I?' (A149). By suffering *for* and *by* the aggression of others, she imagines to be innocent of aggression herself.

But women's search for sexual and moral innocence, and the corresponding denial of her sexual corporeality, are a dead end to a female subject in search of a livable position in the symbolic, as it turns out in 'A Momentary Taste of Being'. In the discourse of inquisition and martyrdom, the abject is as easily spat out as introjected, as Joan of Arc found out when she was sacrificed at the stake for the fortification of the Christian–monarchic order.[48] Lory Kaye's heroic quest for innocence, on the other hand, did not only involve her own (self-)destruction, or the end of the patriarchal–phallic symbolic. Her wish to exorcize (hu)man's aggressive drives extinguished the vitality of *any* version of the symbolic. Dresen justly recalls that the assumed moral superiority of women is, historically speaking, the reversed side of their social and political powerlessness: 'Such a position is a fertile seed-bed for holy innocence, but holy innocence is not a good seed-bed for politically effective and just practices'.[49]

To conclude, insight in the secular sin of innocence provides an important prerequisite for feminist theological discourse (and feminist discourse in a wider sense, for that matter). The sin of innocence is the refusal to acknowledge not only the ambiguity of the world around us but first and foremost the split and composite character of the subject itself. Facing this condition would mean that women start to ponder the meaning of aggression and violence from within. In her discussion of feminism in 'Women's Time', Kristeva also urges us to do what Lory couldn't, that is that

> the implacable difference, the violence be conceived in the very place where it operates with the maximum intransigence, in other words, in personal and sexual identity itself, so as to make it disintegrate in its very nucleus.[50]

Epilogue to Chapters III and IV

> And all he could say was that he did not know. He was guilty therefore, of innocence. Was there anything so loathsome as a wilfully innocent man? Hardly. An innocent man is a sin before God. Inhuman and therefore unworthy. No man should live without absorbing the sins of his kind, the foul air of his innocence, even if it did wilt rows of angel trumpets and cause them to fall from their vines.
>
> Toni Morrison[51]

Although I have seriously tried to look to Lory's interests in these chapters, it has not been possible to really live up to this challenge. Thematizing the repression and the reemergence of the maternal has not been sufficient for bringing into vision a vital oppositional female position in the symbolic. The following question, therefore, forces itself upon me: *why* does this text, this science fiction story, not produce any hopeful outlook on female subjectivity? Why is is that the only future perspective is to be found in the foggy contours of posthuman embryos? This can be rendered into another question: why does Lory seek refuge in an imaginary wholeness that means her own erasure as a subject? Why does she refuse to conceive 'the implacable difference, the violence in personal and sexual identity itself' (Kristeva)?

In the first reading of the text, in Chapter II, it was my well-considered choice to follow (critically) Aaron's perspective, as he is the observing and speaking subject of the overt plot. In the next two chapters, however, the assumption of a less visible mother/daughter plot and the instrument of the psychomachia were applied to get closer to Lory's perspective, to her 'crazy plot'. This effort has been fruitful, inasmuch as Aaron has been dealt with no longer as an oppositional male figure but as the dominant side of the same female figure. In this sense, Aaron and Lory Kaye are together the very emblem of split and composite being.

Notwithstanding this considerable change in approach, I have to face the fact that until now almost anything I said about Lory, any explanation, any judgement, has *still* been guided by Aaron's eyes. But is this focalization as inevitable as it seems? Admittedly the text almost forces the reader to follow its track. Yet it must be possible to switch one's interest. Who is the 'willfully innocent' protagonist? Is it really only Lory, as Aaron thinks? Or is it also Aaron himself, or rather, (I as) the reader of the text that leads me to identify too easily with him? Considering the complexity of these queries, it is time for a more radical change of perspective. Instead of attempting to reinterpret what Aaron sees on my own terms (Chapter II), or to distil the symptoms of a maternal desire from the text (Chapters III and IV), in the next chapter I will aim explicitly at, using a well-known expression of theologian Nelle Morton, a 'hearing into speech' of Lory.

V. (Counter) Apocalypses

Resuming 'A Momentary Taste of Being' differently

Just before the cargo-module in which the alien has been confined is opened—all of the crew members are watching the actions of the investigation team on the videoscreens in keen expectation—Aaron suddenly experiences 'an odd oceanic awareness' (A137). In Freudian psychoanalysis, oceanic awareness is the (revived) feeling of the symbiotic–semiotic oneness with the mother, in other words, the imaginary return to paradise discussed repeatedly in the previous chapters. During this experience Aaron is affected by a flow of thoughts which contains an important textual indication for the reading of 'A Momentary Taste of Being'.

> Here we are, he thinks, tiny blobs of life millions and millions of miles from the speck that spawned us, hanging out here in the dark wastes, preparing with such complex pains to encounter a different mode of life. All of us, peculiar, wretchedly imperfect—somehow we have done this thing. Incredible, really, the ludicrous tangle of equipment, the awkward suited men, the precautions, the labor, the solemnity— Jan, Bruce, Yellaston, Tim Bron, Bustamente, Alice Berryman, Coby, Kawabata, my saintly sister, poor Frank Foy, stupid Aaron Kaye—a stream of faces pours through his mind, hostile or smiling, suffering each in his separate flawed reality: all of us. Somehow we have brought ourselves to this amazement. Perhaps we really are saving our race, he thinks, perhaps there really is a new earth and heaven ahead ... (A137)

In the phrase 'a new earth and heaven' we remotely hear the echoes of the biblical Book of Revelation. In the context of Tiptree's science fiction cosmology, the commonplace expression becomes to point to what can be called an apocalyptic longing, a longing for the actual revelation of the end of times and the beginning of a radically new era. Considered in the light of Aaron's prior views, however, such a desire is quite remarkable. Until now we have come to know Aaron as a mild sceptic, doubting very much humanity's ability to change fundamentally so that its 'animal part' would be eliminated. He even fears the very striving after such a change, for it could easily turn into its own reversal, the very destruction of humankind. Remember his accusation against his sister that she would liquidate ninety per cent of the human race to achieve her utopia of a 'true humanity'. He does not truly seem to believe in the possibility of 'a new earth and heaven'. Once again the tension between the two parts of the Aaron/Lory psychomachia comes to the fore.

This tension—as I argued before—is not a simple opposition. The Kaye double is a wavering figure. Devoted to the reality principle as he may be, in the instance before the release of the alien Aaron's hope for the unbelievable shows itself to be stronger. And what's more, for a while Aaron is fascinated no less than his sister by the promise of wholeness radiated by the alien light. But the devastating events belie any of his momentary hopes. He is the lonely reporter not of the saving of the human race but of its vanishing. What he experiences at that instance must be to him an incomprehensible ordeal rather than the dawn of a new age. Yet the text unmistakably displays an apocalyptic orientation, sustained, as is my assumption, by the Lory-side of the psychomachia.

Until now I have not completely succeeded in granting Lory's part in the text. Over and over again it was Aaron's perception, either of the events on the *Centaur*, the incestuous past, or, finally, Lory herself—her appearance, her views and her behaviour—blotted out his sister's viewpoint. I will suggest, in contrast, that an interpretation of Tiptree's text as a form of apocalyptic imagination is a tool for the excavation of Lory's submerged story. This should not be construed as an attempt to champion a definite and authoritative truth over and against Aaron's presupposed false outlook. Nor do I strive to harmonize contradictions and tensions into a new metastory with one objective outlook. What is at issue in this reading is the significance of the silent voice, the repressed account of the text. This interpretive goal reminds us, by analogy, of Nelle Morton's ethical and spiritual appeal to 'hear women into speech'.[1] This refers to a type of listening which urges someone to speak, no matter how stammering at first, as opposed to the common logic which demands direct and clear statements in order to be heard.

But what does it mean to read 'A Momentary Taste of Being' as a form of apocalyptic imagination? In popular speech, the notion of apocalypse is usually identified with cataclysm and the end of the world, although the Greek *apokaluptein* means to unveil or to reveal, an ambiguity which will prove crucial to my argument in this chapter. The obvious reference point of apocalyptic imagination is the Book of Revelation (or Apocalypse), the contents of which will be briefly sketched in the next section of this chapter, where I will also argue that it is in particular chapter 12 of the biblical text which resonates in 'A Momentary Taste of Being'. However, the more or less clearly detectable echoes of the biblical text in textual signs and imagery form just one dimension of the narrative's apocalyptic orientation. They are at the same time bedded in a more general apocalyptic pattern which can be found not only in the science fiction genre but in Western history at large.

The *Wirkungsgeschichte* of the Book of Revelation, as Catherine Keller remarks, has been 'wide, disparate and contradictory'.[2] Aside from the profusion of its visionary images in religious and non-religious visual and literary arts, music and even performance art to the present day, Revelation occurs principally as an apocalyptic *pattern* operating throughout Western history. In modernity, apocalypticism appears in religious and non-religious guises, with marginal and mainstream positions, with progressive and reactionary implications. Yet these divergent movements and manifestations share a basic apocalyptic pattern, the traits of which are summarized by Keller as follows:

> This pattern, always adjacent to suffering, rests upon an either/or morality: a proclivity to think and feel in polarities of 'good' versus 'evil'; to identify with the good and to purge the evil from oneself and one's world once and for all, demanding undived unity before 'the enemy'; to feel that the good is getting victimized by the evil, which is diabolically overpowering; to expect some cataclysmic showdown in which, despite tremendous collateral damage (the destruction of the world as we know it), good must triumph in the near future with the help of some transcendent power and live forever after in a fundamentally new world. Because the pure and permanent state of the desired identity and its community can never be achieved, such scripts are characterized by an explosive futurism. Most often within this pattern, the extremes of innocence and of vice are coded as impersonally feminine, while the active agencies of good and of evil are figured as masculine heroes and their enemies.[3]

These beliefs need not always take shape in spectacular scenarios of final cataclysms, but can also be found in ideological proclamations of 'the end of' some historical condition, in which echoes of the apocalyptic myth can be overheard. However mitigated, they nevertheless recall the apocalyptic pattern of a final showdown between the forces of light and darkness. The emphasis of such ideologically inspired apocalyptic visions lies clearly on the negative moment—'the end of …'. Nonetheless some of their prophets also refer to the positive element of the apocalyptic pattern when they express their belief that the end of the present time also heralds a new aeon. A utopia of social equality and justice, for instance, or the New World Order and the global victory of the free market, or on the other end of the spectrum, a Green Paradise or a world in which sexual differences are reconciled in the ideal of androgyny.

Many science fiction stories, according to my perception of the genre, can be taken to be narrative revisions of the apocalyptic pattern. As works of the imagination, science fiction texts emerge from the socio-political, religious and cultural context of which they are a part, while they transcend this context as well. They partly reflect their cultural environment but at the same time comment on, transform and distort it. While this applies in a sense to every literary genre, its specific devices, conventions and special effects make science fiction transform reality in its own idiosyncratic way. Whether it is by means of extrapolation or analogy, its imaginary worlds express the fears, desires and hopes of twentieth-century industrialized and techno-scientific culture. Fears and hope which, indeed, are to a large extent apocalyptically tainted, in particular in the North American post-World-War-II context of nuclear anxieties, cold war paranoia, the marriage of Christian fundamentalism and right-wing politics, and post-cold-war cultural confusion and capitalist globalization. Precisely because science fiction is characterized by the creation of imaginary worlds and possible futures, it is a genre in which the apocalyptic pattern is given full play. It offers all the space wanted for the either conscious or unconscious exploration of the meaning of apocalypse for the conception of human relations with each other and the cosmos.

Before actually going into 'A Momentary Taste of Being' again, I will give ample consideration to science fiction's apocalyptic orientation. In doing so, I intend to satisfy the twofold purpose of providing an interpretative key for the interpretation of 'A Momentary Taste of Being''s apocalyptic imagination, as well as contributing to postmodern feminist theological discourse on apocalypticism. To that purpose, I make use of the two meanings of the word apocalypse: catastrophe and revelation. My wish is anything but to present an overview of the genre and its individual works as such. Instead, I address myself to two divergent theoretical approaches to science fiction in relation to apocalyptic discourse, which by and large correspond to the denotations of apocalypse. First, various views of science fiction which focus on representations of catastrophe, end of the world, and survival will be discussed. The other approach, in contrast, deals with the interpretation of science fiction from the angle of apocalypse as revelation, elaborated in *Apocalypse and Science Fiction*, a provocative study by Frederick Kreuziger, who understands science fiction as 'secular soteriology', and science fiction's (virtual) revelation as a revelation of meaning. In this manner, the category of apocalypse functions as a link between science fiction and theology. This is an approach which requires careful consideration and, for that reason, I shall not confine myself to presenting Kreuziger's study as a framework for understanding 'A

Momentary Taste of Being' but also critically assess it from the viewpoint of religious studies.

Situating Tiptree's text in connection to science fiction's apocalyptic imagination means also taking into account its historical context. That is to say, not only the heightened apocalyptic discourse in the contemporary public arena in the United States, as mentioned above, but also the emergence of the women's movement in the late 1960s, and of feminist science fiction as part of it. Together these aspects form a background against which, as I hope to show, Tiptree develops an idiosyncratic apocalyptic idiom in 'A Momentary Taste of Being'. Important parts of Tiptree's text remain fully in the dark if this double background is disregarded. In two sections I seek to shed light on two such obscured corners. They are each of a different nature, though: while the one hides a subplot of the narrative text, Lory's silenced story, in the other references—mere textual allusions—can be found to ancient myths, connected to Revelation, which disclose yet another dimension of Tiptree's text.

I shall conclude this chapter with some speculative thoughts, rooted in the interpretations of the text but at the same moving beyond them, towards a 'counterapocalyptic' prospect of disclosure.

Echoes of the Book of Revelation

Although apocalyptic ideas and images are far from the monopoly of the Christian Western world, in the predominantly protestant North American context, and the type of science fiction it produces, they certainly are rooted in the Judaic–Christian tradition. Apocalypticism in this tradition is a radical form of eschatology, in the form of a collection of myths and doctrines on 'end things' (*eschaton* = last, extreme). Through it, the hope is expressed for the kingdom of God which is understood as a perfect situation either within history, at the end of history or as an after-death heaven. Apocalypticism can be seen as a heightened hope for the kingdom of God, an impatient longing for complete discontinuity with the present world, for a judgement on history, a demand for total transformation— not one day, but today. It is a matter of urgency, for the present time is experienced as a time of crisis, a time that calls for decisions (*krisis* = 1. judgement, 2. separation).

In apocalyptic writings, the end of history is pictured in visionary language. In a religious context *apokaluptein* means the revelation by God of the end of the world. The Book of Revelation is not the only apocalyptic biblical or apocryphal text but it is certainly the most famous and influential. Dated from the end of the first century AD, it is the expression of the vision of Christ bestowed on John of Patmos, in which he is ordered to convey its prophetic words to the seven churches of Asia Minor. The words are meant to encourage and admonish Christians who have experienced harassment and persecution under Roman rule (Rev.1–3). As such, the text, as Keller rightly remarks, 'reveals not a divine investment in catastrophe but a hermeneutic of crisis ... enabling a beleaguered community to interpret its place within historical crisis meaningfully'.[4]

Besides the inaugural vision and the letter septet, the book of Revelation is constituted of three more parts. The second is the vision of God, sitting on a heavenly throne, offering a scroll with seven seals to Christ, the Lamb, followed by the opening of the seals, seven angels blowing seven trumpets, and seven bowls of wrath (Rev. 4–9; 11:15–19; 15:1; 15:5–19:10). Breaking seals, blast of trumpets and pouring out of bowls each fortell a new calamity, like death (represented by the famous four horsemen), famine, wars, plagues like the ones visited on the Egyptians in Exodus, falling stars and geological disturbances. Between times we hear songs of praise to God and the Lamb (7:9–17; 11:15–18). After the emptying of the bowls of wrath the big city of Babylon is called up, represented as a majestic whore, who is to be destroyed by the beast on which she rides (16:9–19:10). The fall of this female Babylon at the same time commemorates the Babylonian exile of the Jews and offers a promise of redemption from the oppression by the Roman empire and its emperors.

The third component of Revelation is enveloped in the text of the seven seal scroll (10:1–15:4). It contains the vision of a small prophetic scroll, in which a woman and a dragon battle over power, a horrendous beast with ten horns and seven heads rises from the sea and another one marked with the number 666 from the earth, and the fall of the beast/Babylon/Rome is proclaimed.

The last part of Revelation contains the visions of judgement and salvation (19:11–21:9).[5] The heavens open for the King of Kings riding on a white horse and clothed in scarlet, a sharp sword is coming from his mouth. He is the Lord of Hosts, the heavenly legions following Him on white horses and clothed in white linen. They catch the beast and his false prophet and throw them in a pool of fire and sulphur. Next an angel descends from heaven to lock satan, the devil, in a deep pit to allow for the millennium, the thousand-year epoch in which the ones reign who were decapitated because of the word of God, and who do not bear the sign of the beast. At the end of this period, satan will be released from his prison, and he will gather the people from all four corners of the earth to attack Jerusalem. But all of them are devoured by fire—the prelude to the Last Judgement.

The dead are standing in front of God's throne, books are opened, and the dead are judged by virtue of what is written in the books. The ones who do not appear in the book of life are thrown into the pool of fire. And so the first heaven and the first earth had passed, and 'there was no longer any sea' (21:1). But John sees a new Jerusalem, a new holy city, descending from heaven, 'made ready like a bride adorned for her husband' (21:2).

It is in particular the third component of Revelation which has produced one of the most remarkable textual resonances in 'A Momentary Taste of Being'. Let me first bring back to mind the female figure, the *'immensely tall, eternally noble woman'* (A83) in Aaron's second dream, who was discussed as the Lady of the Beasts in Chapter II. She was presented as a mythical woman, a queen or goddess who in her close connection to the animals symbolizes, in the description of Estella Lauter, a 'purposive, active ordering of the drives'. Next I explained how this integrative strength fell pray to dissolution—or, the 'working out of the beast'—in the state of chaos and entropy into which the *Centaur* moved. Presently, a specific embodiment of this Lady of the Beasts is introduced: the woman in Revelation 12. The crucial text is Rev. 12:1–6.

> After that there appeared a great sign in heaven: a woman robed with the sun, beneath her feet the moon, and on her head a crown of twelve stars. She was about to bear a child, and in the anguish of her labour she cried out to be delivered. Then a second sign appeared in heaven: a great, fiery red dragon with seven heads and ten horns. On his head were seven diadems, and with his tail he swept down a third of the stars in the sky and hurled them to the earth. The dragon stood in front of the woman who was about to give birth, so that when her child was born he might devour it. But when she gave birth to a male child, who is destined to rule all nations with a rod of iron, the child was snatched up to God and to his throne. The woman herself fled into the wilderness, where she was to be looked after for twelve hundred and sixty days in a place prepared for her by God.

Besides the battle over power between the woman and the dragon, the third part (10:1–15:4) pictures the beast with ten horns and seven heads rising from the sea and another one from the earth, and finally the proclamation of the fall of the beast and its image.

This imagery first draws attention to another narrative by Tiptree. Not only does a substantial part of her fiction consist of end-time stories, some of these stories contain bold revisions of biblical apocalyptic imagery. Especially noteworthy is 'On the Last Afternoon' (1972), in which Mysha, the last inhabitant of a settlement on a colonized planet, is caught between two powerful agencies. He is crushed between the promise of transcendence and eternity incited by an alien creature, the noion (probably from the Greek *noein* = to think, to understand) and, on the other hand, a herd of horrific beasts emerging from the sea. Their form and the way these sea monsters are mating—the males tearing the heads of the females from their bodies afterwards—convincingly recall the beast rising from the sea in Rev. 13:1–10. As this beast has received its power from the dragon (Rev. 13:2), it is somehow connected to the woman in Rev.12. And to the Lady of the Beasts in Aaron's dream.

I will return to this woman later. Meanwhile, we need to obtain more knowledge about science fiction as a genre with largely apocalyptic features, in order to facilitate the assessment of 'A Momentary Taste of Being''s apocalyptic character.

The apocalyptic imagination of science fiction: the spectre of doom

End-time narratives

Science fiction's preoccupation with catastrophe is the most obvious perspective from which to discuss the genre's apocalyptic imagination. Since Hiroshima and Nagasaki, apocalyptic anxieties have been predominantly generated by the 'bomb', although after the global events of 1989 the nuclear threat seems to have lost some impact as a cultural signifier. But besides the nuclear scenario, the modern imagination is offered a wide range of horrors that are virtually devastating to the world, from overpopulation to genetic manipulation in human, animal and plant life, and from ecological destruction to civil and ethnic wars. All of these horrors have been explored in one way or another in science fiction's near-futures. The elaborate depiction of global catastrophes, alternating with devastating invasions of extraterrestrials or magnified animals, appears to confirm what anthropologist Louis-Vincent Thomas suggests, namely, that science fiction is a literature of *fear*. His contention is that science fiction stories reveal fantasms of fear and guilt that smoulder in the unconscious layers of 'a society sick with its own progress'.[6]

Thomas, like Keller, points out the persistence of the apocalyptic pattern in the Western mind, even though the different tenors of the eschatology of the Judaic–Christian apocalyptic myth and the present spectre of the apocalypse cannot be overlooked. John's Revelation shows what Thomas names a model of *annihilation–punishment*, in which a vindicative God punishes humankind for its disobedience and vices. Today it is no longer God who punishes but it is the god-forsaken human being itself that provokes the mechanisms leading to its own fall. The apocalypses of science fiction appear as the product of what Thomas calls, using an expression from Michael Serres, the same 'thanatocracy' that is responsible for the arms race and other devastating manifestations of Western civilization. This kind of science fiction, which, as Thomas suggests, perhaps could be better labelled as 'science affliction', grotesquely stages the excesses of technological and political power. Whether in the guise of masochistic digression, exorcism or warning, writer and reader alike 'find the same morbid satisfaction from the glorification of guilt and the vision of punishment'.[7]

While Thomas clearly includes himself in this 'morbid' writer and reader interplay, such a paradoxical revelling in the depiction of the destruction of earth and/or humanity is a thorn in the side of science fiction writer and critic Stanislaw Lem. In the chapter devoted to end-time stories in his lengthy study *Phantastik und Futurologie*, he asserts that 'science fiction pictures in false sounds what in view of the content need no longer be false'.[8] In his opinion, hardly any skilled and morally sound story about the end of the world has been published after H.G. Wells' *The War of the Worlds* in 1897: 'What once was a vision, an innovation, a myth—as in Wells—and later was able to become a warning, now is tedious entertainment'.[9] Moreover, the majority of this fiction of catastrophe suffers from an immoral lack of sensibility towards the real threats of the post-World-War-II period, as if an author were allowed to sacrifice the entire humankind just for fun or to provoke the readers.

Lem's often eloquently phrased contempt for the literary and moral qualities of most catastrophe stories seems to have more rhetorical than explicative value. Nevertheless he provides us with some thought on this fascination for the catastrophic which is worth considering, as it appears to show affinity with discussions of the downward narrative dynamic of 'A Momentary Taste of Being' in previous chapters. Lem's assertion is that apocalyptic science fiction displays, albeit in a much hazier and much more veiled manner, a motive that can also be found in the works of De Sade. It is the motive of the systematic descent into the 'abyss of anti-creation', the desire to make culture gradually regress through the animal stage to sub-animal levels. However, De Sade's aim, as Lem asserts, was not a simple reversal, not an unambiguous reduction to a natural state of creatures who had reached the apex of culture. In fact, his programme was more ambitious since these noble creatures with their vices had nevertheless to be preserved in order to be the spectators of and witnesses to the systematic conversion of paradise into hell. Thus, 'without ceasing to be an angel, the angel has to take part in the satanic actions, alternately, he has to be both'.[10] And ultimately paradise is created in order to make hell, the abyss of anti-creation, possible.

Although science fiction's stories of the end of the world, in Lem's opinion, seldom offer really creative visions in this respect, the Sadeian motive of anti-creation nevertheless seems to be at work in them.[11] Thus, the explanations provided by Thomas and Lem about the predeliction for the picturing of catastrophe each represent one side of the same coin. While the former stresses the masochistic indulgence in guilt and punishment, the latter points out the Sadeian drive towards cultural and subjective transgression and dissolution. Together these drives indeed seem important complementary forces behind the catastrophic imagination of science fiction. They converge at the representation of what Thomas delineates as:

> the collapse of the homo sapiens and the ego (the one of the cogito), followed by the manifestation of the anti-power, the anti-knowledge in which life triumphs over the harmony of the world, in the victory of instinct over reason, and of the species over the individual.[12]

Yet one wonders *whose* anxieties, death drives, sense of guilt and hunger for punishment find an outlet in science fiction's fantasies of doom? *Who* exactly projects either fear of or desire for the violent annihilation of culture onto the imaginary worlds of the (near) future? To answer this, let us take into consideration that the community of science fiction writers, lay readers and professional critics has until recently been predominantly *male*, while both Thomas and Lem also exclusively refer to male-authored texts. I propose to take Thomas at his word and to read the revisions of the apocalyptic pattern in science fiction as accounts of the disappearance of the *homo* sapiens. To read them, that is, as expressions of the collapse not of reason and the subject *per se*, but of the *masculine* and self-reflexive Cartesian character of the 'ego of the cogito'.

The excessive fantasies of the catastrophe stories seem entangled in a rather ambivalent project. They are so profoundly affected by the violent and destructive sides of Western Enlightenment, that they use the most violent narrative strategies to effect its very destruction. For this reason I think 'A Momentary Taste of Being' belongs to this genre. Even though it is written from a position in the symbolic different from the male-authored fantasies, it reflects a shared obsession for the breakdown of Western culture. In this sense, Tiptree, like the other writers of catastrophe stories, appears, willy-nilly, as a kind of modern apocalyptic anti-prophet.

Survival fiction
We can say that the first three structural elements of the apocalyptic mythical pattern preponderate in the doom stories discussed by Thomas and Lem: the belief that the world is corrupt; that its catastrophical end is imminent; and that the one proclaiming the end is seen as prophetic. Moreover, the end is no longer merely imminent: the imagination has

moved beyond the painting of the dystopic and toward the actual representation of catastrophe. Most often the result is pictured as either total (sometimes even repetitive) destruction or the absorption of reason by the non-rational or the irrational, which is projected on the figure of the alien, the mysteries of the cosmos or an anti-civilization of mutants.

So-called survival fictions, of which both science fictional and canonized literary works are a part, rather take the fourth element of the apocalyptic pattern as their point of departure. This is the hope for a new age or new world beyond the final showdown, in which injustice has been purged and the cosmos renewed. To what extent, on the level of literary imagination, is this hope fulfilled? In the first place, the fictional post-apocalyptical worlds give expression to the fact that the twentieth-century cultural order is shaken to its very foundations. Auschwitz and Hiroshima remain the emblematic horrors of the breakdown of a culture whose technological reason has speeded up its forces to the extent of a possible total destruction. Ensuing from it is the awareness of the impossiblity of the realization of a new heaven and a new earth and, in correlaton with it, the impossiblity of *narratives* in which utopian societies are created. What then are these post-catastrophical fictions like? What kinds of world, and what kinds of narrative are involved?

In an essay on postmodern and postnuclear narrative, Mária Minich Brewer raises the important point that survival fictions written by non-feminist and feminist authors differ considerably from each other. In non-feminist narratives, the disorientation with respect to reality and to the possibility of a coherent narrative about reality frequently leads to a nostalgic reassertion of the Oedipal plot in the imaginary post-apocalyptic world. On the one hand this fiction is marked by a style of fragmentation: it consciously distances itself from the closed and self-sufficient vision of reality which ends in the destruction of what is excluded as other. A closer investigation of the manifest text, however, discloses still another layer: in the chaotic post-catastrophical world great efforts are put into the regeneration of the phallocentric symbolical order. Such narratives evolve around a solitary male survivor, and turn out to be stories about initiation, a rite of passage into masculine sexuality.[13] Women appear only as servants or exotic objects of desire in these all too familiar heroic quests that lie at the heart of the Oedipal plot.

Post-nuclear and other survival fictions by non-feminist writers thus appear too often as a collaboration of writer and protagonist to set 'the defective Oedipal machine' in motion once more. As if the very imagining of the nuclear holocaust has not already put into question the obviousness of the symbolic order that 'determines *his* place in the phallogocentric system'.[14] Brewer, therefore, is but one of the critics who turn to feminist authors using the defamilarizing conventions of science fiction to explore the possibilities of a different worldview. Robin Roberts even suggests that the total destruction of the patriarchal or world produces a 'blank canvas' on which 'women can recreate society in their own image'.[15] It would be better, however, to acknowledge that not even a science fiction imagination can accomplish a total escape from the old symbolic order.[16] For that reason I believe that a divine-like female creation in her own image is less transformative than what Brewer describes as 'the invention of an alternate fictional world in which the other (gender, race, species) is no longer subordinated to the same'.[17]

In these worlds, catastrophe is the referent of a type of writing that divides a 'past–present' from a possible 'present–future'. Discontinuity and difference are its crucial categories: discontinuity with the Oedipal narrative that dictates rivalry between biological and symbolic fathers and sons and determines women as lack, and difference as a radical recreation of language, subjectivity and culture. Situated on the border between the end and a survival beyond the end, feminist post-catastrophical science fiction texts address themselves, as Brewer rightly points out, to the question of survival in a double sense: 'for women, it is at once a matter of surviving the patriarchal narrative of exclusion *and* the fable of catastrophe that it programs'.[18]

As discussed in previous chapters, the type of catastrophe pictured in Tiptree's imaginary world—the cosmic reproduction—is so peculiar that it is hard to determine whether its main focus is survival or destruction. Destruction of the phallic–patriarchal symbolic and its imagination seems the very prerequisite for surviving its narrative, although survival in this case is not represented in the form of an alternate human culture but rather as *some* aspect of the human which continues in the generation of something unknown. Tiptree's text tells us neither anything decisive about which aspect it is that survives nor about the character of the posthuman creatures. What these creatures represent with any degree of certainty is a break from the past: this is what Brewer refers to as difference and discontinuity with the familiar patriarchal organization of language and subjectivity.

The apocalyptic imagination of science fiction: the hope for salvation

In the previous section the central issue was the meaning of representations of catastrophe and end-time scenarios in science fiction. Subsequently, I will focus on a rather differently tuned view of science fiction as apocalyptic imagination. The guideline for this approach is the already mentioned study

Apocalypse and Science Fiction: A Dialectic of Religious and Secular Soteriologies
by Frederick Kreuziger.[19] It is remarkable, to start with, that Kreuziger sees
science fiction as a literature of *hope*, contrary to Thomas for instance, who
qualified it as literature of fear. And yet, both Thomas and Kreuziger take
their starting-point for discussing the genre in twentieth-century
secularized culture dominated by science and technology. In addition, both
refer to biblical apocalypse as a model for interpreting science fiction.
Largely divergent, however, is the meaning of this model for their
assessment of science fiction as apocalyptic literature. Thomas equals
apocalypse to final catastrophe and reduces the biblical myth to the aspect
of Last Judgement and punishment of God, recaptured in a secularized
way in the doomdays of science fiction.

In Kreuziger's approach, on the other hand, the appeal to Revelation—
and to apocalyptic thinking in a more general sense—widely exceeds the
diagnostic aim of Thomas' cultural criticism. The most conspicuous thing
in Kreuziger's study is the absence of catastrophe and the destruction of
the world in a literal sense. Destruction is understood as a metaphorical
phenomenon, effecting a transformation of the mind. In other words, it is
not the representation of nuclear or any other cataclystic threats which
functions as science fiction's prime apocalyptic signifier: in Kreuziger's
view, science fiction *as a genre* tends toward the apocalyptic. What we see
here, in short, is a shift from the understanding of 'apocalypse' and 'apocalyptic' as representation of catastrophe and the end/new beginning of the
world, to apocalypse as a *theoretical category* for approaching science fiction.

As I will go on to clarify, this means in the first place a shift from the
thematical content and the imagery to the *structure of language*. At this point
Kreuziger's approach turns out to converge largely with Brewer's in that
both emphasize the structure and concatenation of narrative, rather than
its content. For that reason the crucial category of discontinuity in Brewer
overlaps to a large extent with the notion of *disjunction* used by Kreuziger.
Both terms, I would say, refer to an awareness of *crisis*: the fiction under
discussion is thought to be expressing the idea that the contemporary
culture is in urgent need of radical transformation. For Brewer, the critical
point and the aim of transformation is the representation of difference,
sexual and otherwise, beyond the phallocentric symbolic and the Oedipal
plot. Kreuziger's approach too is characterized by a political commitment
to cultural change but, in addition, it is motivated by a theological objective.
By reading science fiction as popular literature tending towards apocalyptic,
he seeks to bring the genre into action as a model for the resocialization
and repolitization of what he considers a self-sufficient and spiritualized
Christian theological discourse. His aim is reassessment of the often
maligned biblical apocalyptic and, consequently, renewed systematic

reflection on apocalyptic thinking as the horizon for a contemporary critical theology.[20]

I shall pay ample attention to Kreuziger's approach because it offers an important insight into both the possibilities and the limits of connecting literary and theological discourse in the understanding of science fiction as apocalyptic imagination. As such Kreuziger's study is a two-pronged instrument for me. First it offers indications as to how to read 'A Momentary Taste of Being'. Critical evaluation, on the other hand, of its theological assumptions allow me to give more relief to my own, partly dissenting, view on apocalypse as theological horizon, which I will tentatively sketch in this section and resume at the end of this chapter.

Apocalypse: the language of future expectation
The subtitle makes the objective of Kreuziger's study explicit: to provide 'a dialectic of religious and secular soteriologies'. A soteriology is a theory of salvation (= the Greek *sootería*). In a narrow sense salvation is identified with the redemption by Christ from sin. In a less specific and more positive sense, salvation or redemption refers to well-being and joy, to salutary effects and healing properties, bestowed on people by a power that is experienced as transcending oneself. The secular soteriology in Kreuziger's study is of course science fiction, while the religious soteriology refers to biblical apocalyptic, not only in the restricted sense of the book of Revelation but also as a particular genre or type of language. The notion of apocalyptic is applied as the link between both discourses: 'Apocalyptic ... becomes the genre which opens both science fiction to a "theological" reading, and intertestamental/biblical apocalyptic to a "popular reading".'[21]

By characterizing science fiction as popular literature tending towards apocalyptic, Kreuziger stresses the importance of the early science fiction and its self-understanding, that is the 'pulp' origins of the genre in the 1920s and 1930s in the United States.[22] Its subcultural character of close connections between writers, readers and publishers in 'fanzines' has deeply influenced the further development of the genre: it was, according to Kreuziger, basically popular literature, and has remained so during the development of the genre until the present day. The early science fiction was historically both a product and a particular response to the Depression: it reflects not only the economic and social crisis of those days but also the belief that science and technology will *save* humankind. And precisely the experience of crisis and the concomitant longing for immediate salvation connect science fiction to biblical apocalyptic. They both 'look for salvation and deliverance by something or someone beyond present reality (of which it despairs)'.[23] In the case of science fiction this saving agency from beyond may be captured in terms simply of the future, or in terms of extra-terrestrial life.

Crucial to this understanding of apocalyptic is the notion of *expectation*, that is, the expectation of the reader, or rather the community of readers. Its counter-term, connected in the first place to the skills of the author, is extrapolation, speculation about something unknown from facts that are already known. The point of reference for Kreuziger, here, is *New Worlds for Old* by David Ketterer, who sees science fiction as an outstanding example of the apocalyptic imagination of North American literature.[24] According to Ketterer,

> Apocalyptic literature is concerned with the creation of other worlds which exist, on the literal level, in a credible relationship … with the 'real' world, thereby causing a metaphorical destruction of that 'real' world in the reader's head.[25]

'Credible' in this definition should be taken not only in the sense of plausible but also as 'effecting faith', for 'an act of faith and an act of reason may be equally and inextricably involved in the acceptance of any unseen world'.[26]

While crediting Ketterer for considering the apocalyptic character of science fiction in the light of its 'credibility', Kreuziger nevertheless wants to radicalize its implications. He proposes to shift the attention from the extrapolative skills of the author to the expectations of the reader. According to him, it is not extrapolation but expectation which is responsible for the metaphorical destruction of the known world in the reader's mind.

> Apocalyptic, then, does not so much reveal the writer's intentions (to dream, fantasize, escape, or inflict his/her paranoia onto a hapless world) as it reveals the reader's expectations and hopes.[27]

The implication of this shift, subsequently, is a *remythologization* of apocalyptic, a shift from individual to collective readership, for science fiction is 'a social and socializing' literature.

Kreuziger posits the motto 'What you expect is mostly a matter of how you expect' as 'a philosophical and theological principle for the critical investigation of science fiction, apocalyptic, and indeed of the whole of a biblically grounded hope'.[28] One could say that his theory aims at delineating a *right way of expecting the future*. Apocalyptic language involves three types of future expectation: simple, modified and disjunctive expectation. These types of expectation express how people relate to what Kreuziger refers to as the dialectic of promise (vision) and fulfilment (reality) of salvation.

Both biblical and secular apocalyptic opt for the promise, because what good is a promise if it can be fulfilled? Only a sustained dialectic between promise and fulfilment causes people to look criticially at the present. But is science fiction always capable of sustaining this tension or dialectic? In the language of simple expectation, the dialectic collapses into fulfilment; the future is expected simply as a continuation of the present. 'Change, in this language, is a fact of reality; it is not a function of human consciousness and/or interpretation'.[29] Modified expectation already functions less simply. In this language the future exists as a depth-dimension of the present. This depth-dimension is known because of promise, whence the future is allowed to exercise a critical function in relation to the present. The future is not the object of fulfilment but the instance of hope.

Most 'promising', however, is the disjunctive expectation; in it the structure of apocalyptic can be isolated. Its semantic structuring is performed by such words as 'but', 'however', 'nevertheless', 'on the contrary', all of them indicating a break, an interruption, a shattering of the expected end and meaning of the story. From the perspective of temporal structuring, the best qualifier of disjunctive expectation is *imminent* expectation. It signifies a breakdown of the usual configurations of time as conjunction or cause/effect logic. Imminent or disjunctive expectation is the medium through which the radically new breaks into the present. Its language is the language of crisis or, in other words, of the tension between promise and fulfilment. And its importance lies in the twofold purport of crisis:

> Apocalyptic … is not only occasioned by crisis, it also, in its own way, occasions crisis by acting as a critical counter to a shallow reading of the present moment and the present world and its structures.[30]

From this description of apocalyptic language in general ensues Kreuziger's quality standard for science fiction, which appears to be literary and theological at the same time. What characterizes 'the best of science fiction' is the capacity to hold out the tension between promise and fulfilment, a quality which marks 'true apocalyptic literature'.

> It is only when science fiction as true apocalyptic literature moves beyond excessive concern with fulfillment that it allows promise to exercise its critical role: to provide a critique of all final solutions.[31]

To have science fiction assume genuine apocalyptic potential, Kreuziger explains, the difference between knowledge and meaning is crucial. While the (technological or scientific) knowledge science fiction contains 'is already dated by the time the ink dries', its stories may always offer new meaning. Not knowledge but meaning saves. An apocalyptic story is 'not about revelation; the story is the revelation, which not only gives knowledge, but also meaning'.[32] Yet science fiction more often than not fails the standard of 'true apocalyptic literature' when its stories promise the unlimited but deliver only the limited: the very human knowledge of science.

Of course, Kreuziger asserts, biblical apocalyptic was better fitted to reveal (ultimate) meaning to its readers. The horizon of the promise of salvation was God, while science fiction only has to offer 'flawed' symbolizations for expressing transcendence. Kreuziger distinguishes the model of the 'future history' and the 'we are not alone' model in science fiction. The first model narrates the end of the cosmos, time and history, humankind, and meaning, and the beginning all over again of the cycle. In the second model, the promise is maintained that somewhere in the universe other intelligent life exists with which contact will be established in order to give a fullness to human life it now lacks. On the whole Kreuziger is in favour of the second type of stories. While the future history model simply extrapolates possibilities based on present (scientific) knowledge, the 'we are not alone' model represents an openness to the radically new. This means that two different forms of expectation are involved. In the future history model, expectation is immanent, whereas in the 'we are not alone' model expectation is imminent or disjunctive. Unfortunately, however, too often the means (science) becomes the end also in the latter model: contact with the alien gets reduced to a drama of technical expertise, or of technical virtuosity in science fiction films.

> Contact, in that kind of story, however, is never of the kind which stands in critical relationship to the contact with the 'other' always imminently expected in our own lives, whether it be with the dark side of our being, with the other person, or with a transcendent principle or being we call God.[33]

Although, fortunately, counterexamples can be given—to his own example of Stanislaw Lem's novel *Solaris* the filmic version by Tarkovsky can be added without hesitation—Kreuziger's objection to the shallowness of alien encounter stories seems valid enough.[34]

Yet it is in this very criticism of the representation of the alien in science fiction that a problematic aspect of Kreuziger's approach becomes manifest. The quoted passage may be illustrative for this problem. It is suggested, on the one hand, that the imminently expected alien may have different faces. It may be a saving/salutary agency, which is a meaning-giving source; we may also look in the face of the dark side of our being. In the case of the former, we are dealing, according to Kreuziger, with myths of salvation. The latter face of the alien, in contrast, points to fantasies of anxiety or horror. These, however, are consciously left out of the picture by Kreuziger since his views are based on a strict distinction between positively oriented science fiction in which desire (expectation) prevails as propelling force and, on the other side, science fiction horror, 'nightmare fantasy', in which fear leads the narrative.

To me, this seems a rather artificial division. Questions raised by such division are: Is desire only a positive force, and is it never mixed with fear? And, moreover, isn't the alien the outstanding *ambivalent* figure in science fiction of any kind? This is the case at least in 'A Momentary Taste of Being', as I have pointed out time and again in the previous chapters. The belief that 'we are not alone' may indeed be conceived as a promise of salvation, even more so if we understand this to refer not only to the alien other but, as Kreuziger indicates, to the ensuring community of believers as well. Sometimes, however, the virtual presence of the other can be a threat of doom as well. I rather tend to think that the very absence, or rather, repression of ambivalence as to this promise is indeed a contentious point in Kreuziger's project.

Or: 'What is awaiting us?'

The model favoured by Kreuziger for the interpretation of biblical and secular apocalyptic is that of a dialectical hermeneutics, in which both 'genres' throw light on each other in order to revitalize an apocalyptic horizon in modern theology. This approach takes as its (problematic) point of departure the belief that texts are actually able to reveal meaning. To clarify this, let us first go back for a moment to David Ketterer, who concludes *New Worlds for Old* in this manner:

> In whatever displaced, disguised, secularized, or antagonistic relationship, the religious element remains a constant identifying characteristic of the apocalyptic imagination.[35]

This so-called religious element is identified with the desire for the revelation of a 'genuine, hitherto hidden, reality'.[36] The reality referred to thus is revealed in the immanence of textual worlds created by means of the extrapolative skills of the author. Kreuziger, in turn, has displaced the disclosure of the hidden reality to the reader's attitudes of expecting. Moreover, instead of Ketterer's 'religious element' he uses the more open notion of 'meaning'; we find a search for meaning in science fiction—for 'answers to many of the oldest, the most important, and the most exciting questions mankind has ever asked'.[37] Despite these displacements, Kreuziger's view nevertheless still rests on the same supposition of a genuine hidden reality.

This reality, of course, should not be naïvely mistaken for a supernatural world. In Kreuziger's vision, the hidden reality is the kingdom of God, which is not an abstract hereafter but a metaphor for a radically new and salutary meaning which breaks into reality. The question of God, and the kingdom of God, cannot be treated apart from the social, political, cultural and religious life of people. And for that reason, as is Kreuziger's contention, the collapse of God-language in modernity, the so-called 'death of God', does not imply the collapse of apocalyptic language, as many people would have it. What remains after the death of God is the *promise* of salvation, which is a promise without content yet not an empty promise. What Kreuziger means by this is probably most saliently expressed in the following lines:

> That today it is no longer customary to speak of God as the giver of the promise in no way denies the fact that the promise as something received somewhere along the line (if only through the exercise of critical reason) is of vital concern for those who work for the emancipation of humankind. The death of the gods of rationalism, enlightenment, positivism, pragmatism, capitalism, of science and technology—all these deaths are the occasion for the flowering of apocalyptic, for each death in its own negative way clarifies the understanding of the promise. Apocalyptic, thus, is engaged in a constant and unending re-reading of history in order that someday the whole story may be told.[38]

The conception of apocalypse in Kreuziger's study is, as I would summarize it, that, no matter how hopeless, iniquitous and meaningless the present may seem, we need to rely on the promise that there *is* (textual and ontological) meaning, and that history *does* make sense. There is a *telos*, a purpose and an end, not in the trivial sense of the fulfilment of a history of (technoscientific) progress, but in the sense of a promise of meaning. It is an approach critical towards ideological and political claims, for it guards against identifying actual historical developments with fulfilment. Unlike the prophets of contemporary American fundamentalist apocalypticism, Kreuziger, I would say, understands the promise not as a biblical Guarantee soothing a (self-)chosen people, but as a metaphorical expression of belief that there is truth in the future. Thus promise, for Kreuziger, is able to exercise the critical role of providing a critique of all final solutions. Trust in the promise, or, in his words, imminent expectation provides 'a meaningful interpretation of the course of historical events'. It does so by 'transforming expectation and waiting into an openness to the radically new, the coming of which exceeds all hope and yet is grounded in it'.[39]

For Kreuziger, hope and expectation are grounded in the belief that 'some day the whole story may be told': no matter how veiled and marked by the negativity of history the true story may seem, there *is* a promise, and therefore, ultimately, a salutary plot. I agree that openness to the radically new is what qualifies the best of science fiction. Yet I see the need to make a reservation as to the very nature of this radically new. That is to say, whether the radically new is salutary or destructive is not a truth that will reveal itself but is a matter of political and ethical judgement. What is ignored in Kreuziger's vision of imminent expectation is the fact that the radically new *has* already revealed itself over and over again in twentieth-century history. The novelty of the radically new, however, has not manifested itself historically as a saving but as a destructive faculty, witness the succession of technoscientifically structured wars and genocides that have deeply scarred the twentieth century. It is this fact, and the accompanying feeling of *loss* of expectation, with which an important part of both science fiction and theology since World War II try to deal. In my opinion, therefore, the apocalyptic awareness as horizon of contemporary theology Kreuziger advocates is flawed by the exclusion of negativity.

I would like to oppose to this the critical question put forward in an essay by Hermann Häring on the theological and philosophical implications of the apocalyptic imagination and the concept of the Last Judgement in post-World-War-II postmodernity. The apocalyptic question, he states, is not 'what may we expect, but: what is awaiting us?'[40] In other words, the future is not the object of an immanent utopia towards which we can direct ourselves but something unknown which directs itself towards us. Apocalyptic hope thus largely exceeds the anthropological framework: it refers to the question of whether despite the historical and virtual catastrophes in the twentieth century, there is salvation inside, along with, or after the demise that threatens our world. Häring's view implies the opposite of a fatalistic 'waiting for Godot'. In his understanding it is not only a humane but even more so a religious and ethical task to develop, on the one hand, an awareness that our society suffers from an 'apocalypse-blindness'[41] and, on the other, the faculty of *imagining*, instead of moralizing or rationalizing. By imagining, Häring means the deployment of the senses and the imagination, of contemplation and intuition, to anticipate both the destruction and the hope that are virtually present in our reality:

> In my view, everyone must become acquainted with the idea of a possible end, in order not to be blind to the injustice that heavily burdens the world: the suffering of the victims and the useless revenge, the howls of derision throughout milleniums, from Cain to Hitler, from Nero to Stalin.[42]

Only from here, Häring argues, it becomes possible to hope for what theologically is called 'a new creation', which is an entirely *extra*-empirical category and signifies *unexpected* salvation. Hence it makes perfect sense, I feel, that he concludes his plea for an apocalyptic imagination by referring to Walter Benjamin's rejection of any politico-theological project of realizing the future in history. After all, Benjamin reminds us that the Jews were concerned about the future not as an object of control but because they believed that 'every second of it was the small gate through which the Messias could enter'.[43]

To return to Kreuziger, then, I think his altogether important consideration of apocalyptic language could gain from modification by a more postmodern viewpoint such as Häring's. Kreuziger's modern theological project, unlike for instance Häring's, is still grafted on a metaphysics of divine presence. That is to say, on the assumption that there is a ground of being, a divine foundation which, however veiled (or secularized) in modernity, can be revealed and known. I think that the 'death of God' is not an accidental inconvenience, however, a death, as Kreuziger more or less suggests, which could be undone by killing the false gods of modernity (rationalism, capitalism, technology and so on). Compare this to Häring's thought, on the contrary, that the death, or rather the absence, of God is no less than a catastrophe for those who believe in God. And he wonders why this experience of God's absence, unlike the other catastrophes of the twentieth century, is so seldomly phrased in apocalyptic language. The question about the divine after the death of God is one of the issues that will be tentively tackled in the concluding chapter. At present I will confine my argument to the apprehension of science fiction as apocalyptic imagination. To reach a conclusion, I think Kreuziger offers an innovative model for relating science fiction and apocalyptic discourse to the extent that it moves beyond apocalypse as the mere narrative thematization of a mythical pattern of catastrophe and renewal. Its importance lies in the category of *disjunctive expectation*, for it points to a structure of narrative in which the seemingly logic and normal order of language and time are shattered. It expresses the desire to open up a hermetic (story of) reality; it advocates a fundamental openness to the future, in other words. Unlike Kreuziger, however, I do not conceive disjunctive expectation as the belief in a revelation of meaning but as an urge, motivated by an experience of crisis, to imagine the impossible and the unexpected, in *both* its horrific and hopeful aspects.

In this sense, disjunction closely resembles the categories of difference and discontinuity put forward by Minich Brewer: notions indicating experiments of the imagination, which, indeed, can signify experiments of hope and longing for a transformation of reality. Thus, disjunction would no longer be a soteriological sign, of either a religious or a secular kind, but a device of the literary and theological imagination. In science fiction, this imagination vacillates between confirmation and disruption of the conventions of, respectively, popular literature and myth. Between, to put it differently, the belief in narrative, subjective and collective coherence and, on the other hand, their postmodern defeat. Science fiction is as much a remythologization, as Kreuziger would have it, as a demythologization of apocalyptic. It desires salvation as much as it distrusts and despairs of it. And it creates meaning and plot as much as it deconstructs them.

In the most evocative works of science fiction these contradictory inclinations motivate the very textual dynamic. I consider 'A Momentary Taste of Being' as one of these works. In the following sections, I will discuss Tiptree's text as an example of science fiction which clearly demonstrates an apocalyptic imagination. An imagination, moreover, which cannot be understood in isolation from its specific feminist character.

The apocalyptic imagination of 'A Momentary Taste of Being': Lory's apocalypse

In order to explore 'A Momentary Taste of Being''s apocalyptic orientation, I will bring together the two approaches of the relation between science fiction and the apocalyptic frame of reference discussed in the previous sections. This means paying attention to the narrative representation of elements of the apocalyptic pattern, and in particular the elements of crisis, catastrophe and survival/renewal. These elements are intermingled with the textual organization of disjunctive expectation in the modified manner defined above: as a collapse of the traditional temporal and narrative order to open up the imagination for the impossible and the unexpected. I hope to show that these two aspects of the apocalyptic imagination, the thematical and structural, are closely related. Together these intersecting searchlights will assist me in tracing the possible meanings of 'A Momentary Taste of Being' when Lory's viewpoint is taken as point of departure. As we shall see, this results in the first place in a new understanding of the negative outlook of the story. Nevertheless the disjunctive force also creates fissures in the text through which we can catch sight of a possibly more positive tenor.

There are two major disjunctive moments in the text. First I want to bring back to mind the scene described at the beginning of this chapter. All the crew members are watching the videoscreens showing the cargo-module with the alien confined inside. Aaron is flooded by emotions of an oceanic kind, mellow and proud feelings towards his fellow crew members, and hence by apocalyptic expectations of a positive kind: 'Perhaps we are really saving our race ..., perhaps there is a new earth and heaven ahead

...' (A137). Then the alien's module is opened and the alien's beautiful luminescence flows out. With astonishment, Aaron watches the research team taking off their helmets. The next moment—

> he is jostled hard. He blinks, recovers balance, looks around. Jesus— he's in the wrong place—everybody is in the wrong place. The whole corridor is jamming forward of where it's supposed to be, staring at that marvelous glow. (A139–40)

I suggest reading this passage as a signpost in the text, indicating a radical shift in perception. Both Aaron and the reader are being shaken up in order to experience a destruction, both literal and metaphorical, of an old order of understanding and the emergence of a new dimension of the text. Aaron is being confronted with the alien life-form and its seductive light, while the reader starts to uncover Lory's silenced story.

Even more telling is the disjunctive organization of the text itself. To assess this moment of disjunction it is necessary to focus on Aaron once again. What we see then is a profound gap between the composed, confidence-building, rational physician from before the manifestation of the alien light (part i–iii) and the boozing, cynical and utterly confused person afterwards (part iv). In this last part, in which Aaron is recording, Aaron, the narrative, and language itself have *all* lost linearity and coherence. While in the first three parts there were constant switches from internal (Aaron) to external (impersonal, non-distinct) focalizing agency, in part iv only the internal focalisator remains. Any distance between narrating and observing agency has disappeared now, there is no buffer zone any more between Aaron's story about reality and reality itself— hence the last sentence 'I don't dream anymore'. Aaron has lost any hold on the self and the world. He has turned from a more or less stable subject that clings to his own story, identity and perspective into a desintegrating subject without any fixed point. Sometimes he and Lory telescope into each other, Lory becoming the familiar and he himself the alien. Sometimes they dissociate again: 'Comment on me. Call me Lory—no, we aren't going to talk about Lory, either' (A158).[44]

The language in part iv, moreover, has still barely narrative properties, while instead deliriously associative utterances predominate. In this stylistic rupture between parts iii and iv, and the concomitant change in representation of the subject, the apocalyptic—or disjunctive—force of the narrative is embodied. The configuration of time is shattered: the future breaks into the present and thus interrupts the supposed linear succession of past, present and future. A radical difference between pre- and post-alien time is established, with the latter presenting a tangle of time dimensions that resists unwinding. In the post-alien time the past and the future exercise a constant critical power on the present. The reason for this is that in the contact with the alien light a story has surfaced which can no longer be excluded or repressed from the dominant story.

In the previous chapters I referred repetitively to Aaron's awareness of the alliance between the alien and Lory: 'Lory! She's in league with that thing ..., this is her crazy plot' (A141). Until now I have ignored the words following in the quotation: "He has to stop it. Kill it!" (A141). I ignored their violent implications. They cannot be avoided any longer. Lory's plot must not be killed but, on the contrary, admitted the right to exist. To that purpose we have to return to the beginnings of the narrative. It leads us down to the Interview/Observation chambers in *Centaur*'s quarantine ward.

'Psychic rape'

After her return from the scout's mission to the assumed paradisaical planet, Lory was interrogated twice by the *Centaur*'s security officer, Frank Foy. The situation is as follows. Because of possible contamination, Lory is held in an isolation ward. She is wired up to a sensor bank by Aaron's lover, Solange, who is wearing an anti-contamination suit. Aaron watches his sister from an observation room with viewscreens on two walls. The screen in front of him is activated two-ways: it shows the four men of the interrogation team in a separate room (Frank Foy, Captain Yellaston and the subcommanders Tim Bron and Don Purcell); the other screen focuses on Lory, who sees only a blank screen.

Aaron's attitude toward the interrogation is rather ambivalent. Although he ironically admits that the questioning is necessary 'for the safety of the tribe' (A69), Lory's position of subjection makes him feel very uncomfortable: 'It's a disgusting scene, Aaron thinks; the helpless, wired-up woman, the hidden probing men. Psychic rape' (A69). His repugnance is in particular focused on Foy, whom he reproaches for his harsh impersonal attitude along with the pleasure he seems to derive from the questioning. Solange seems to be Foy's reverse: 'Empathy is Solange's speciality' (A70), although later her empathy is qualified as an *'impersonal receptivity'* (A79, my italics).[45]

Harshness and empathy thus appear as two complementary, traditionally masculine and feminine (or paternal and maternal) connoted aspects of the same process of distilling the truth from a (human or textual) object. This process is presented as scientific and objective ('impersonal'), directed at insights with a universal interest ('necessary for the safety of the tribe' A67). Though reluctant, Aaron also acknowledges this, despite his feelings of compassion for his sister and his spontaneous dislike of Foy (his *foe/foil*). The immediate goal of the interrogation is to detect virtual discrepancies between verbal responses and physiological reactions. Put differently, Foy searches for a possible subtext of Lory's text which could contradict the overt story and reveal the hidden truth beneath the deceptive surface. The next step is to put so much pressure on the interrogated person that she will come up with a confession, so that it becomes possible to conflate surface and undercurrent.

During the first session anomalies are simply registered: 'the physiological reactions ... are not characteristic of her base-line truth type' (A71), without an appropriate explanation being available. The second time Lory is put under much more pressure. Again and again Frank Foy asks her why she had welded shut the cargo module with the alien inside and left all tools for opening it behind on the planet. 'I repeat, Dr. Kaye, were you afraid to have a means of unsealing the alien?' (A88). Despite her denial, not only the tapes but all people observing her register that she is lying. Nevertheless, only a few minutes later everyone, including Aaron, settles for her explanation which apparently leads the attention entirely away from the alien: there was a fracas amongst commander Kuh's crew. 'So that is Lory's secret. Aaron breathes out hard, euphoric with relief. So that's all it was!' (A90). Frank Foy is even 'entirely satisfied' and believes that Lory's 'revelation of the, ah, conflict dovetails perfectly' (A101).

Aaron, on the other hand, is not entirely satisfied. After his initial relief, he soon continues to sense that his sister is covering something. 'He distrusts everything; cannot tell' (A123). As a medical doctor he is able to detect the signs of anomaly: Lory has come back from her scout trip with ulcers, while her coppery curls are turning grey. But is he also capable of *interpreting* these signs? And what is even more important, are we as readers capable of interpreting them in a right perspective?

The entire process of Lory's interrogation seems to exemplify the reciprocal connections between sadism and story suggested by Laura Mulvey and Teresa de Lauretis. The former states that:

> Sadism demands a story, depends on making something happen, forcing a change in another person, a battle of will and strength, victory/ defeat, all occurring in a linear time with a beginning and an end.[46]

De Lauretis, in turn, asserts the reversibility of the two terms: not only sadism demands a story to be performed, the reverse is even more true. Narrative demands sadism: 'forcing a change in another person, a battle of will and strength, victory and defeat'. And all of this 'is, to some extent, independent of women's consent'.[47] The interrogation scenes in 'A Momentary Taste of Being' clearly have sadistic connotations in this sense: a passive, wired-up woman is subject to the gaze of a group of men, who try to penetrate her metaphorically ('psychic rape'). Sadism demands a story indeed: Lory's secret must be revealed, Lory has to be made to confess. Conversely, the reader may be tempted to take these scenes as mirrors or models for his/her interpretative labour, being seduced into a sadistic practice of extracting a confession from the text. Nevertheless I do not agree with De Lauretis' pessimistic claim that story necessarily demands sadism.

Her view is rooted in the assumption that all narrative relies on the model of a mythical hero in search for knowledge, which represents a transformation from childhood in adulthood. The narrative space is marked by a boundary or obstacle between an internal and an external sphere the hero has to cross. The closed space he penetrates and has to emerge from (i.e. the obstacle) is morphologically female 'and indeed, simply, the womb'.[48] Hero and space/obstacle are by definition connoted masculine and feminine, respectively. In crossing the boundary, and defeating the obstacles he finds on his way, the mythical subject becomes a man: 'the active principle of culture, the establisher of distinction, the creator of differences'. Even when the mythical subject is personified as a woman, she is connoted masculine, for femininity means mere passivity and inchangeability: 'she (it) is an element of plot-space, a topos, a resistance, matrix and matter'.[49] The question arises, however, if subjectivity in narrative is as inevitably male as suggested in De Lauretis' circular or 'claustrofobic'[50] reasoning. Wouldn't a non-oppositional relationship between hero and space, between subject and object, automatically make the traditional opposition of active masculinity and passive femininity invalid too? Crossing a boundary, entry into another space and emergence from it need not necessarily implicate violent penetration of passive matter. Donna Haraway suggests that

> the object of knowledge be pictured as an actor and agent, not a screen or a ground or a resource, never finally as slave to the master that closes off the dialectic in his unique agency and authorship of 'objective' knowledge.[51]

If we follow this viewpoint, the desire for knowledge would no longer be contrary to female subjectivity. And what is more, 'entering and leaving a closed space' could just as well refer to the closed system of binary thinking, the illusion of self-sufficiency, or any system of totalizing claims, *including* that of mythical narrative.

In view of reading 'A Momentary Taste of Being', this different approach advocates an alternative for the interpretive method of the 'psychic rape' and the epistemic closure it aims at. Unlike Frank Foy, I do not believe that it is possible to squeeze a decisive truth or final revelation out of either Lory or the narrative text. Only *partial* disclosures can be attempted, partial implying both awareness of the necessarily biased and limited nature of one's views and accountability for one's affinities. Partial disclosures require more radicality than Aaron could summon up. He felt Lory kept on hiding something, and was right in believing neither in Foy's lie detector nor in his settlement for 'perfectly dovetailing revelations'. Yet he was not able to grasp what was going on behind Lory's social screen.

We need not repeat Aaron's myopia. What is wanted is more *receptivity* to the silenced, dark side of Lory's words. We could use multiple senses and look at its signs in the text in order to hear Lory into speech, so that she will be transformed from a female obstacle in men's quest for knowledge into a female subject with her own story, her own account of truth.

Physical rape

Aaron was not able to interpret Lory's body language. Ulcers, red hair turning grey—recent changes referring to an actual crisis. They need not be referring to an actual event, though. A crisis can also be evoked by the return of a repressed memory. Frank Foy intuitively hit the nail on the head when he suggested that Lory might have been afraid of unsealing the alien during her return flight from the planet. The alien Lory is 'in league' with is many possible things, as we have seen in the previous chapters. It might be understood as a projection screen of fear and desire: a paradoxical force of procreation and annihilation, the maternal semiotic, the abject, a power attributed healing faculties. But the alien is also Lory's suppressed account, the spectre that is haunting the text. *Un*sealing the alien would have meant releasing a subtext that does not dovetail at all, with anything.

No matter how attentive Aaron was to the psychic violence inherent to the interrogation situation, his sensitivity fails him when it comes to the crunch. Or rather, he refuses to face reality: '*I am the doctor* ... The inner voice comments that more than Lory's ulcers are unhealed; he disregards it' (A109). He deliberately disregards the signs. This also happens, most saliently, in the following scene, when all the people on the spaceship have gathered to listen to a speech by Yellaston on the history of human exploration and migration.

> The hall is falling silent, ready for Yellaston. Aaron catches sight of Soli on the far side, Coby is by her with Tighe between them. And there's Lory by the other wall, sitting with Don and Tim. She is holding herself in a tight huddle, *like a rape victim in court*; probably agonized by her tapes being on the scanners. Aaron curses himself routinely for his sensitivity to her, realizes he has missed Yellaston's opening words. (A98, my italics)

But what if Lory is not *like* a rape victim but in reality *is* a rape victim? And more specifically, what if the suggestion of rape refers to the very brother–sister incest, being experienced thus by Lory as a far more ambiguous and violent event than by Aaron?

Although there is no explicit mention of this possibility, I nevertheless believe that the text offers enough allusive evidence to permit the suggested 'what if' reading. (Re-)reading particular textual signs from Lory's point of view, then, requires the 'imaginative poetics' (*inbeeldende poëtica*) coined by Mieke Bal. In an imaginative poetics, one is not 'reading for the plot' (Brooks) but trying to imagine the situation of the woman and its implications for her: reading for the experience. This reading is directed towards making visible what is ineffable and beyond representation. For rape makes the victim invisible.

> In the first place I mean this literally: she becomes invisible because the wrongdoer covers her. In a figurative sense she becomes invisible because her self-awareness, her *subjectivity* is attacked: temporarily stunned and in many cases even definitely nullified. Finally, rape cannot be visualized because the experience is both physically and psychically an *inward* experience, the rape takes place inside. In this way also the rape is invisible, 'imagined' by definition; it cannot exist as a hard fact, only as experience and memory'.[52]

In rape indeed, as I believe with Bal, the victim is silenced, her identity as speaking subject is denied. The consequence is that speaking about rape is considered the privilege of men too. Male voices articulate not only their own visions but those of women as well; women speak through male voices. Very often the story of the man is still the only available story in our culture (and most other cultures): the story of seduction. The counter-story, the woman's experience of rape, is culturally repressed, and must therefore be retrieved from silence.[53]

How at the same time shocking and confusing these insights are when related to 'A Momentary Taste of Being'! Our attention is as never before attracted to the fact that the audible voice guiding us through the text is a *male* voice, and that the story Aaron is telling about his and Lory's youth is the culturally accepted story of seduction. It is founded on the memory of mutual seduction, of shared intimacy and sexual pleasure, an incestuous and therefore transgressive love. Although repressed for years this love has a seductive power that is still haunting him.

> Lory the non-sex-object, sure. Barring the fact that Lory's prepubescent body is capable of unhinging the occasional male with the notion that she contains some kind of latent sexual lightning, some secret supersensuality lurking like hot lava in the marrow of her narrow bones. (A82)

And he adds that on Earth he had watched 'a series of such idiots breaking their balls in the attempt to penetrate to Lory's mythical marrow'. Which 'occasional male' is he speaking about? Which 'idiots' does he have in mind? Is he not simply speaking about himself, disclosing his own violent attempts to 'penetrate to Lory's mythical marrow', which may well be read as a trivial euphemism for 'rape'? Any distrust of the reader, however, is nipped in the bud for her attention is immediately lead off by Aaron's next thoughts:

> He knows the secret lightning in Lory's bones. Not sex, would that it were. Her implacable innocence—what was the old phrase, *a fanatic heart*. A too-clear vision of good, a too-sure hatred of evil. No love lost, in between. Not much use for living people. (A82–3)

In the previous chapter, I joined Aaron in this specific view of Lory, questioning her striving for 'innocence of sin'. A striving that is ironically producing its own reverse: the secular sin of innocence, the refusal to accept that 'the implacable difference, the violence be conceived in personal and sexual identity itself' (Kristeva). I think that such a criticism on moral absolutism certainly is valuable. In a concrete situation like Lory's, however, it could tend to ignore real pain underlying it. And I as a reader may run the risk of repeating such blindness or even wilful denial. Indeed I have to admit that Aaron's opinions about Lory have a truly averting power, for they ward off the ghost of sexual violence incited just before. Nevertheless, as I have mentioned at various occasions in this study, ghosts have the inclination to return. Sexual violence tends to be socially invisible while its painful memory keeps on haunting its victim, and, at least in the case of 'A Momentary Taste of Being', the possible aggressor as well. Only by naming it, by breaking the silence, sexual violence can become manifest after all.

Unfortunately, Lory does not speak up as a subject herself. She has always let her body do the talking: her boyish and breastless body bears witness to the refusal to enter womanhood as it is primarily associated with pain. Ulcers and grey hair, on the other hand, mark the adult woman's refusal to keep the pain (the alien) entirely concealed inside. She even challenges her brother to discover her story:

> I really brought it [the alien specimen] back for you, Arn. I wanted us to look at it together. Remember how we used to share our treasures, that summer on the island? (A92)

But Aaron turns away quickly, acting 'like a man kicked in the guts' (ibid.). He refuses to read the story behind the visible signs. And so the possibly oppositional female voice is silenced.

In an essay about novels on incest written by contemporary Dutch authors, Liesbeth Eugelink observes that these texts break with the Romantic portrayal of brother–sister incest as characterized by spiritual union and equality.[54] In Chapter II, I questioned the relevance of the Romantic model, by means of Yourcenar's description of it, for understanding the Aaron/Lory incest. This incest appeared to be appreciated in a highly ambivalent manner. On the one hand, in the way Aaron remembered their sexual initiation on the spruce island we found a repetition of the Romantic ideal. Yet, at the same time, this ideal is thwarted if not ridiculed in that the relation between Aaron and Lory is also an infertile closed system, in analogy to the *Centaur*'s closed and contraceptive system. The novels discussed by Eugelink also show, to a greater or lesser extent, an ambivalent relation to the Romantic ideal. This ideal is still present in the motives of the special bond and of the social and geographical isolation of the brother and the sister. On the other hand, these novels are also affected by the public debate of the last decades, in which incest is primarily dealt with as sexual abuse. The voluntariness and equality of the brother–sister relation is no longer taken for granted in these novels. The space for the expression of experiences outside the Romantic dream is created by giving up the male-dominated narrative viewpoint. The Dutch novels are in line with other twentieth-century writings inspired by the Romantic tradition on incest, in which the sister's perspective is increasingly introduced.

As we know, this, by contrast, is the thorny point of 'A Momentary Taste of Being': the sister's voice is silenced. The reader is left with the uneasy question of why a female author, who, moreover, at various occasions claimed herself to be a feminist, allows the sister's experience, Lory's plot, to be 'killed' (A141). But then again, this may not be an apt question at all. One can speculate endlessly on the reasons for the pervasiness of male protagonists in Tiptree's fiction. In my opinion, it makes more sense to simply conclude that, for whatever reason, many of Tiptree's stories cannot bear to articulate *directly* the pain and the desire of women, and therefore require more reading between and behind the lines ascribed to male voices. Moreover, I want to suggest we leave for a moment the narrative approach used so far, in favour of the psychotextual framework employed in Chapters III and IV. That is to say, instead of Aaron and Lory as protagonists in the story, they are considered as the two sides or aspects of a female psychomachia, the subject at war with itself. What surfaces from the text in that case is an unsettling double-account *within* the subject, in which desire and violence, guilt and pain with respect to the incest are colliding and merging by turns. The Romantic account is projected on the brother-side, apparently a more acceptable perspective, while the possible other story, the sister's, is not exactly wiped from the narrative but at least submerged.

Beyond pain

And yet, is Lory's account as inaccessible, or cryptically present, as suggested? It should not be overlooked that the tragic relationship between Lory and Aaron is taking place within a science fiction framework. The author has more than mere 'realistic' means and settings at her disposal to produce certain effects. In 'A Momentary Taste of Being', the mysteries of the cosmos themselves are brought into action to realize Lory's 'crazy plot'. In the end Lory's plot appears to be superimposed on Aaron's. Her silence turns out to be much stronger than Aaron's speech: the release of the alien causes a blinding and dumb striking apocalypse. From Lory's vantage point, the purifying powers of the cosmic catastrophe put an end to a human 'order' in which the brother rapes the sister. 'Sex equals death,' Yellaston and Aaron concluded from the terrifying events of the cosmic insemination. The implications of this statement, understood in a broader cultural context, have been discussed extensively in Chapter II. In the present context, however, it might be translated as 'sexual abuse equals the death of female subjectivity'. The death of humanity, consequently, would mean also the end of sexual violence.

In an article on Tiptree's work, Lowry Pei points out what she considers to be a strange paradox. In 'A Momentary Taste of Being', as in many other stories, we are warned against people like Lory 'who throw the word "humanity" around too much, promising salvation that is actually death'.[55] But, Pei objects, are the stories themselves less fanatical? They 'cry out against fanaticism, sexism, death, yet at the same time they resolve conflict by means of final solutions which are themselves the stuff of nightmare'. Pei even wonders if this is not the very project of the stories: to elimate people, to get rid of the human race? She decides that there are two sides in Tiptree's fiction: besides the fanaticism of idealistic killers like Lory Kaye, there is also 'much of Aaron Kaye, who resists the pull of beautiful annihilation in order to remain stubbornly human to the end, caring for the dying even though they do not notice'.[56]

Like my own to a greater or lesser extent in the previous chapters, Pei's analysis seems to be in the grasp of Aaron's point of view, the reasonable, well-balanced half of the Aaron–Lory dyad. It is the manifest, easily legible plot. An imaginative poetics, however, seeks to disclose the traces of pain that are hidden beneath the manifest level of meaning. From Lory's point of view, the beautiful annihilation brought about by the alien is not a perverse lure, as it is for Aaron, but the expression of a longing for salvation: it could mean the end of pain. The difference between Aaron and Lory is marked by this hidden experience of pain. Aaron's is a narrative of transgressive and shameful but no less sweet pleasure; Lory hides inside a narrative of pain. These narratives cannot be dialectically reconciled into one 'dovetailing' pleasure-and-pain tale. The terrifying radicality of 'A Momentary Taste of Being' does not allow it. Its apocalyptic end forces Lory's story upon Aaron's, meeting reluctance first but granted recognition by the latter eventually:

> Little sister, you were a good sperm, you swam hard. You made the connection. She wasn't crazy you know. Ever, really. She knew something was wrong with us ... (A162)

What we witness in 'A Momentary Taste of Being' is the execution of Lory Kaye's Last Judgement on history. It is not history in an abstract sense, however, but a well-defined and specified history of doom: an experience of the barest face of male-identified power: sexual violence. Through Lory's alliance with the alien this history is radically put to an end; the cosmic insemination turns out to be the instrument of Lory's wrath. Aaron was not wide off the truth when he thought his sister would 'liquidate 90% of humanity to achieve her utopia'. He did not recognize, however, that her longing for utopia was hardly a moral and political testimony but rather a cry from a tormented heart. Small wonder her utopia is a 'noplace' rather than a 'good place', and a true humanity is a humanity/*man*kind delivered from the evil of drives, the 'beast worked out':

> No hurting anymore, never. They [Kuh and his people] came back so gentle, so happy. They were all changed, they shed all that. It's waiting for us, Arn, see? It wants to deliver us. We'll be truly human at last. (A149)

In fact salvation equals annihilation, and eschatological fullness—the 'new earth and heaven ahead'—appears to be a devious illusion: ultimate reality is set in the 'icy wastes' (A155).[57] The hidden account of Lory's pain proves a terrifyingly negative force in the narrative. The sounds of the *carcajada*, the sardonic laughter in the face of unrelieved pain, have faded. What we hear is a war howl.

The extent to which the text's overwhelming negativity is embedded in a female experience of pain turns 'A Momentary Taste of Being' into a curious example of science fiction apocalypse. What makes Tiptree's text so disturbing is its lack of an identifiable positive vision beyond the end. While so many other writers take up the collapse of culture as an opportunity to create feminist survival fiction, in 'A Momentary Taste of Being' cultural crisis apparently provokes a leap beyond the human. Instead of alternatives for the Oedipal plot and different relations between the human sexes, uncanny cosmic creatures come into existence, for which humans are sacrificed ('die to form') and of which nobody knows if 'they [are] brutes or angels' (A160). It is as if the experience of crisis is so vehement that it obstructs the chance that anything human could still make sense.

It involves a crisis with as many cultural as individual implications. Reading the story from Lory's perspective makes evident, furthermore, an analogy between Aaron's violence against Lory and the 'rape of the earth' by its 'teeming billions'.

> He munches, absently eyeing the three-di shot of the early clean-air days. What are they eating there now, each other? ... As he gets up, the image of Earth catches his eye again: their lonely, vulnerable jewel, hanging their in blackness. Suddenly last night's dream jumps back, he sees again the monster penis groping toward the stars with *Centaur* at its tip. Pulsing with pressure, barely able to wait for the trigger that will release the human deluge— (A74–6).

In addition, the semantic fullness of the 'wastes' referred to in the text speaks volumes for ecological concern as one aspect of 'A Momentary Taste of Being'. Not only is the final act set in the 'icy wastes' but in fact the whole story is, as illuminated in the epigraph, taking place 'amid the Waste'. The story's wastes are metaphorical landscapes, certainly, the wastelands of the self-deceptive mind and the deserts where no hopeful relations between the sexes can bloom. But they refer also to literal waste, the waste products of the twentieth century's global capitalism. In the *Centaur*'s dining-hall a sign says: 'THE CENTRAL PROBLEM OF OUR LIVES IS GARBAGE. PLEASE CLEAN YOUR SERVERS' (A103). With the outlook for the promised land someone has taped over GARBAGE and replaced it by BEAUTY. A waste of hope, apparently. For human beings themselves turn out to be nothing more than what overpopulated megacities like Calcutta, Rio de Janeiro and Los Angeles testify: waste, unused sperm, the products of 'nature's notorious wastefulness' (A162).

> Born too soon or too late—too bad. Rot away unused. Function fulfilled, organs atrophy ... End of it all, just rot away. *Not even knowing*—thinking they were people, thinking they had a chance ... (A162)

The cosmic Queen in 'A Momentary Taste of Being'

We need to catch our breath. To say that 'A Momentary Taste of Being' does not offer any positive prospects for humanity, let alone for women in particular, seems an understatement. Yet I think it also contains signs of hope; that pain and catastrophe are interwoven with the hope for transformation in the narrative's dynamic. I am well aware that I run a risk of sounding cynical with this claim—what hope is left in Tiptree's text? These uncanny ghostlike creatures? In the previous chapters, in particular in the context of 'A Momentary Taste of Being' as *choric* fantasy, they formed an important perspective for investigating the story's limits of hope. While the negative thrust—the *end* of violence and pain—is the most obvious, the vision of a life beyond the human, no matter how uncertain and terrifying, apparently does offer some consolation. The posthuman implies in the first place *dis*continuity with the existent; whether its human remnant will contribute in a positive manner to this new creatures is a question only the future can decide about. I shall come back to this issue in Chapter VI.

For the present, I want to highlight a rather different figure of transformation that can be retrieved from the text. There is still another hidden aspect, besides Lory's story of pain and annihilation. My intention is to connect 'A Momentary Taste of Being' to a tradition of cosmic mythological imagination that may be more salutary to women than the solution of a final apocalypse. As stated above, we can find reminiscences in the text of the Queen of heavens in Revelation 12 and her adversary the dragon, which are both called up by the Lady of the Beasts in Aaron's Dream. This mythological figuration too bears the traces of violence but it nevertheless has an empowering force. Its textual excavation may revive the hope that shimmers, against all the odds, at various places through the surface of 'A Momentary Taste of Being'. It is not an easy task, because the negativity of Tiptree's text, Lory's negativity, is a persistent counter-force. Yet it is a matter of survival not to give up this interpretative struggle too soon.

For the interpretation of Rev. 12 I lean on Catherine Keller's 'feminist–theological midrash' of the text.[58] By presenting her discussion as a feminist Midrash on a Christian biblical text, Keller extents the proper sense of Midrash, which refers to the collection of rabbinical comments on the Hebrew Bible. Thus, her interpretation is a comment on the Bible which differs from both exegesis, which situates the text in its original context, and allegory, which generalizes without any context. A Midrash implies a contextual and constructive development of the text starting from and in behalf of a particular community.[59] Keller understands the woman of Rev. 12 as a *Fremdkörper* in Revelation, as an alien so to speak. Not only in Keller's estimate, but also in that of other feminist theologians, Revelation is the most patriarchal and dualist biblical book: 'Here Christian glorification of sacrifice and martyrdom unite with historical determinism'.[60]

Rosemary Ruether goes so far as to extend this to Christianity in a wider sense: 'as the heir of both classical Neo-Platonism and apocalyptic Judaism, [it] combines the image of a male, warrior God with the exaltation of the intellect over the body'.[61]. In the concluding section, I will clarify this harsh criticism a bit more; at present it suffices as a background picture for the contrasting appearance of the heavenly woman in Rev.12. This woman, Keller indicates, is the first sign in Rev.12–19, the book of the seven signs, and the only one that is good—all the others are evil. She is not an ordinary woman, and it would be shortsighted to understand her as, say, an allegory of the suffering of women. She is a Queen of heavens, an epiphanic figure, a cosmic and even divine woman, who in some baffling way managed to settle in this masculine book. Her attributes are all the elements of cosmic light: the sun, the moon and the stars. Keller sees her as both cosmic immanent spirit and parthenogenic mother-goddess, but emphatically dissociates her from matriarchal utopias as well as archetypical femininity. She is neither Mother Earth nor the Goddess of the Moon. Because she is astral, solar, and lunar at the same time, she transcends traditional gendered identifications.

Notwithstanding her powerful image—or maybe because of it—the woman has a rough time. First she is tormented by terrible labour pains, then a dragon comes to devour the child she is about to bear, while the son is carried off to God's throne right after his birth. 'For a goddess it would be extremely difficult to give birth inside the Bible, and especially in this book! No wonder she is in big agony.'[62] The immediate separation of the son from the mother is executed for the purpose of his identification with the powerful and absent Father god. The child will become a warrior-god who 'is destined to rule all nations with a rod of iron' (Rev. 12:5). As Keller sees it, '[t]he sudden alienation from physical and emotional love in the arms of a woman leads logically to the paternal throne of absolute power and to the theocratic fascism that preaches the millenium'.[63]

Finally, the woman flees from heaven into the desert (the wastes), which, surprisingly, is pictured as a place of survival and divine protection. Immediately a cosmic war between masculine powers breaks out (Rev. 12:7–12): a dualistic battle of archangel Michael and his angelic armies against the dragon and its armies. Of course the last party is defeated by the first, and the dragon, 'that ancient serpent who led the world astray, whose name is the Devil, or Satan' (12:9) is thrown down to the earth. But without delay, the dragon–snake starts to hunt for the woman again (12:13–18). However, the woman receives two eagle's wings to fly back to the safe desert. This means, Keller explains, that the symbol of special power and elevation that, like the symbol of the sun, in the patriarchal biblical context was usually reserved for men is bestowed on the woman. The last sentences of Rev.12 (15–18) read as follows:

> From his mouth the serpent spewed a flood of water after the woman to sweep her away with its spate. But the earth came to her rescue: it opened its mouth and drank up the river which the dragon spewed from his mouth. Furious with the woman, the dragon went off to wage war on the rest of her offspring, those who keep God's commandments and maintain their witness to Jesus. [13:1] He took his stand on the seashore.

Woman and dragon seem absolute adversaries. But, Keller wonders, are they really? What if the dragon–snake's pursuit of the woman is aimed not at her destruction but at reconnecting with her? This takes us back to the first verses of Genesis, to the beginnings of a history the Apocalypse strives to conclude.[64] In the previous chapter, I expounded Keller's views on the transformation of the monstrous mother-goddess of the Babylonian *Enuma Elish*, Tiamat, into the Hebrew *tehom*, the deep, in Gen. 1:1–2. Keller recalls the battle between old and young gods, resulting in the slaughter of Tiamat by the warrior-god Marduk, who splits Tiamat's body in two to create his own new heaven and new earth out of it. In Gen. 1, the maternal dragon was pacified a long time ago, she need not be openly killed any more. Nevertheless a long tradition connects the primeval waters *tehom* with the female monsters of the Sea: Tiamat, Leviathan (Is.27:1, Job 3:8), Rahab (Psalm 89, Job 26:12, Is.51:9–10), who must be conquered and controlled. It is suggested in the Book of Revelation that the repressed female–maternal danger has returned, as the snake–dragon seeks to sweep the woman along in its own flood. But the earth comes to the woman's rescue by absorbing the water. Later, in Rev. 21:1, we read that a new heaven and new earth have come, 'for the first heaven and the first earth had vanished, *and there was no longer any sea*' (italics added).

Together with the elimination of the sea, however, the cosmic woman seems to have been removed as well: 'The city [the new Jerusalem] did not need the sun or the moon to shine on it, for the glory of God gave it light, and its lamp was the Lamb' (Rev. 21:23). As Keller elsewhere summarizes:

> The oceanic womb of life, construed in various Hebrew scriptures as a monster to be contained, is now eternally vanquished, replaced by the purely paternal creation. But even the relatively austere diversity of planetary bodies is eliminated, and a glory-light of immaterial transcendence shines on the desired future.[65]

At this point, the woman and her offspring are fully integrated into the evolving framework of Christian monotheism. The cosmic power she represents has been displaced to the heavenly Father. Could this power possibly re-emerge, somehow, in Tiptree's text? I believe we meet the cosmic woman of Revelation again in Aaron's second dream; we see the same epiphanic woman/goddess, a Queen of heavens walking on earth. It is not a glorious resurrection, however. At first, dragon or snake—as symbol of sexuality—reappear (or 'reincarnate') in the ape and the tiger, in intimate relationship with the woman but chained: under control. Then, most remarkably, the woman tries to set them free—to give up her libidinal power—and urges them to go away from her. But unlike the dragon–snake who started to haunt the woman to gain their reunion after he was separated from her, the ape and the tiger simply cease to be ... Renouncing her own desire and sexuality results in the loss of vitality; the woman of Aaron's dream begins a death chant.

Possible cosmic attributes ('dark jewels'), moreover, have become detached from her body and are dispersed all through the text. The sun has been displaced to Yellaston, the 'yellow sol', reappropriated thus as an exclusively male symbol. A multiplicity reduced to what Luce Irigaray calls 'the economy of the Same':

> [Yellaston is about to speak] The rostrum is at the middle, where the speaker's whole figure will be most visible. It's empty. Beyond it is a screen projecting the star-field ahead; year by year Aaron and his shipmates have watched the suns of Centaurus growing on that screen, separating to doubles and double-doubles. Now it shows only a single sun. The great blazing component of Alpha [Centauri] around which Lory's planet circles. (A97)

As in Revelation, where the glory of God makes sun and moon redundant, the woman in 'A Momentary Taste of Being' has been deprived of her cosmic powers. No wonder she is grieving and in despair! Light and warmth have vanished: the cosmos is grey and icy now. Apparently her cosmic light sources have been appropriated by patriarchal powers, as was the case with the woman in the Apocalypse. But where have all these double and double-double suns gone that Aaron and his shipmates were observing before the one single sun took over? The Lady of the Beasts appears to be a sign of the alien. The overwhelming light that is radiated by the alien life-form reveals that there is still more light in the universe than the One can contain. It is Aaron who clearly experiences this. After the dream 'he is acutely aware of a direction underfoot, an invisible line leading down through the hull to the sealed-up scouter, to the alien inside' (A83–4). Later this awareness takes shape more explicitly in an odd displacement of the planetary constellation surrounding the biblical image of the Queen of heavens in Rev.12:1, who *'is robed with the sun, beneath her feet the moon'* (my italics).

> He fancies he can feel a chill on his soles. Imagine, he is in a starship! A fly walking the wall of a rotating can in cosmic space: *There are suns beneath my feet.* (A119, italics in original)

It is not just Lory who sees the alien light as a promise of salvation and wholeness, of the promise that 'we are not alone' ('You'll see, it will all be gone, the pain … Arn, dear, we'll be together' (A141)); for a short but very intense moment Aaron does so too:

> The beauty of it floods Aaron's soul, washes all fear away. Just beyond those bodies is the goal of man's desiring, the fountain—the Grail itself maybe, the living radiance! (*ibid.*)

What is actually conveyed in the narrative by means of Aaron, however, is not that the light brings salvation and wholeness but that it *disrupts* reality; it does not eliminate the pain, but transfigures it. The alien remains invisible, and in this sense 'A Momentary Taste of Being' tells us that indeed we *are* alone. Yet the alien's beacon lights sometimes glow in the dark, not probably leading us to a Gold Coast (or paradisaical planet) but rather to the wastes of our twentieth-century world, in which signs of hope and despair are lit by the same flash. The figure of the Lady of the Beasts, or the Queen of heavens, represents one of these beacons, sending out her ambiguous light which is both destructive and healing. She 'paces besides a leaden sea', Aaron's dream says, while later Don Purcell sees (the hand of the Almighty on) the Deep. Has the sea dried up completely eventually, like at the end of the Book of Revelation, have the wastes conquered the cosmos definitely? Not necessarily. The epigraph of Tiptree's narrative suggests that even amid the waste there is a well of being. And also according to my interpretation, the oceanic womb of life has reappeared in various guises in the textual layers of 'A Momentary Taste of Being': as chaos producing order, as the mythical Deep, as the semiotic *chora*. A highly ambivalent power, indeed, both destructive and (pro)creative, both *well* and *waster* of being, annihilating one life in order to generate another.

One aspect of the cosmic woman remains to be discussed. Does the child of the woman in Revelation somehow re-emerge in 'A Momentary Taste of Being'? One is inclined to say that the woman in Aaron's dream did not bear a child at all. But why not to understand Aaron as her virtual child? After all, it is *his* dream (which was also elaborated in Chapter IV, in relation to the desire for the mother). The son in Revelation was sent to God's throne to be trained to become a ruler with an iron staff.[66] Aaron too, before the break in the narrative events that is reflected in the textual

order, basks in the protective power of Big Daddy Yellaston's throne, and
he has used the 'iron staff' against Lory. After the collapse of masculine
power and subjective stability, however, the only solace left to him is his
medical identity.

> I visit my patients daily. Most of them are still sitting. Sitting at their
> stations, in their graves. We do what we can, Lory and I. *Making gentle
> the life of this world* ... (A160, italics in original)

I consider it a sign of hope that the staff of Aesculapius is tougher than the
iron staff: due to its emblem the monstrous snake still crawls through the
text. Where in the Apocalypse the snake–dragon, the heir of the Babylonian
sea-monster, was fought and slain once and for all by the warrior-god, in
'A Momentary Taste of Being' it unexpectly returns in the last desperate
acts of compassion.

Apocalypse as dis/closure

'I don't dream anymore.' Aaron's loss of dreams marks the end of illusions
not just about a happy ending but about any *single* ending. As a feminist
version of the myth of apocalypse, 'A Momentary Taste of Being' is, on
the one hand, undeniably driven by what Frank Kermode in his famous
collection of lectures of the same name has called 'the sense of an ending':
the apprehension of a (narrative) conclusion as well as the meaning or
purpose of a conclusion.

Kermode stated that we need fictions of the End to make sense of the
world we live in. Without an imagining and interpretation of an end (and
a beginning, for that matter) we would get stuck in ceaseless transition.
Kermode, and following in his footsteps Ketterer and Kreuziger,
understand modern fiction about the end according to the biblical model.
The Bible presents the ideal fiction of concord: Genesis and Apocalypse are
in harmony with each other, while Apocalypse traditionally is considered
to epitomize the whole book. In modernity, we still feel the need of concord,
Kermode claims, even if the fictions have become more varied and self-
conscious. 'In the middest we look for a fullness of time [*kairos*], for
beginning, middle and end in concord.'[67] The interval between 'the *tick* of
birth and the *tock* of death' needs to be made meaningful lest we go under
in ceaseless time (*chronos*). Unlike in the Book of Revelation, however,
today the end is no longer conceived of as imminent but immanent: the
end is not the closure of common history but a personal death or crisis, or
a reference to epoch. Kreuziger, then, has modified both Kermode's
assumption that the modern sense of an ending has become immanent,
and Ketterer's that modern apocalyptic literature implies the metaphorical

destruction of the 'real' world in the reader's head. His view, as we have seen, is that due to science fiction's character as popular literature, the expectation of an ending has become imminent again, comparable to the biblical expectation of salvation in Revelation.

My assumption, however, is that 'A Momentary Taste of Being' differs both from Kermode's modern fiction and Kreuziger's science fiction as remythologized secular apocalyptic, in that the story's sense of an ending does not provide any certainty: is there really an end, does the end make sense at all, are there more ends than one? And what if the beginning(s) cannot be certified—the beginning of what?—how could any concordance, either real or fictional, be achieved? The unfathomability of the alien appears as the ultimate sign of the narrative's indecidibility. But at the same time we are dealing with *feminist* science fiction. It means that the absence of fictional concordance, or narrative closure to put it in different terms, becomes the very tool that enables a reader to open up narrative and subjective space for women. The feminist fictions, both narrative and interpretive, that thus come into existence are not to be misconstrued as the slurry and putty that stop the gaps in favour of a deferred fictional closure. Above all they are to be understood as imaginative and theoretical experiments with the possible.

Feminist postmodern fictions, of either a literary or a theological character, distance themselves from the model of a concord beginning and end guaranteed by a secular or religious transcendent agency. Consequently, the meaning of apocalypse also changes considerably in view of a feminist assessment. One may even seriously wonder if it were not better to dispense with the notion of apocalypse altogether.[68] Yet I wish to defend the critical power of apocalyptic discourse insofar as it implies a radical and sensitive confrontation with the horrors of our time and the imagination of hope against all the odds. To elaborate this to some extent, I will turn again to Catherine Keller, whose thought experiments on the apocalyptic I find truly inspiring.

Let me first recall that Western history is embedded within the apocalyptic narrative, by which I mean—in keeping with Keller—a general pattern rather than the specific biblical text. As stated earlier, it is a narrative that is operative especially in moments of social and cultural crisis: of destabilization, despair and transformation. The last decade of the twentieth century, therefore, was likely to display not the end of apocalyptic thinking but 'the accelerating, near simultaneous encounter with its many faces: judgement and promise, secular and religious, patriarchal and egalitarian'.[69] Keller conceives of the present moment as *kairos*, a fullness of time, which is, however, understood not as a concord fiction but as 'a moment of the crisis of converging difference', or in a different theoretical framework, the crisis of postmodernity. This crisis manifests itself, in theory and in history, as the threat *and* opportunity of difference.

> Perhaps the depolarization of the superpowers has not so much disempowered the apocalypticism of this epoch—conclusive or creative—as much as it may allow its diversification and its contextualization in the real life of real communities, who, in their communing and their antagonisms, do indeed create the future. The struggles for national-ethic identity, peoplehood, nonracialism, and liberation all manifest the insurrection of difference against the hierarchies of sameness.[70]

Keller decides that the postmodern value of difference is a 'positively apocalyptic theme for the not-yet-being of a small and overpopulated planet'. It offers a 'negation of negation', that is, a resistance against closed political and ideological systems, and a positive disclosure of what is becoming. The Christian Apocalypse, however, remains a problematic model for a theology that understands itself as postmodern discourse, and for feminist theological discourse in particular.

> Yet the 'master'-images of biblical eschatology are irredeemably male-identified and often misogynist. They cast the messianic force in the image of the raging patriarch, who in his Christian apocalypse takes the form of the bloodiest warrior–messiah in the Bible.[71]

The divine warrior is not an apt model for feminists, not just because of violence *per se*, but because he operates within a fantasy of ultimate and dualistic victory. It rests on an unambiguous opposition of good and evil, seeking final solutions, and it is in the conclusiveness of this 'either/or' that the danger of the apocalyptic impulse is located. In Keller's view, feminist theology, in its awareness of the 'unsettled and unsettling ambiguity of women's differences, relationships, and loyalties', has no choice but to leave behind all visions of purity and conclusiveness. She urges feminist theology to join the postmodern resistance against the authoritarianism of any single end to history.

Theologically speaking, the sense of a single end, and its corollary the denial of difference, multiplicity and complexity, depend upon the image of a controlling and transcendent deity. The impact on Western culture of faith in history's end and in its divine guarantee is still palpable. It has resulted in demonization of multiplicity, passivity toward the fate of the earth, and desacralization of both the earth and what Augustine called 'the fleshly varieties': 'woman's flesh, colored flesh, worker's flesh, the flesh of the animals and the elements, all repressed, oppressed, and suffering flesh'.[72] Furthermore, the image of the transcendent creator who is also the endtime judge has fostered passive acquiescence towards authority, paving the way for the totalitarian powers in modernity.

As an antidote to this life-threatening apocalypse of despair, Keller wishes for an 'apocalypse of dis/closure' or 'counterapocalypse'.[73] It is anti-apocalyptic inasmuch as it opposes or parodies apocalyptic images which have frozen into archetypes of closure, such as Last Word and Final Solution, and into deadlocked antagonism and moral dualism. Instead, an apocalypse of dis/closure implies both disruption of any closed social system of epistemic, economic or ecological dominance and an open-ended process of revelation. Let me add to this Haraway's similar view that,

> It's not a 'happy ending' we need, but a non-ending. That's why none of the narratives of masculinist, patriarchal apocalypses will do. The System is not closed; the sacred image of the same is not coming. The world is not full.[74]

Both advocate a radical yet engaged openness to the future. An openness which is related, as Keller recalls elsewhere, to openness in the biblical sense: opening one's mouth to tell what was hidden, opening one's ears to hear the language of images, and the opening of the grave to reveal life itself.[75]

As I understand it, dis/closure indicates a decoding and deciphering (figuring out) of what may count as a truth when and for whom, rather than the unveiling of a decisive truth which lies hidden behind a veil but is nevertheless already existent. At the same time, dis/closure points to the possibility of unexpected, unthought and as yet non-achieved disruptions of reality. Apocalypse as dis/closure means an affirmation of difference, neither as hierarchical dichotomy nor as liberal monadism, but as multiplicity and complexity which disclose themselves in the fragility, finitude and strength of the for better and for worse interconnected 'fleshly varieties'.

Hoping for inhuman(e) miracles

Difference, as I would render it into the language of science fiction, refers to both the 'fleshliness' *and* the alienness of the alien. Thus, the alien refers to what differs fundamentally from the known (images of) world and self but can nevertheless be experienced only in relation to the known. The disclosure of the alien knows no conclusion. The dissolutions and disruptive transformations of known selves and known worlds it brings about do not necessarily contain a promise of meaning and salvation. We have seen that transformation in 'A Momentary Taste of Being' indicated primarily a fantasy of the end of Western history, an end both dreaded and longed for.

Whether the ghostly posthuman creatures offer any hope for the 'fleshly varieties', and for women in particular, can be answered in a positive way only if we move beyond the limits of Tiptree's story. But I want to take these limits very seriously. I have not resorted to science fiction's reservoir of utopian imagination or the experiments of feminist survival fiction, because for me the significance of 'A Momentary Taste of Being' is to be found precisely in the display of crisis and despair. Moving to the vulnerable and explosive edges of meaning it opened up the imagination to the unexpected and impossible alien, not as a comforting guarantee that 'we are not alone' but as a disruptive sign of hope in a redefinition of our relationship to otherness.

Hope is a precious thing, even if, or maybe precisely because the only horizon of our hope is an undetermined future. I want to conclude this chapter by returning for a moment to the desperate and fragmented Aaron Kaye in order to attempt to make him look at the alien in a new manner, to disclose to him a vision of hope beyond the end. This vision can be found at the conclusion of Stanislaw Lem's famous book *Solaris*, which shows several remarkable correspondances with 'A Momentary Taste of Being'. *Solaris* is the story of the vain attempts of a small group of scientists in a space station to make sense of a beautiful planet which is covered by an ocean-like plasma. The ocean is not a salvific alien but a mysterious power which transforms memories of dead people into incarnations ('f-products'), who look like humans but behave like ghosts. The ocean is represented as a being with *choric* and divine connotations, and with destructive and generative powers. A being, however, which remains ultimately beyond grasp.

One of the 'returned dead' is Harey, the lover of narrator Kris Kelvin. Harey and Kelvin become again involved in a love-affair, which, however, is doomed to fail because in fact it is a relationship between a guilt-ridden man (Harey had committed suicide) and his unfulfilled hopes. Finally, Harey voluntarily disappears again by means of an annihilation device. After his first grief and feelings of hostility towards the ocean, Kelvin nevertheless decides not to return to Earth but to stay close to the ocean. He neither believes nor not-believes that this makes any sense. His concluding words read as a counterpart of Aaron Kaye's last words. They display an equally strong yearning for the lost other (part), but, unlike Aaron, Kelvin is still dreaming. I would like to quote these sentences as an important postmodern expression of hope for the unexpected.

> I did not believe for a moment that this liquid colossus, which has had many hundreds of people perish in it, and with which for decades humankind has in vain sought to establish some contact and which

without noticing me has swirled me away like a piece of dust, that this colossus would care about the tragedy of two people. But its activities would lead to some goal. Of course I was not entirely convinced of that. However, leaving would mean to ignore this probably small, maybe even imaginary chance that was hidden in the future. So I was to live for years among contraptions and objects both of us had touched, to breathe in for years the air still carrying the memory of her breath? Why for heaven's sake? With a view to the hope for her return? I was beyond hope. But inside me a vestige of it was still alive—expectation. Which fulfillments, ridicules, and catastrophes were still awaiting me? I did not know, and therefore I persevered in the unshakeable belief that the time of inhuman(e) miracles was not over yet.[76]

The tenor of Lem's novel differs substantially from the film *Solaris,* directed by Andrei Tarkovsky (1972). In this film, Kelvin leaves Solaris, which is shaped like a mother's breast, to return home to his father's house to conclude a symbolic narrative of Christian transformation (conversion) and atonement. Although my aim is far from reinventing any such traditional narrative, Tarkovsky's version does evoke the question of whether there is a possible religious discourse which grants the postmodern *Gelassenheit* and hope for the unexpected, such as expressed in Lem's novel, while allowing at the same time for a more sensual and dynamic understanding of the divine. This question will be posed again at the end of the last chapter, where it is linked to a consideration of 'A Momentary Taste of Being' beyond its own textual boundaries.

VI. A Momentary Taste of Being

... A momentary taste
of Being from the Well amid the Waste—
James Tiptree, Jr

Being joins the terrible syncopated dance [of life and death] of its own accord, the dance we must accept for what it is, conscious of the horror it is in key with. If our heart fails us there is no torture like it. And the moment of torment will always come: how would we overcome it if it were to fail? But all of being ready and open—for death, joy or torment—unreservedly open and dying, painful and happy, is there already with its shadowed light, and this light is divine: and the cry that being—vainly?—tries to utter from a twisted mouth is an immense *alleluia*, lost in endless silence.

Georges Bataille[1]

Looking back on the future

We have come to the end of my wo/andering through Tiptree's science fictional heterotopia. We have been plunged into strange spatio-temporal settings—an interstellar spaceship, the vastness of outer space, indefinite time—and confronted with uncanny events. By reading Tiptree's narrative in the light of a variety of theoretical discourses, heuristic images and intertexts it has proved possible to unlock various possible layers of the text. Aaron Kaye's plot, the alien mother/daughter plot, Lory Kaye's plot—plots which were all anti-plots at the same time. Plots with cosmological, sexual, intra-psychic, moral, mythological, religious and historical dimensions. Plots, moreover, which were detected in readings which are partial and perspectival explorations—sometimes complementary, sometimes colliding—rather than successive stages in a straightforward process of uncovering meaning.

The divergent interpretations in the subsequent chapters basically evolved around what I consider to be the three salient issues of the text: namely, the painful quest for female subjectivity, the figuration of the posthuman and a multiple vision of the divine. What we have seen is that these issues are absorbed in a vehement current of negativity, that is, of violence and annihilation: in the first reading the grotesque annihilation of masculinity dominated the scene; a desperate desire for primordial oneness was excavated in the second reading; the abject directed the focus in the third; and apocalyptic–destructive strategies were central object of the last reading. And yet, for the attentive listener the negative basic sound conveyed overtones of hope as well. Germs of hope developing in the text's counter-currents.

This sixth chapter is devoted to further elaboration of these three questions—female subjectivity, the posthuman and the divine—*beyond* the boundaries of 'A Momentary Taste of Being'. The figuration of the posthuman will function as a hinge between the other two questions. On the one hand it is understood as negativity in the formation of (female) subjectivity; on the other, it points to the unfathomability of the alien. In this quality, the posthuman can be interpreted as a *sign* of both sexual difference and the divine. In winding up the explorations of 'A Momentary Taste of Being' at this station, I seek to come to terms with the negative slant of Tiptree's text and explore the limits of hope it contains. In doing so, I plan to derive from them my own contribution to feminist theological discourse on female subjectivity in its relation to the divine: you may take this as a tentatively positive vision of a momentary taste of being.

Female subjectivity: Writing beyond the death drive

'[A]nother of those women disillusioned with meanings and words, who took refuge in lights, rhythms and sounds.'[2] The women referred to here by Julia Kristeva, in *Des Chinoises*, are female authors who have committed suicide—Virginia Woolf, Marina Tsvetaeva, Sylvia Plath, to whom many more could be added. James Tiptree, for example, or Alice Sheldon? Was her suicide foreshadowed in her work? Perhaps. This is not, however, the type of plot I am after. For 'A Momentary Taste of Being' itself has turned out to be a most unsettling stage of a female life-and-death struggle. Its strongest dynamic force may very well be what Kristeva described as a desire 'to dissolve being itself, to free it of the word, of the self, of God'.[3] A desire *not to be*, not to come into being as a female subject, rather than to die.

What is at stake in the lives and the writings of authors such as the aforementioned is, as Kristeva sees it, a wellnigh impossible dialectic between a woman's attempts to identify with the masculine, paternal order, and, on the other hand, to give in to 'the call of the mother's *jouissance*'. I think this results in an aporia because by doing the first she censures herself as a woman, whereas 'the invasion of her speech by these unphrased, nonsensical, maternal rhythms, far from soothing her, or making her laugh, destroys her symbolic armour and makes her ecstatic, nostalgic or mad'.[4] As Kristeva rightly says, however, this is an aporia we should refuse. Nevertheless Kristeva very much doubts whether a different identity is possible for women 'within the framework of patrilinear capitalist society and its monotheistic ideology (even when disguised as humanism)'.[5] For it is precisely in monotheism—the paternal Word—that sexual difference was installed as a 'fight to the death between the two races (men/women)'.[6]

Kristeva originally wrote these words, which may sound somewhat overburdened now, in 1974, at about the same time that Tiptree must have been working on 'A Momentary Taste of Being'. In my view, both authors share a similar feminist interpretation of the *Zeitgeist*. Several of Tiptree's stories of the same period picture in the most horrific literalness possible the mortal battle between men and women that Kristeva suggests in her theory (think of 'The Screwfly Solution' and 'Houston, Houston, Do You Read?'). 'A Momentary Taste of Being', however, stands out among such stories: here the battle between the sexes is directed *inwards*. The female subject—the author, the reader—wages her quest for the creation of a female voice in the symbolic through the story's double figure, Aaron and Lory Kaye, who form an awkward cross-gender configuration of female identification with and evasion of the paternal symbolic.

Most disturbingly, the female voice of 'A Momentary Taste of Being', turned out to be expressing first and foremost a strong death wish, a desire not to be. Or, in psychoanalytic terms, a drive towards a condition of stasis and nondifferentiation, 'that which precedes and therefore surpasses any identity, sign, order or belief'.[7] It manifests itself via the father's daughter Lory, with her boyish body and harsh judgement, as well as the father's son, the unmanly Aaron. In their picturings of the paradisaical planet and the alien life form, Lory and Aaron testify alike to the absorbing beauty of colours, fluxes and lights that remind us of the semiotic *chora*. Yet the influx of the semiotic—this alien yet deeply familiar force—ultimately manifests itself in the text as much a violent usurpation as a joyful disruption of the symbolic. Not only does Lory lose identity and speech, but ultimately Aaron too experiences the most frightening dissolution of self in a delirious fragmentation of language and loss of powers of communication. Here Kristeva's assertion seems to be illustrated that a woman has nothing to laugh about when the symbolic order collapses.

However, I want to raise the question: isn't there more to the text? Is Tiptree's apocalypse really devoid of any laughter? What if we emphasize the other side of the boundary between life and death, the writings instead of the suicide? Let us not forget the *imaginary* character of the dissolution of the Aaron/Lory figure and the decline of humankind altogether. The apocalypse of 'A Momentary Taste of Being' is a fantasy staged by dint of unconscious and conscious motives. I detect, then, in this fantasy besides—indisputably—the silence of powerlessness and pain also the echoes of

Tiptree's use of the grotesque, the sardonic *carcajada*. 'A Momentary Taste of Being' certainly pictures the tragic impossibility of being a mother's daughter in the paternal symbolic. But at the same time it bears witness to the unscrupulous satisfaction of the imaginary destruction of this symbolic.

The narrative shows, thus, violence as a two-edged sword: violence *against* and *by* women. Let me unravel this by focusing once more on what I consider the uncanny core of the story: the submerged memory of incestuous sexual initiation. First I want to stress again that it is impossible to settle its truth once and for all. The text does not allow for it, and my choice of method aimed to sustain the tensions its ambivalence produces and make them fruitful for textual readings and theoretical reflection. Should we decide that the memory of incest is to be read as an angry and hurt epitomization of masculine sexuality in its crudest forms? If this interpretation is followed, the imaginary destruction of humanity can be understood as a fantasy of counter-violence, as the revenge of the victim— violent but to some extent justifiable. The suffering from sexual embodied existence may be so profound that it evokes a fantasy of destructive transcendence of the body. Destruction and self-destruction are paired here, like in the kamikaze tactics of terrorist groups. In this perspective, the female death drive appears as the result of the more original violence in which the maternal is sacrificed for the sake of a paternal–phallic symbolic. This violence is repeated over and again in sexual and social violence against women in any type of patriarchal order. It is a sacrifical violence, moreover, which may be interiorized by women, reflected, for instance, in the image of Lory's repression of her own female corporeality, as I have explained in the comparison of Lory's relation to the figure of Jeanne d'Arc.

As I argued in my reading of 'A Momentary Taste of Being' in Chapter V concerning the excavation of Lory's story: the suggestion that Tiptree's text can be read as a fantasy of female counter-violence is both textually plausible and ethically valuable because it seeks to listen and bear witness to women's silenced voices of pain. And yet, this approach is not entirely satisfactory to me, as it tends to posit Lory as *innocent* despite the actual violence enacted by her upon both the symbolic order and herself. Attributing innocence to her would, paradoxically, deprive her of her subjectivity after all since an illusionary female innocence denies the fundamentally split condition of human existence. For this reason I want to save the ambiguous meaning of the memory of incest in 'A Momentary Taste of Being'. Could Lory not have been at the same time a victim of a masculine culture which condones violent transgression, as well as a subject of her own desire? If we grant such a possibility, then the narrative confronts the reader with a female death drive of a different inclination than that suggested above. In this case, the memory of incest may be said to express an autonomous female desire for transgression into extra-cultural nondifferentiation, that is, a desire to give in to the call of *jouissance*. A desire, however, which in the text was displaced onto the male part of the psychomachia to ward off the dangers, considering women's vulnerable position in the symbolic, of a dissolving self.

The proposal to understand 'A Momentary Taste of Being' as an expression of female pain *and* of female violence would fit in with Tiptree's own radical outlook on life. To clarify this, I will go back for a moment to the interesting article by Lowry Pei referred to previously. In an attempt to come to terms with the 'fanatical' character of Tiptree's stories, Pei recalls a passage from a 1971 interview with Tiptree, quoted in the famous introduction to *Warm Worlds and Otherwise* by Robert Silverberg:

> I'm one of those for whom the birth and horrendous growth of Nazism was the central generation event. From it I learned most of what I know about politics, about human life, about good and evil, courage, free will, fear, responsibility, and What to Say Goodbye To... And, say it again, about Evil. And Guilt. If one of the important things to know about a person is the face in his nightmares, for me that face looks much like my own.[8]

To be the face in one's own nightmares is, Pei elaborates, 'to dream "all sweet Auschwitz" from the point of view of both the SS and the Jew'.[9] The reference to Auschwitz is taken from one of Tiptree's earliest stories, 'Mama Come Home' (1968):

> There's rape and rape, you know. The brutal violation of the body, that's bad enough. But there's worse—the atrocities done to the vulnerable body in order to violate the spirit, the savage mockery of sex that joys in degrading the living victim to a broken *thing* ... All sweet Auschwitz.[10]

It is a story written in a hilarious tone, replete with allusions to James Bond films, about giant women from another planet visiting Earth, going around doing media shows and attacking men sexually. The male narrator is also raped by them, and is thus metonymically put in relation to Tillie, the woman he is in love with, but who was gang-raped as a girl and there-after waged 'permanent guerilla war inside' against all men. The odd thing is that Tillie, except for her height of course, is the giantesses' look-alike.

In a far more blunt manner the own face in the nightmare is investigated in 'The Psychologist Who Wouldn't Do Awful Things to Rats' (1976), which I consider as one of Tiptree's most brilliant stories. The story's male protagonist is, like Sheldon at that time, an experimental psychologist, the Jewish Tilman Lipsitz, nickname Tilly, who tries to be gentle to the laboratory rats because they remind him of his helpless people in the concentration camps in Nazi Germany. During a drunken vision he sees a rat king (young rats with their tails entangled) transforming into a King Rat. Lipsitz expects redemption from the King Rat, 'joy and healing', 'a second morning of the world', for:

> Maybe somewhere there is a reservoir of pain, he muses. Waiting to be filled. When it is full, will something rise from it? Something created and summoned by torment? Inhuman, an alien superthing ...[11]

After the vanishing of the hallucination, however, he starts to kill his rats with cold pleasure.

These stories and many others confirm, Pei's conclusion that for Tiptree humankind

> is ruled by drives, that reproduction and sexuality are a scourge, a fatal affliction that few if any escape, that sexuality and violence are inextricably linked, that civilization and annihilation are next-door neighbors and on the whole the world would be better off if we weren't here.[12]

In a more compassionate version of Tiptree's tragic vision, the human being could be summarized as 'an eternally divided, paradoxical double, seeking community and love and killing it in the moment it is found'.[13] Although I concur largely with Pei's interpretation of Tiptree's work, I think it is important to include the question of difference. A narrative like 'A Momentary Taste of Being' shows not only that the human subject is internally divided but also that this split is not embodied in a universal manner but according to one's different position in the symbolic. From the multiple differences in 'A Momentary Taste of Being', the one that concerned me most was *sexual* difference. The resulting impasse has been all too often from women's weak position in the phallic–paternal symbolic which I have delineated by means of the Aaron/Lory psychomachia: either to be a loyal father's daughter who, storing her grief inside, shuts her mouth about the violence committed against *and* by her, or to be a mother's daughter who in death-driven speechlessness indulges in her own (self-) destructive power.

Beyond the death drive
Notwithstanding this dilemma which runs through the pages of 'A

Momentary Taste of Being', once again the act of writing should be
emphasized. In the very creation of the literary text the death drive, the
urge to take refuge in non-being, is counterbalanced by the desire to
become a female subject, to voice a sense of being. I think a similar paradox
may be involved here as the one described by Elisabeth Bronfen at the end
of *Over Her Dead Body*, a compelling study of the aesthetic representation
of the dead feminine body. The central question of Bronfen's study is the
following. Considering that women's (historical and imagined) deaths have
always been either the object or the inspiration of literary texts, how can
women inscribed within this cultural convention carve out a space for their
own authorship? The difficulty for women in creating their own symbolic
system is that woman/women is/have been constructed as man's other,
that is to say, as that which is not the centre of a social or representational
system.

> Hers is a position of non-coherence, of the void or an empty space
> between signifiers precisely because she is constructed as the
> vanishing point and the condition of western culture's fictions of
> itself; as the object and foundation of representation; as the telos and
> origin of man's desire to represent his culture; as the object and sign
> of his exchange with life and death, of his socio-economic exchanges
> and of his creativity.[14]

Bronfen's conclusion about the exemplary texts by women writers she has
analysed is that they 'self-consciously install the cultural paradigm that
links femininity with death in the same gesture that they critique it'.[15]
These texts demonstrate the more or less conscious strategy used by the
hysteric of oscillating between complicity and resistance. 'By using distance
and comedy they take conventions to excess only to transform them into
the macabre or the grotesque.' However, whether this excess produces a
comic or a tragic mode, it simultaneously confirms the tropes and clichés
by which femininity and death become conflated. 'In a sense these texts
compulsively repeat so as to disclose the point of non-existence beyond
which a woman writing as yet can't move.'[16]

What is taken to excess in Tiptree's narrative is the masculine code,
voiced most distinctly by the figure of Yellaston, that sex equals death and
that women are to blame. The science fiction conventions of travel in outer
space, entropy and the alien encounter are deployed to represent the
dissolution into non-being, the 'death' of the female subject *as well as* the
culture that suppresses the female voice and violates her embodied
subjectivity. In the same movement in which the grotesque testicle-Earth
and the monster penis are erected in Aaron's dream their decline in the
rest of the narrative is prepared.

'The dance on the boundary between life and art is once again shown to be coterminous with a game between life and death.'[17] Could this be demonstrated better than in Aaron's desperate efforts to continue writing his log that probably nobody will ever read? He is recording the uncertain reality of the un-dead, of the ghosts that eternally hover between life and death, never ceasing to haunt him as the signs of his repressed part/past. I think Aaron's logging represents a not merely desperate but indeed brave attempt to go on writing after the collapse of the quasi-refuge that the phallic cultural order offers to women. Moreover, it shows the courage to render account of the power of the death drive, this pull towards beautiful annihilation and semiotic bliss, while acknowledging the need for resisting it.

Aaron's log, ultimately, is directed not to an immanent reception but to the readers *outside* the narrative universe. But what we see in his writing strikes the reader as very painful, for it reflects the tragic bias of Tiptree's text: the very disillusion/dissolution of the writing subject that was constituted with great difficulty in the narrative text. 'I don't dream anymore' (A163) is the conclusion. What makes this twice as painful to me is the gendered division according to which the process of perishing is staged. The strongest desire to live is projected on the male guise of the writing female subject, while its female guise is appointed the carrier of the death drive.

Would it be overstepping the mark to suppose that this split reflects to some extent the tensions of Sheldon/Tiptree's own authorship? As we know, this authorship was characterized by paradoxical literary and social strategies, like a male pseudonym and cherished anonymity, which aimed at creating a female subject position in a genre that until just a few decades before was considered typically masculine. However, while Tiptree's writing identity is unique for its colourfulness, its struggle for recognition on its own terms may be representative of that of women authors of her generation.[18]

In the almost 25 years that have gone by since 'A Momentary Taste of Being' was written we have witnessed considerable changes. Women writers have emerged to positions of prominence in the science fiction genre, even though science fiction as such is still not included in either modernist, postmodernist or feminist literary canons. Furthermore, it is highly debatable whether the cultural context in which science fiction is produced still corresponds to Kristeva's generalized description in 1974 of the 'patrilinear capitalist society and its monotheistic [religious and secular] ideology'. In the first place, the political situation providing the background of both 'A Momentary Taste of Being' and *Des Chinoises*—the cold war and the policy of détente, leftist fascination for Mao's China—has radically changed. What we are confronted with at the end of this second millennium are the conditions of post-industrial capitalism with its world-wide social, political and cultural rearrangements tied to hardly surveyable scientific and technological developments. Science fiction in particular is engaged in dealing, on the level of the imagination, with what Donna Haraway indicates as 'transitions from the comfortable old hierarchical dominations to the scary new networks' that can be called 'the informatics of domination'.[19]

It would be interesting to discuss in what ways exactly the 'comfortable' material and ideological domination of the masculine over the feminine under white capitalist patriarchy has been (and is being) transformed by the global power structures of the information age. This, however, largely exceeds the aim of the present study. The point I wish to emphasize at the moment is that the political, social and cultural shifts of the last twenty years (feminism, not only but most visibly in the Western world, being one of them) actually *have* destabilized the traditional economy of the sexes relying on the sacrosanct 'paternal Word'. To paraphrase Lefanu, there are more chinks in the world machine in which women nestle nowadays. While in Tiptree's 'The Women Men Don't See', the source of the metaphor, women remain invisible and still have to spend all their energy on survival (see the introduction to this study), at present we use the chinks in the armour to open up spaces for the acquisition of a positive female subjectivity and to enact it not only in the social but also in the symbolic.

By the notion of positive female subjectivity I refer, once again, to a vision of women who are desiring, speaking and acting in their own myriad ways. According to this vision of a symbolic revolution, women appear neither as non-man—or man's 'other'—nor as pseudo-men, nor as models of the New Woman. Instead, they are selves that are never set and finished but always becoming, never whole and one but always split and composite; and *as such* they embody, experience and imagine sexual difference. Understood thus, sexual difference is not an essentialist reduction of a woman to a fixed 'feminine' body, but an affirmative yet open-ended exploration of how real-life women experience and signify the difference between women and men, the differences among women and the differences within each woman. In this sense, sexual difference is, as Rosi Braidotti states, the expression of women's ontological desire: the desire to be.[20]

I think 'A Momentary Taste of Being' is defined as much by a desire and will to be as it is by a drive towards non-being. Feeding on the exchange of life and death, its writing discloses a vehement battle of a female subject simultaneously at war with herself and with a culture which still assesses sexual difference primarily as a violent abyss or lack rather than as a creative possibility of empowerment. In my evaluation, this battle remains undecided. At first sight, the negative slant of 'A Momentary Taste of Being' is the absolute winner: the exhaustion of patriarchy dragged down the vulnerable female subject with it (or was it the other way round?). The narrative thus lacks a positive view of sexual difference, and sexuality for that matter, as affirmation of the desire to be. The experience of violence and suffering seems to oppose any utopian dimension of the imagination. And yet, there is a vision of future life in 'A Momentary Taste of Being'. Admittedly, it would be outlandish and over-optimistic to intimate that these science fictional images of posthuman being empower sexual difference. They are indeed too shadowy and ghostlike, too fond of the threshold between life and death to embody a substantial utopian promise. Nonetheless I think it is via these uncanny creatures that the question of sexual difference can be further explored.

Posthumanistic contours

To begin with, such exploration requires that the significance of the figuration of the posthuman species in Tiptree's story be extended so as to include a theoretical category. In that sense, it points to a process of incarnation of posthumanistic thinking in a world in which, to avoid misunderstandings, not so much humanity as Western humanism has reached its point of depletion. Earlier I have called the posthuman as it appears in 'A Momentary Taste of Being' a category of the future. It is not a sublimated repetition of the human, not a projection of a more-than-human, as exemplified by the celestial Starchild of Kubrick's *2001*. Nor does it signify the victory of the in-human—whether imagined as technological domination, brute force or whatever.[21] Instead, the posthuman implies a new look at the present from the perspective of the future, of what is not yet. Just as the postmodern is a rewriting of the modern rather than its opposite, as Jean-François Lyotard recalls, the posthuman is a redefinition of the human. Like the zygotes of human sperms and alien ova in 'A Momentary Taste of Being', the posthuman conjures up the ghosts of the past and evokes the spirit of new states of being.

By humanism I mean the idea that the Human is the highest value and indisputable gauge. The ongoing erosion to which this humanist ideal is liable does not imply, however, indifference to the suffering and well-being of human beings. On the contrary, I would say. Rendering account of the limited, dependent and divided being of the human may generate more respect for the fragility of life than a pathetic defense of the Human. That is to say, the old universal of the autonomous and isolated individual is replaced with the radical singularity of a subject that is a fundamentally interrelational being.

The humanist vision, moreover, is closely linked to the assumption of a rational, self-defined, unified and universal subject of knowledge and moral judgement. More and more, this has been demythologized as a Western, white, masculine subject frantically holding on to the foundering illusion of his cultural and epistemological superiority. In opposition to this vision, a feminist posthumanistic discourse, as I favour it, would acknowledge the internal contradictions of the subject as ir/rational being. It investigates the power relations in which any subject is embedded because of her or his sex, colour, age, social–economic situation, religion, education, geographical background, corporeal condition, sexual privilege and so on. It thinks through the interdependence of the human with the non-human: the animal, the mineral, the cosmos, the machine. Finally, posthumanistic thinking would take into account that there is a dimension of reality which is ultimately beyond grasp and defying the human faculty of rationalistic comprehension, a dimension which might be referred to as the divine.

To summarize, then, what I understand the posthuman in 'A Momentary Taste of Being' to point to—but not to signify—is a posthumanistic horizon. As such these posthuman beings are characterized by continuity as well as discontinuity. They are still partly human. But the human is fused with the non-human, with something alien. The germinal posthuman beings evolving from this fusion therefore point (back) to a frightening yet radical moment of transformation. What is shed in this transformation is a view of humanity which strives to 'work out the beast', which denies the violent, irrational, desiring and death-driven components of human being (our 'ghosts') only to project them outside on some 'other' being.

What the transformation brings about, however, is deeply uncertain. The suggestion of a posthuman paradise would only revive the pitfalls of humanism. What are they like, 'the creatures that generated us, that we die to form', Aaron Kaye wondered, 'Are they brutes or angels?' Probably we can only hope that the posthumanistic insight that human beings are *both* will contribute to the increase of cultural and political practices of negotiation and control of personal and structural violence. This concerns more in particular the devastating reality of sexual violence, not only in its crudest physical manifestations but also in the organization of sexual difference according to the phallocentric symbolical order. That the power of imagination is essential to these practices I hope to have illuminated during this study of 'A Momentary Taste of Being'.

Sexual difference
Yet, once again, Tiptree's narrative does not provide us with a positive

vision of a different organization of sexual difference. Rather the posthuman in 'A Momentary Taste of Being' is a marker of *negative* difference: it expresses a desire for a total dismantlement of traditional arrangements of sexual difference without making positive images available yet.[22] In Tiptree's literary feminism, 'at once so bitter and so radical' (Pei), such as expressed in our story, the dissipation of masculine aggressive libidinal energy apparently demands the liquidation of any familiar categories, not only of the sexes but of the human altogether.

At this very point, Jean-François Lyotard's thought experiment concerning the significance of the death of the sun becomes highly relevant. In the *causerie* 'Can Thought Go without a Body', Lyotard deploys the idea of the absolute limit to human thinking which is the death of the sun—in say 4.5 billion years—to ponder on the meaning of corporeality. It is a striking text because it can be read as a counter-narrative to Tiptree's tale. While both texts converge on their imagination of a cosmic apocalypse, their appreciation of sexual difference from the post-catastrophical viewpoint is rather different. Let me first convey the contents of Lyotard's vision.

To start with, it recalls that the alternative for a feeling of *après nous le déluge* (of matter) is the project that contemporary technological sciences are already working on. It entails the simulation of the material circumstances in which thinking will still be possible after the radical transformation of matter, which the catastrophe of the extinct sun is all about. To that purpose a *hardware* needs to be developed that is analogical to the human organism yet independent of terrestrial conditions of life. The *software* of these machines is, in plain words, the human capacity to think and use language. Thinking and body are inseparable in this process for 'each one is analogous to the other in relation to their respective (sensual, symbolical) environments, while this relation itself, in turn, is analogous in both cases'.[23]

This being stated, Lyotard subsequently presents a spokeswoman (*Elle*) to expand on the consequences of these analogies. If we wish a post-solar thinking to be something else than the obsolete 'miserable dichotomized skeleton', one of the crucial issues is that of sexual difference (*la différence sexuelle*) as it is inscribed on the body and in the unconscious. The unbridgeable difference between the sexes is conceived by Lyotard as paradigm of the incompleteness of bodies and spirits, a deficiency which causes both suffering and desire. The way I understand Lyotard, he suggests that sexual difference, rather than technology in itself, is to be approached as the very neg-entropic force of the universe: 'Your thinking machines should not only feed themselves on radiation, but also on the unbridgeable discord (*différend*) between the sexes'.[24] While the difference between the sexes can never be fully grasped, it generates endless thinking. Nonetheless it would be incorrect to see it as a kind of primordial explosion, a challenge to thinking, comparable to the catastrophical explosion of the sun. Lyotard decides that this is not the status of sexual difference since it 'is implied in the secret of bodies and thoughts and [thus] generates endless thinking. Sexual difference means the annihilation of the One.'[25] According to him, reflection on the complexity and inevitability of the division between the sexes is a vital prerequisite for post-solar thinking. If this is neglected, 'the *Exodus* in space will be propelled by entropy after all'.[26]

At first sight, the philosophical and science fictional speculation reflect each other extremely well. The exodus of the spaceship *Centaur* was truly driven by increasing entropy and the approaching death of the sun. 'A Momentary Taste of Being', to be more specific, is a fantasy about the entropy of a 'spermatic' libidinal economy, the emasculation of masculine sexual–aggressive drives, and the unmasking of phallic–patriarchal power. Entropy has been given a particular interpretation here, referring to the end of a *certain* history, not, as in Lyotard, of human history *per se*. Thus it turns out that the metaphor of entropy is deployed in rather diverging manners in the respective generic forms of Lyotard's philosophical causerie and Tiptree's science fiction. In Lyotard's cosmological fable, the reader is exposed to the theoretical implications of an ever so abstract death of the sun. In Tiptree's narrative, however, the sun does not represent an absolute limit to thinking but an actual power structure. That is to say, the story's sun is at once more metaphorical and more real than the sun in 'Can Thought Go without a Body?': Yellow Sol/Yellaston is the embodiment of sexual and symbolic phallic power. And it is the death of this 'sun' that is exposed in Tiptree's story of entropy and dissipation.

My belief that the pain experienced by actual women because of patriarchal power runs through the pages of 'A Momentary Taste of Being' makes it perfectly comprehensible to me that the imagined post-apocalyptical time of the narrative does not emphasize new figurations of sexual difference. The echoes of the old ones are still too powerful to run the risk of involuntarily repeating them. In contrast with Lyotard's fable, therefore, it's up to unstable posthuman beings rather than the refurbished human sexes to express the striving for negative entropy.

In a comment on Lyotard's cosmological essay, Braidotti shows herself somewhat disappointed with its imaginative powers. According to her, Lyotard's vision is tainted with a romanticized notion of the role of sexual difference in moving beyond the alleged crisis of the paternal metaphor in the age of modernity. It displays a melancholy longing for an imaginary symmetry between the sexes instead of a more radical attempt to 'force the issue of sexual difference to some sort of catastrophe or head-on collision'.[27] Well, at least nobody can deny James Tiptree the quality of radicality up to the catastrophical. Unlike Lyotard, she is not, in Braidotti's phrase, 'lingering in a twilight zone, sitting mournfully among the debris of the old universe, waiting for a rebirth of sorts'.[28] 'A Momentary Taste of Being' as well as Tiptree's more overtly feminist stories such as 'The Screw Fly Solution' or 'The Women Men Don't See', to name just a few, are narrative testimonies to the factual and historical *dis*symmetry between the sexes. For that reason, let me reiterate the point that the birth of the posthuman in 'A Momentary Taste of Being' cannot remotely look like a rebirth of any familiar categories of the masculine and the feminine. Rather it is Tiptree's writing itself which provides a taste of sexual difference in a posthumanistic age—a type of women's writing which wrecks the need for solace but dares the imagination towards the unexpected, the not-yet-dreamt.

The tragic heuristic

In a nutshell, the insights to which Tiptree's text has urged me on so far are the following. Firstly, that women's quest for subjectivity involves to a greater or lesser extent a struggle between life and death drives and that violence is an intrinsic part of this struggle. This, I need to emphasize, by no means calls for a trendy celebration of female aggression, but for critical acts of analysis and sublimation. Secondly, my reading of the text suggests that a posthumanistic frame of mind, besides engendering a view of the human which critically incorporates its violent and non-rational components, instead of exorcizing them, also constitutes an uneasy horizon of sexual difference. Finally, that women's drive toward non-being can be simultaneously reinforced and counter-balanced in the very act of writing and imagining, and that the grotesque and the tragic are constantly alternating in this writing process.

My concern thereupon is how feminist theologies are to digest these insights. The female desire to be and the meaning of the death drive and of violence in relation to female subjectivity bring us in the first place to the field of theological anthropology, that is to say the contemplation of human existence in the light of the orientation towards what may be called the divine. I situate myself among feminist theologians who take a post-theist stance, that is to say, that the divine is disconnected from the image of a foundational and substantiated God pitted against the finite. Instead, the divine is to be conceived as a power which becomes manifest in and by the finite itself.[29] Yet there are still many ways of imagining such a power, of naming and interpreting divinity. It is by interrelating the issues of female subjectivity and the naming of the divine as they emerge from

my interpretation of Tiptree's 'A Momentary Taste of Being' that I make
a tentative move to explore these questions in the last sections of this study.
It may come as no surprise that as well as to feminist theological texts, at
times I will turn to literary texts as resources to illuminate my
wo/anderings.

Let me emphasize again at this point the importance of recognizing the
subject's fundamentally divided being. This is to be understood not in the
sense of a consciousness at war with its conscience, but rather as the
Kristevan drama of contradictory symbolic and semiotic forces which are
continuously enacted in each individual and every culture. The subject
always balances, so to speak, on the edge of the symbolic and the semiotic,
anxiously looking for the safety net above the abyss. Subjective existence
does not only involve reason and the construction of order, for interwoven
with them are the unresolvable ambiguities of desire, the flows of life and
death drives. Our yearning for an original wholeness and innocence is as
ineradicable as it is groundless. I think this is an insight which deserves
fuller consideration, not just in (feminist) religious studies.

Interestingly, Amy Hollywood arrives at a similar recommendation by
dint of the rereading of *Wuthering Heights* in the light of Kristeva's theory
of the formation of the subject. In her essay 'Violence and Subjectivity',
Hollywood employs the meaning of violence as a key to Emily Brontë's
text.

> Like Kristeva over a hundred years later, Brontë offers a picture of
> the violent underside of all our subjectivities, as well as providing a
> compelling counter-myth to the prevalent Christian discourse of
> innocence, fall, guilt, and redemption.[30]

Obvious limitations prevent me from expanding on Hollywood's
illuminating interpretation of *Wuthering Heights*, but I would like to
reproduce her assessment of the figure of Heathcliff.

> The force of his emotional and physical presence, in an age marked
> by increasing feelings of vascillation [*sic*] and dis-ease with the self—
> in point of fact, abjection—is a source of mythological fascination for
> some Victorian and many modern readers. Willing to explore the
> depths of violence and evil in his faithfulness, Heathcliff goes beyond
> the Romantic Satan in that he acknowledges violence as violence,
> evil as evil, and *still* finds them preferable to the cultural world that
> has taken his love from him.[31]

In other words she suggests that one should read Heathcliff as an emblem
of the insight that each subject of either sex hides inside the 'potentialities

of *victim/executioner*' rather than as a character.[32] We are all psychomachias, I would say, tragic—and at times comic—doubles: 'I am Heathcliff', Cathy asserts; 'Call me Lory', Aaron Kaye echoes.

By analogy to 'A Momentary Taste of Being', the return of the repressed at the end of Brontë's novel, with the corollary of the re-emergence of the ghosts of Cathy and Heathcliff, is marked first and foremost by the violence of the drives. Likewise, the return of the repressed should not be understood only as a threat, for, as Hollywood claims, it also represents a hope and a promise. With Hollywood, I see this hope as the attempt— apparently as painstaking for a female Victorian gothic author as it is for a twentieth-century female science fiction author—to inscribe a myth or narrative beyond the Christian scheme of Paradise/Fall/Salvation that would help shape a new and powerful subjectivity. Nonetheless, the ambivalence between 'threat and promise always remains, for as the novel shows us, such power and violence are both liberating and destructive'.[33] I deeply agree with Hollywood that we do well to deal with ambiguity and tension rather than to resolve them smoothly in either an eschatological frame (presupposing a *telos* of salvation[34]) or in the projection of evil completely outside the (female) subject.

> It is how we negotiate and control violent drives and our need for freedom that must be subject for discussion, rather than how to do away with violence entirely, an impossible task that can lead to the worst kinds of oppression.[35]

Here indeed we are also reminded of both the critical analysis of women's fantasies of innocence by Grietje Dresen, and of Toni Morrison's literary exposure of the sin of innocence, briefly introduced from her novel *Tar Baby* at the end of Chapter IV. Morrison's novels offer a series of sophisticated and emotionally and historically probing narrative essays in which the triad of Paradise, Fall and Salvation is transformed into a myth of the *fortunate fall*. While judging harshly the injustices of white culture and the devastating reality of slavery, Morrison also scrutinizes, compelled by empathy and compassion this time, the motives and actions of her black protagonists. The specific features of black and gendered experiences are incorporated into Morrison's various elaborations of the biblical pattern. In this manner the novels have the triple effect of conjuring up the ghosts of white racist history, empowering black people and producing a moral statement on a universal existential level. They picture 'the necessary and potentially redemptive passage from a garden state of debilitating innocence to painful self-knowledge and its consequences'.[36] Morrison's protagonists involuntarily suffer from evil and injustice inflicted on them by others and still have to deal with their own contradictory fears, desires *and* actions. They are divided selves, by historical fate and by human nature. The most terrifying and heart-breaking example is Sethe in *Beloved*, the mother who committed infanticide to save her daughter from the hands of the slave-owner.[37]

Sethe, like the other characters in Morrison's novels, in a way is a tragic heroine, inevitably confronted with choice, in which every decision entails a loss. For Katherine Sands, *Beloved* is one of the (literary) resources for a feminist theology with a sensibility to the tragic, which she begins developing in a study with the telling title *Escape from Paradise*. 'Tragic conflicts expose the limits of the principle of noncontradiction and they efface all innocence, human and divine.'[38] In Sands' advocacy of a tragic heuristic I find a promising impulse to the theological and ethical consideration of the subject's ambiguity, violence and our irreversible fall from innocence. Tragedy, as Sands understands it, is the inevitability of our involvement in evil. Tragedies are stories—or a style of story-telling— that highlight elemental conflicts of truths, which, differently put, are also conflicts of powers. Her attention may concern any narrative of profound suffering. Starting with what she calls 'prereflective wonder about suffering as suffering and power as power', tragedy in her definition becomes religious, while 'it is the translation of wonder into inquiry, discernment, and action that renders tragedy theological'.[39] Greek tragedies form but one model of a 'rendering of religious myth as *heuristic drama* in which moral questions can be directed to elemental power',[40] elemental powers being the vital, integral dimensions of life in a particular context. 'Tragedies illuminate the way in which such elemental conflicts afflict humanity with evil—that is, with negative moral judgments of the tragic characters.'[41]

A tragic sensibility, in my view as well, befits a postmodern feminist theology, as the latter raises fundamental questions not only about the human but also regarding 'elemental power', or divinity. It enhances theologies founded on questions instead of doctrinal claims. 'Tragedies foreclose the faith that forecloses questioning.'[42] The tragic heuristic Sands proposes, therefore, is neither a world view or new universal nor a new justificatory metanarrative or modern theodicy but 'a set of questions'. Tragedies involve three major functions, which are also pertinent to a theology that matters. First, they have a *mystical* or illuminative dimension in which elemental powers are acknowledged. The tragic convention of questioning the divine not only implies the naming and honoring of the deities, but it also permits their indictment.

> If as postmoderns we are learning to think of our deities as our own creation, tragic consciousness stands as a reminder of how creativity gets out of our hands, how sociality is as much a condition of blindness

and constraint as a promise of freedom and enlightenment. Like the divine, sociality is both within and beyond our control.[43]

Secondly, tragedies have an *aesthetic* or expressive dimension, which reaches beyond the confines of analytical reason, for '[a]rt stretches the cramped world, colors the black and white, and teaches even grief to sing'.[44] Sometimes sensibility to the tragic may also mean the apprehension of disturbing beauty in the midst of evil and violence. Sands illustrates this with Morrison's Sethe, in *Beloved*, who remembers with horror the scarring beauty of the sycamore tree in which black children were hanged.

> Theology needs to articulate both the scarring and the healing powers of the aesthetic, avoiding on the one hand an amoral aestheticism and on the other hand a moralistic disrespect for the autonomy of art as a differentiated function of community.[45]

Thirdly, tragic discourse has a *moral* or transformative function. Sands levels criticism at all notions—be they Platonic, Kantian or feminist—of an absolute and unconditional moral good, including idealized views of nature and the divine. From a tragic awareness, moral judgements are 'strategic, contextual judgments about how the diverse goods of life might be integrated and necessary suffering minimized in a particular place and moment'.[46] Moral assessment is thus dislodged from any secure metaphysical or transcendent foundation. In a world of suffering and radical conflict, like the present one we live in, morality should aim at the continuance of the world, which far from being an innocent faith is 'a *practice* of compassion'. A practice, that is, of intellectual compassion, in which the plurality of truth is taken seriously, and moral compassion, in which the plurality of values is honoured. Unlike in a liberal support of plurality, however,

> the heuristic purpose of tragedy is to discern in the moment and for particular historical agents what is within our control and what is not, forming responsible judgments on the one side while holding compassion and desire open to what remains beyond.[47]

To what extent can we assign the functions of tragedy to Tiptree's 'A Momentary Taste of Being'? And what significance does it thus have for a theology that is sensitive to the tragic? The first two functions of tragedy, the mystical and the aesthetic, I shall address in the last section of this chapter. What about the moral function of 'A Momentary Taste of Being'? More specifically we may wonder whether the overall apocalyptic inclination of Tiptree's text allows of a tragic heuristic. How much room for moral compassion and responsible judgements is left open in a narrative text heading so directly towards a 'final solution'—an 'anti-salvation' we might say—to humanity's fall, that is, the dominance of spermatic economy? Its apocalyptic tendency notwithstanding, I do think the tragic dimension of 'A Momentary Taste of Being' is obvious too. Or perhaps we should say that the irresolved inner tensions and contradictions of Tiptree's text precisely make for its tragic character.

On the one hand phallic sexuality and patriarchal social relations are directly and indirectly designated as evil. This implies a feminist repetition of a long tradition of dualism in Western discourse, in which evil is hypostatized and at times demonized. Behind the narrative's imagination, however, is not mere rational analysis, I assume, but also pain, anger and empathy about real-lived experiences of sexual violence and other injustices because of the dissymmetry between the sexes. The painful paradox itself of the attempt to counter, and maybe even undo, lived violence with textual violence already attests to the grief of tragedy. Yet on a more explicit level Tiptree's text also thematizes the tragic deconstruction of absolutes. That is, as already highlighted, where the psychomachia of Aaron and Lory Kaye is concerned. The Lory-part of the double is hurt by life and love and seeks impossible redemption by annihilation. By believing in absolute goodness she makes herself guilty of the sin of innocence. The Aaron-figure, then, is a tragic (anti-) hero with a vengeance. While seeking moral sanity that is based on the truly tragic insight that humanity inescapibly involves passive and active affliction with evil, and that paradise is a dangerous place, he nevertheless becomes 'wilfully innocent' by dismissing Lory's submerged story as a 'crazy plot'. In the end, subsequently, he willy-nilly makes the decision to resist the lure of the alien—absolute (de)light—saving consequently his own existence but facing the unbearable loss of communal life.

'A Momentary Taste of Being''s propensity for the tragic is on the verge of fatalism with regard both to men/humankind's sexual-aggressive drives and to human fate in the face of elemental (cosmic) power. The text does not show much compassion for its protagonists. Instead it relentlessly investigates the subject's ambiguous moral motives and self-delusionary choices, blowing up the inquiry to the size of cosmic tragedy and, at times, cosmic grotesque. I would want us to honour such harsh self-investigation as displayed in Tiptree's text, but to exercise more consideration for the Earth-scale moral dilemmas into which we might run.

But then again, it is the very cosmic proportions of 'A Momentary Taste of Being' that motivate its mystical and aesthetic functions of tragedy.

Transformation in the divine

How could what I read as 'A Momentary Taste of Being''s mystical dimension illuminate an understanding of the divine which is no longer conceived of as an omnipotent, separate reality or entity, but as a power which becomes manifest from within and by the finite itself? Assuming that the finite itself gets redefined in a postmodern vein as a split, multi-layered and internally contradictory process, deprived of any ontological foundations or transcendent referent. To get a clearer idea of the possible significance of the narrative's alien landscape in this respect, I would first like to expand a bit on the kind of representation of the divine to which I am critically addressing myself. In broad outline it is an image of the divine as *goodness*, which tends, in some feminist theologies, to replace the obsolete omnipotent Father god of the Judaic–Christian tradition. A representative example of such a vision may be the introduction provided by the editors of *Weaving the Visions*, Judith Plaskow and Carol Christ, to a section of articles called 'Naming the Sacred':

> Recognizing that female as well as male images can perpetuate models of domination and power-over, feminists both in and outside traditional religions are seeking ways to imagine sacred power as present in the whole complex web of life, not as power-taker but as empowerer.[48]

More concretely, this empowerer is interpreted by Plaskow and Christ as a dynamic force or energy of transformation, combining individual, social and spiritual aspects, which is in this manner also a power of creation and envisioning, of reconnection and healing.

No matter how inspiring the affirmation of finite being implied in this view may be, especially *vis-à-vis* the theological traditions of abhorring the flesh and the finite, I do wonder about the equation of the divine with the power of (re)conciliation, oneness and goodness. Does it not tend, thus, to neutralize tragic conflicts and fundamental splits into the idea of a 'web of life'? In addition, is transformation in the divine simply to be equated with moral growth and increasing social justice? A brief consideration of a kindred example of feminist naming of the sacred might further clarify my hesitations. In *A Feminist Ethic of Risk*, Sharon Welch strongly advocates the immanence of the divine, which she understands as the 'resilient, fragile, healing power of finitude itself'.[49] By denouncing the claims of classic theism, it is possible to circumvent the pitfall of theodicy, of having to defend divine omnipotence in the sight of the triumphs of evil in history. In Welch's view, therefore, it is neither necessary nor liberating to posit a foundational power or substance outside the finite, for the healing power of right relations itself *is* the divine, or grace as she also names it.[50] Grace, or a surplus of relationship, love and joy, is not the gift of God or the Goddess: 'it is all there is or need be of the divine':[51]

> The words *holy* and *divine* denote a quality of being within the web of life, a process of healing relationship; and they denote the quality of being worthy of honor, love, respect, and affirmation.[52]

Divinity is fragile, as the triumph of evil in the atrocities of twentieth-century history demonstrates. Yet, Welch asserts, there are innumerable states and actions that are worthy of being called divine, to be found in work for justice in movements seeking social and cultural transformation as well as in personal and sexual relationships. 'Attentiveness to the web of life, to the exuberance of children, to the beauty of nature, provides a sense of peace, of belonging, of exultation, of ecstasy'.[53]

Although I agree that grace as Welch defines it—beauty, joy, healing, and right relations (justice)—may form part of an experience of divinity, I wonder whether the identification of the divine with goodness, even if not as ontic structure but as moral quality, is acceptable. In this manner goodness is made an absolute—something which reality always belies. Let me once more quote Sands, who maintains that the

> religious and moral risk of tragic consciousness ... is to encounter elemental power/truth in its radical plurality, unmooring the good from any metaphysical anchor, so that it becomes *an entirely human, entirely fragile creation.*[54]

From an epistemic angle, moreover, I am in serious doubt as to whether grace indeed is 'all there is or need be of the divine'. It is at this point that the significance of 'A Momentary Taste of Being''s imagination comes to the fore. Let us continue focusing on the posthuman figuration as signpost of a posthumanistic horizon. In the first place the figuration implies still embryonic revisions of the human beyond the self-contained and self-reflexive Western (male) norm. As a part of this process of refiguring the image of subjectivity, here and there on this horizon one can also detect traces of a new sensibility for transcendent or sacred dimensions of reality. I want to stress, however, that this sensibility nevertheless risks—in our late twentieth-century consumer societies—being subsumed in either humanistic hedonism or facile moralism. In contrast, I propose to take Tiptree's posthuman species as not only an uncanny marker of the impossibility to fixate sexual difference but also as a sign of the *unfathomability of the divine*. The spaceship *Centaur* set off on an exodus from the wastes of the world to search for a paradisaical promised land. Its people's quest, however, was not fulfilled, but rather disrupted. Instead of finding what they were looking for, *they* were found.

Let me call to mind Aaron Kaye's recollection of the divergent interpretations of the experience of the alien light.

> It may be of great significance that they all saw it different, the egg-things I mean. Don said it was god, Coby saw ova. Ahlstrom was whispering about the tree Yggdrasil. Bruce Jang saw Mei-Lin there. Yellaston saw death. Tighe saw Mother, I think. All Dr. Aaron Kaye saw was colored lights. Why didn't I go, too? Statistical phenomenon. Defective tail. My foot got caught ... Lory saw utopia, heaven on earth, I guess. (A160–1)

To this range I have added my own naming of the human–alien encounter: I suggested that it can be taken as a reference to the divine. Thus, the divine is what is alien to the human yet can be experienced and named only with the help of known categories from the collective and individual histories of humankind. These categories, in turn, become redefined by the very experiences they signify. From the crew members we hear a variety of conventional names for the ecstatic experience of immersion in the alien light: namings which have prominantly figured in the various readings of the story.

The names have ambiguous and contradictory connotations, largely dependent on the giver of the name. In the name *god*, uttered by white American army commander Purcell, we hear the echoes of familiar patriarchal images of the divine. But it also discloses older matriarchal images which underlay it. *Yggdrasil* is the Scandinavian tree of life but also the sign of apocalyptic decline of the gods: resumption and refutation of mythological thinking at once. *Death*, coming from Yellaston, refers to a masculine fear of/desire for dissolution of the self. Yet from another angle we see the unclaimable regenerative power of matter in Coby's qualification *ova*. And in Bruce Jang's vision of Mei-Lin we see the return of one's lost beloved. *Mother* refers to an experience of semiotic bliss, of *jouissance*, and the either consolidating or disruptive impact of maternal powers on the symbolic. The dream of the kingdom of God on earth, finally, resonates In Lory's *utopia*, aroused by the suffering and longing in history yet bound to turn into its destructive reverse once sought to be actually realized.

What we as readers, together with Aaron Kaye, cannot fail to notice, however, is that, in retrospect, the posthuman demonstrates not only the partial but also the necessarily flawed character of each of these names, for they do not negotiate the alienness of the divine. The posthuman zygotes/ghosts are the result of a transformation of the familiar human into an uncanny posthuman. Being configurations of the human and the alien, they point to the available names of the divine so as to allow humankind to partially and provisionally domesticate alienness. On the other hand, they point even more to an *un*bridgeable difference. However, I would argue that Tiptree's text in its entirety does negotiate the strangeness of the divine.[55] It does so in the type of *transformation* that is pictured in the text.

The transformation that undeniably takes place through and as a result of the human–alien contact does not establish unity and coherence; on the contrary, it disrupts and leads to disintegration so as to generate an unknown future. This disruptice force of transformation as it comes to us from the text I would like to interpret as a manifestation of divinity. I observe two inseparable movements in this transformation: the dissolution of old identities, orders and sufferings, and the transcending towards an unknown state of sexual, cultural and spiritual change. Death and annihilation are closely connected with life and generation in 'A Momentary Taste of Being''s narrative. Yet this should not be misconstrued as an image of cosmic balance or sublime complementarity. Neither, I want to emphasize, are they the multiple aspects or plural faces of an inclusionary divine empowerer of the web of life. Nor do destruction and generation, more dynamically, indicate a rebirth in a mythical and non-tragic eternal cyclus. I read the zygotes rather as the uncanny witnesses to—and textual signs of—an unsettling transformation that is so extraordinary in its movements from the sublime to the ridiculous and vice versa that we would want to call it divine.

It is unsettling, first, because there are no guarantees whatsoever, only a passionate hope, that these beings indeed point to a transfiguration of pain and violence, and not just to a repetition in disguise. The dynamic of annihilation/generation which the posthuman beings represent is unsettling, moreover, because it discloses the *horrific side* of transformation. Transformation may indeed be seen, in keeping with many feminist theologians, as a manifestation of grace, of the gift of experiencing oneness with a bigger whole. 'A Momentary Taste of Being', on the other hand, shows transformation in the divine not only as a power of sweetness and joy but also of painful and horrifying rupture. Maybe it is somehow like when Teresa of Avila writes in her *Book of Life*, 'I saw myself dying in a yearning to see God and I did not know where to look for this life save by death'.[56] Teresa's 'death' is not the transcendence of her body into a spiritual realm but the embodied experience of death and birth at once, which is a no less painful than joyous experience of being touched by divine grace.[57] Thus the moment of rupture, of 'death' and dissolution, is paradoxically the very moment of coming into being. It goes beyond a traditional dynamic of conversion, in which a subject submits to a (divine)

Other. Rather it is a movement/moment in which the boundaries between self and other, between inside and outside, familiar and alien, human and divine have lost their meaning. In this movement, therefore, *both* terms get unsettled and open to redescription afterwards.

In my view, it is also such an intensely ambivalent and dynamic movement/moment of transformation that is taking place in Tiptree's text during the crew's indulgence in the alien light. The sweet/horrific experience of that moment is what the text refers to as 'a momentary taste of being'. After having crossed the time-gap between a twentieth-century agnostic science fiction text and a writing of sixteenth-century Christian mysticism, I want to bridge another distance for further clarification of the possible meaning of the story's momentary taste of being. This time I seek refuge with a modern, not particularly Christian author. In the part of her memoirs called *A Sketch of the Past*, Virginia Woolf—who, according to Kristeva, as noted at the beginning of the second section, should be associated primarily with the drive towards ultimate *non*-being—wrote with passion about what she called 'moments of being'. For Woolf, non-being was attached in the first place to the inevitable ordinariness of everyday, 'a kind of nondescript cotton wool'.[58] Within the cotton wool of non-being, however, exceptional moments of being may arise, sudden violent shocks. Some of these moments of being, Woolf recalls, brought about utmost satisfaction, like the experience of discovering wholeness in a flower bed. But others, such as the confrontation with aggression in herself and her brother or the suicide of an acquaintance of her parents, 'brought with them a peculiar horror and a physical collapse'.[59] Woolf defines her authorship in relation to these moments of being. While in her childhood they were passively received as the blows of an enemy lurking in the dark, later she started to see them as a revelation of some order which can be made real and whole only by being put into words.

> *Hamlet* or a Beethoven quartet is the truth about this vast mass that we call the world. But there is no Shakespeare, there is no Beethoven; certainly and emphatically there is no God: we are the words; we are the music; we are the thing itself. And I see this when I have a shock.[60]

The act of writing means connecting the severed moments of being with each other so as to imagine a wholeness that takes away the pain and the power to hurt. Woolf weaves the fragments of being, the horrific and the beautiful ones, together into a wholeness that is healing and which feeds the emerging self. She believes in the power of creating 'a real thing behind appearances', a pattern behind the cotton wool of non-being.[61]

In Tiptree's text, on the other hand, the process of writing bears witness to women's ontological desire in a less confident and balanced way. The divergent fragments of being are not patiently interwoven into a web of life, as in Woolf's work, but assembled in one moment of heightened Being in a fearful process of continuous becoming. One moment of coalescent subjective and cosmic becoming, an overwhelming transformation of the self and the world it was embedded in. Tiptree's momentary taste of being does not offer the solace of Woolf's moments of being, but points to the disruptive and transformative force of elemental power. Tiptree's text voices irony and desperation, but also hope and desire in relation to the well of life, which is material finitude itself in its generative and annihilative ambiguity. A momentary taste of Being does not seem to offer healing of the scattered self. And yet, from the vantage-point of victimized and marginalized being, this overwhelming moment of transformation may signify a departure from the wastes of non-being, with no promised land glowing on the horizon but only the contours of hope. It may be what I want to call the apocalyptic moment, not as the closure or fulfilment of history, but rather in Walter Benjamin's sense of a disclosure of the *possibility* of unexpected salvation, 'the small gate through which the Messiah could enter'.

But let us not forget, finally, that a *taste* of being refers not only to the transience of the moment but also to the intensity of the senses. At this point the mystical and the aesthetic dimensions, as I see them, of 'A Momentary Taste of Being' intertwine. The alien light offers cosmic beauty in the midst of horror.

For women as divergent as Tiptree, Woolf or Teresa of Avila, being is not an abstract spiritual state but a transforming experience equally involving the senses, the heart and the mind. For them, the hearing of the Word is just one possibility among many others for getting in touch with divinity.[62] Tasting may be the most intimate, and therefore most ambivalent of these ways, since the flavours of bitterness and sweetness easily mingle.

Being *touched* by the divine, then, may feel feathery as snowflakes or hot as lava. It is a deep sensation of both the skin and the eye. In his record, Aaron notes that 'there does seem to have been momentary physical contact, apparently through the forehead' (A159). In the practice of yoga, the forehead is the site of the *Ajna*, the sixth of the seven *chakras*, the centres of cosmic energy. More specifically, it is the place between the eyebrows, which controls the autonomous nervous system and corresponds with the ganglion of the sinus cavity, and probably the pineal gland. On a spiritual level, the *Ajna* is the seat of the mystical 'third eye' of Shiva and hence, for the yogi, the site of clairvoyance as well as ordinary insight, the power of concentration and connectiveness. In the imagery of

'A Momentary Taste of Being', the forehead must have been the point where the strong light emanating from the alien matter actually touched the humans as a terrible transformative force.

This alien light resembles the image of the 'obscure light' in the Western mystical tradition.[63] But it also draws our attention to even more surprising connections, such as the following passage from *The Famished Road*, the Booker-Prize-winning novel by the Nigerian-English writer Ben Okri.

> But deep inside that darkness a counterwave, a rebellion of joy, stirred. It was a peaceful wave, breaking on the shores of my spirit. I heard soft voices singing and a very brilliant light came closer and closer to the centre of my forehead. And then suddenly, out of the centre of my forehead, an eye opened, and I saw this light to be the brightest, most beautiful thing in the world. It was terribly hot, but it did not burn. It was fearfully radiant, but it did not blind. As the light came closer, I became more afraid. Then my fear turned. The light went into the new eye and into my brain and roved around my spirit and moved in my veins and circulated in my blood and lodged itself in my heart. And my heart burned with a searing agony, as if it were being burnt to ashes within me. As I began to scream the pain reached its climax and a cool feeling of divine dew spread through me, making the reverse journey of the brilliant light, cooling its flaming passages, till it got back to the centre of my forehead, where it lingered, the feeling of a kiss for ever imprinted, a mystery and a riddle that not even the dead can answer.[64]

In search of new insights and questions about subjectivity, sexual difference and the divine in a postmodern vein, I came across James Tiptree's 'A Momentary Taste of Being'. I have made use of divergent hermeneutical keys and theoretical frameworks to introduce just this small part of James Tiptree's science fictional world. A world that may strike us as 'alien'. Yet I am convinced that it turns out to be less alien if one focuses on the desire and hope for the transfiguration of pain and violence which underlie the idiosyncratic imagery. Then it becomes possible to see how the power of the imagination crosses the boundaries between literary and academic genres, between sexes, cultures, decennia. Not to create false universalisms or cultural indifference but to get a taste of the unexpected and the unimaginable.

Notes

Introduction

1 Mary McClintock Fulkerson, *Changing the Subject: Women's Discourses and Feminist Theology* (Minneapolis: Fortress Press, 1994), p. 362.

2 Discourse is to be understood in the Foucauldian sense as practices of reading and writing, which are, in every society, organized and controlled by procedures of exclusion, internal rules and procedures of selection. Discourses do not discover or express the truth but rather effect and produce each truths of their own. Examples of important feminist discussions of theology as discourse are offered by, besides McClintock Fulkerson, *Changing the Subject*: Rebecca Chopp, *The Power to Speak: Feminism, Language, God* (New York: Crossroad, 1989); Jonneke Bekkenkamp, *Canon & Keuze: Het bijbelse Hooglied en de Twenty-One Love Poems van Adrienne Rich als bronnen van theologie* (Kampen: Kok Agora, 1993).

3 Grietje Dresen, 'Mijmeren', *Tijdschrift voor Vrouwenstudies* 2 (1981) 1, 88–95. p. 95.

4 Grietje Dresen, Unpublished paper for symposium 'Over grenzen gesproken', Catholic University Nijmegen, 21 October 1993.

5 See Wouter Hanegraaff, *New Age Religion and Western Culture: Esotericism in the Mirror of Secular Thought* (Leiden: Brill, 1996). Hanegraaff describes New Age in all its diversity as a resumption of nineteenth-century Western esotericism and occultism, rejecting thus the popular belief that associates New Age with 'Eastern religion'.

6 John Clute and Peter Nicholls, eds, *The Encyclopedia of Science Fiction* (London: Orbit, 1993), p. 1231.

7 Ilse Bulhof and Laurens Ten Kate, eds, *Echoes of an Embarrassment: Negative Theology in Contemporary Philosophy of Culture* (Fordham: Fordham University Press, forthcoming).

8 Paula Cooey, *Religious Imagination and the Body: A Feminist Analysis* (New York and Oxford: Oxford University Press, 1994), p. 69.

9 In this approach I feel confirmed by Manfred Geier, 'Stanislaw Lem's Phantastischer Ozean: Ein Beitrag zur semantischen Interpretation des Science-fiction-Romans "Solaris"', in Werner Berthel, ed., *Über Stanislaw Lem* (Frankfurt a/M: Suhrkamp, 1981), pp. 96–163. Geier's triple readings of Lem's novel *Solaris* have inspired and to a certain extent served as a model for my own study of Tiptree's text.

10 Let me refer in this respect to Myriam Diaz-Diocaretz, 'Het woord vergeet niet waar het geweest is: de communicatietheorie van Bakhtin als perspectief voor feministische literatuurkritiek', *Lover* 16 (1989) 1, 8–16, in which M. Bakhtin's important notion of 'dialogism' is tested and further elaborated with a view to feminist literary theory. 'An exploration of language as a dynamic word—in Bakhtinian terms, as *slovo*—appears to be an adequate method for situating the process of writing [and interpreting] in a framework of communication, instead of in an ahistorical system based on the privileging

of the Logos', p. 12.

11 Sarah Lefanu, *In the Chinks of the World Machine: Feminism & Science Fiction* (London: The Women's Press, 1988).

12 Jeffrey D. Smith, ed., 'Women in Science Fiction', *Khatru 3 & 4* (Baltimore: Phantasmicon Press, 1975). The other contributors were: Ursula Le Guin, Joanna Russ, Vonda McIntyre, Virginia Kidd, Raylyn Moore, Luise White, Kate Wilhelm, Chelsea Quinn Yarbro, Suzy McKee Charnas, Samuel Delany and the initiator, Jeffrey Smith.

13 Lefanu, p. 106.

14 James Tiptree, Jr, *Warm Worlds and Otherwise*. With an introduction by Robert Silverberg (New York: Ballantine, 1975).

15 James Tiptree, Jr, *Star Songs of an Old Primate*. With an introduction by Ursula K. Le Guin (New York: Ballantine, 1978).

16 An interesting and by now famous analogy in this respect is described by Allucquere Stone in 'Will the Real Body Please Stand Up? Boundary Stories about Virtual Cultures', in *Cyberspace: First Steps* ed., M. Benedikt (Cambridge, Mass.: MIT Press, 1991), pp. 81–118. Stone describes a case of 'computer crossdressing', in which the totally disabled older woman Julie nevertheless managed to push the keys of a computer with her headstick. Julie projected a personality into the 'net'—the vast electronic web that links computers all over the world—and showed herself a very interesting companion to speak with and confide intimate feelings to. After several years it was revealed that Julie was not a 'free net persona trapped into a ruined body' but merely a computer creation of a middle-aged male psychiatrist. The public reactions of astonishment and anger to this uncovering were very similar to those following the disclosure of James Tiptree's 'paper crossdressing'.

17 Nancy Miller, 'Changing the Subject: Authorship, Writing, and the Reader', in *Feminist Studies/ Critical Studies* ed., T. de Lauretis (Bloomington: Indiana University Press, 1986), pp. 102–20, at p. 106.

18 Maaike Meijer, 'And now her body must decay, now, in me, has she ris'n again: Ida Gerhardt and the Poetic Remembrance of the Mother', *Lover* 19 (1991) 2, 72–8, p. 78.

19 Annelies van Heijst, 'Personen en personages bij Blaman en Dorrestein: Subjectiviteit als "continuing story", *Tijdschrift voor Vrouwenstudies* 15 (1994) 3, 356–69, p. 369.

20 (Auto-)biographical information on Alice Sheldon/Tiptree has been taken from James Tiptree, 'Everything But the Name is Me', *Starship* (Fall 1979), 31–4; Susan Wood, 'James Tiptree, Jr', in E. F. Bleiler, ed., *Science Fiction Writers: Critical Studies of the Major Authors from the Early Nineteenth Century to the Present Day* (New York: Charles Scribner's Sons, 1982), pp. 531–41; Nancy S. Gearhart and Jean W. Ross, Sketch and Interview for *Contemporary Authors* Vol. 108 (Detroit: Gale Research, 1983), pp. 443–50; Charles Platt, 'Profile: James Tiptree, Jr', who is also Lefanu's main source, *Isaac Asimov's Science Fiction Magazine* 7 (1983) 4, 26–49; Mark Siegel, *James Tiptree, Jr* (Mercer Island, Wash.: Starmount House, 1985).

21 Gearheart and Ross, above, p. 444.

22 Platt, n. 20 above, p. 35.

23 *Ibid.*, p. 43.

24 *Ibid.*, p. 45.

25 *Ibid.*, p. 36.

26 Gearheart and Ross, p. 448.

27 Platt, p. 38.

28 In *Extrapolation* Vol. 31 (spring 1990), Joanna Russ published a passage from a letter Alice Sheldon sent her, dated 25 September 1980: 'Just been reading the Coming-Out stories ed by Stabley & Wolfge (with a lot of Adrienne Rich) and it occurred to me to wonder if I ever told you in so many words that I am a Lesbian—or at least as close as one can come to being one never having had a succesful love with any of the women I've loved, and being now too old & ugly to dare to try. Oh, had 65 years been different! I *like* some men a lot, but from the start, before I knew anything it was always girls and women who lit me up.'

29 Alice B. Sheldon, 'Preference for Familiar Stimulation Independent of Fear of Novelty', *Psychonomic Science* 13 (1968) 3, 173–4; 'Preference for Familiar Versus Novel Stimuli as a Function of the Familiarity of the Environment', *Journal of Comparative and Physiological Psychology* 67 (1969) 4, 516–21. References found in Siegel, n. 20 above, p. 43.

30 Platt, n. 20 above, p. 40.

31 Lefanu, n. 11 above, pp. 105–29.

32 *Ibid.*, p. 122.

33 *Ibid.*, p. 124.

34 James Tiptree, Jr, 'The Women Men Don't See', rpt. in *Warm Worlds and Otherwise* (New York: Ballantine, 1975).

35 Lefanu, p. 126.

36 James Tiptree, Jr (as Raccoona Sheldon), 'The Screwfly Solution', rpt. in *Out of the Everywhere* (New York: Ballantine, 1981).

37 As I have nowhere found any indication as to whom this Schonweiser might have been, I assume he is a fictional authority.

38 Gearheart and Ross, n. 20 above, pp. 445–6.

39 *Ibid.*

40 Platt, p. 46.

41 A fine discussion of the theme of transcendence in Tiptree's work is found in Mark Siegel, 'Double-Souled Man: Immortality and Transcendence in the Fiction of James Tiptree, Jr', in *Death and the Serpent: Immortality in Science Fiction and Fantasy* ed. C.B. Yoke and D.M. Hassler (Westport, Conn.: Greenwood Press), 163–73.

42 James Tiptree, Jr., 'Second Going', in *Crown of Stars* (rpt. 1988. London: Sphere Books, 1990).

43 James Tiptree, Jr, 'A Momentary Taste of Being', in *Star Songs of an Old Primate*, 65–163. All future quotations will be noted as (Apage).

44 According to *The New Encyclopaedia Britannica* (1974, 15th edition), myxomycetes resemble both protozoa (one-cellular animals) and fungi. The *Lycogala epidendron* looks like small puffballs, which are mostly orange or yellow but can adopt many colours. Assumed at first to display non-sexual reproduction, at present it is considered to be sexual.

45 Occam's [Ockham] razor (*entia non sunt sine ratione multiplicanda*) is often referred to in science fiction and its criticism as a means of channelling speculations. See, for example, Stanislaw Lem: 'In a literary process a maximum number of events should be achieved by a minimum use of both stylistic (linguistic) means and narrative (material) elements ... This is the artistic counterpart of the empirical principle known as "Occam's razor"',

Phantastik und Futurologie II (rpt. 1964/1977 Frankfurt a/M: Suhrkamp, 1984), p. 46. In addition, think also of the role of Ockham in Umberto Eco's *The Name of the Rose*.

46 Yggdrasil is the cosmic tree in the Scandinavian *Edda*. Another story of Tiptree's, 'Mother in the Sky With Diamonds' (1971), focuses on a spaceship named *Ragnarök*. In Scandinavian mythology Ragnarök is the twilight of the gods and the end of the world. It says that during Ragnarök the tree Yggdrasil will quake, thus causing the passing away of the gods.

47 Salman Rushdie, 'Is Nothing Sacred?', in *Imaginary Homelands: Essays and Criticism 1981–1991* (London: Granta Books, 1991), p. 422.

48 Edward FitzGerald, *Rubáiyát of Omar Khayyam the Astronomer–Poet of Persia rendered into English verse* (rpt. London: Macmillan & Co, 1899). The stanza is number XLVIII of the first edition of 1859. In the second edition, from 1868, the stanza has been modified into: 'One Moment in Annihilation's Waste, / One Moment, of the Well of Life to taste—/ the Stars are setting and the Caravan / Starts for the Dawn of Nothing,—Oh, make haste!' (number XXXVIII).

I: Seed-beds

1 Corinne Squire, 'Science Fictions', *Feminism & Psychology* 1 (1991) 2, 181–99, p. 187.

2 *Ibid.*

3 Maaike Meijer, *De Lust tot Lezen: Nederlandse dichteressen en het literaire systeem* (Amsterdam: Sara, 1988).

4 Helen Carr, ed., *From My Guy to Sci-fi: Genre and Women's Writings in the Postmodern World* (London: Pandora, 1989), p. 7.

5 Squire, n. 1 above, p. 189.

6 Teresa de Lauretis, *Technologies of Gender: Essays on Film, Theory, and Fiction* (Bloomington: Indiana University Press, 1987).

7 Catherine Keller, 'Why Apocalypse, Now?', *Theology Today* 49 (1992), 183–95, p. 193.

8 At this point I use the term postmodern in the first place to indicate the epistemological, ethical, cultural and political practices of continuous questioning of posited truths and foundations with the intention of creating partial (in the double sense of the word) and provisional insights, judgements and narratives. I prefer the notion of postmodernism over poststructuralism because it expresses not only a critical and analytical but also an experiential/existential dimension. Also postmodernism in the sense of aesthetic and literary practices of course bears relevance to the study of science fiction, as it, in addition to the features mentioned above, refers to generic and stylistic eclecticism, the influence of mass media and informatics, and an undermining of the strict line of demarcation between high and popular culture. Cf Andreas Huyssen, *After the Great Divide: Modernism, Mass Culture, Postmodernism* (Bloomington: Indiana University Press, 1986).

9 Jonneke Bekkenkamp, *Canon & Keuze: Het bijbelse Hooglied en de Twenty-One Love Poems van Adrienne Rich als bronnen van theologie* (Kampen: Kok Agora, 1993), p. 2.

10 Carol Christ, *Diving Deep and Surfacing: Women Writers on Spiritual Quest* (Boston: Beacon Press, 1980, 1986²).

11 *Ibid.*, p. 5.

12 *Ibid.*, p. 3.

13 *Ibid.*, p. 3.

14 Bekkenkamp, n. 9 above, p. 4.

15 Christ, n. 10 above, p. 8.

16 Bekkenkamp, n. 9 above, p.45. Not, incidentally, that this view prevents Bekkenkamp herself from giving sophisticated and often beautiful decodings of the poetry of the *Song of Songs* and *The Twenty-One Love Poems* by A. Rich.

17 These differences in context and function of the theological use of literature should not be ignored. A great awareness of how the context influences the function and methods of the feminist theological appeal to women's texts is found in Bekkenkamp, *Canon & Keuze* (n. 9 above). She has developed four context-dependent options for reading 'as a woman' and 'as a theologian': 'The first model fits feminist vicars, as the second and third will suit university teachers who either want to integrate women's religious studies in theological curriculae or claim an autonomous status for them. The fourth is meant for dialogical situations among equals', p. 299. The last-mentioned option suits my own study best, the 'equals' being the discourses of the interdisciplinary field in which I am moving about. A disregard of contexts, on the other hand, flaws Annelies van Heijst's discussion of the appeal to literary texts by feminist theologians, in *Longing for the Fall* (Kampen: Kok Pharos, 1995). Because of its abstract stance I find Van Heijst's view, though astute in several of its critical observations, misleading, not in the least because of the moralistic rhetoric accompanying it. Without paying attention to the function, context and own merits of their appeal to women's writings, Van Heijst rebukes theologians like Christ for not submitting to the methodological test of criticism of literary science. In my view, Van Heijst fails to reflect on the meaning of both *imagination* and *narrative* in feminist theological practices of reading literary texts.

18 Donna Haraway, 'A Cyborg Manifesto: Science, Technology, and Socialist-Feminism in the Late Twentieth Century', in *Simians, Cyborgs, and Women: The Reinvention of Nature* (London: FAB, 1991), p. 181.

19 Mary McClintock Fulkerson, *Changing the Subject* Introduction, n. 1 above, p. 381.

20 Rosi Braidotti, *Nomadic Subjects: Embodiment and Sexual Difference in Contemporary Feminist Theory* (New York: Columbia University Press, 1994).

21 Joan Scott, 'Experience', in *Feminists Theorize the Political*, ed. J. Butler and J. Scott (New York and London: Routledge, 1992), p. 37.

22 Annelies van Heijst, *Leesbaar lichaam: Verhalen van lijden bij Blaman en Dorrestein* (Kampen: Kok Agora, 1993). Paula Cooey, *Religious Imagination & the Body: A Feminist Analysis* (New York and Oxford: Oxford University Press, 1994).

23 Although references to debates about the meaning of the body and embodiment, as well as related debates about sexuality and desire, frequently occur in my study, the inevitable urge to restrict oneself prevents me from addressing myself more in depth to this important matter. I hope to do this more explicitly in the future within the context of the Dutch research programme *Corporeality, religion and gender*.

24 Van Heijst, n. 22 above, p. 36.

25 Cooey, n. 22 above, p. 9.

26 *Ibid.*, p. 122.

27 *Ibid.*, p. 9.

28 *Ibid.*, p. 76.

29 *Ibid.*, p. 78.

30 Other books of pertinence from this viewpoint I would recommend are Katherine M. Sands, *Escape from Paradise: Evil and Tragedy in Feminist Theology* (Minneapolis: Fortress, 1994), chapter 7; Mark Ledbetter, *Victims and the Postmodern Narrative or Doing Violence to the Body: An Ethic of Reading and Writing* (London/New York: Macmillan/St. Martin's, 1996).

31 Tom Woodman, 'Science Fiction, Religion and Transcendence', in *Science Fiction: A Critical Guide*, ed. P. Parrinder (London & New York: Longman, 1979), pp. 110–30. Robert Reilly, ed., *The Transcendent Adventure: Studies of Religion in Science Fiction/Fantasy* (Westport, Conn.: Greenwood Press, 1985).

32 Woodman, above, p. 128.

33 *Ibid.*

34 Sarah Lefanu, Introduction, n. 11, *In the Chinks*, p. 7.

35 Lefanu, p. 21. Compare this view to the much-quoted study of Darko Suvin, *Metamorphosis of Science Fiction: On the Poetics and History of a Literary Genre* (New Haven: Yale University Press, 1979). Suvin's definition of science fiction as 'cognitive estrangement' met with broad consent. This definition, however, implies that science fiction has to be rigorously set apart from all kinds of 'irrational' genres. That is, science fiction has to be safeguarded against all elements of myth, fairy tale and fantastic tale (ghost, horror, Gothic), genres which display what Suvin dismissively calls 'metaphysical estrangement'.

36 See for instance Carter Heyward, 'Crossings', in *Our Passion for Justice* (New York: The Pilgrim Press, 1984), pp. 243–7.

37 Robert Pielke, 'The Rejection of Traditional Theism in Feminist Theology and Science Fiction', in *The Intersection of Science and Philosophy*, ed. R.E. Myers (Westport, Conn.: Greenwood Press, 1983), pp. 225–35.

38 Sallie McFague, *Metaphorical Theology: Models of God in Religious Language* (London: SCM Press, 1983), p. 161. The notion of speculative fiction is derived from Robert Scholes' approach of science fiction as 'structural fabulation'.

39 McFague, p. 169.

40 *Ibid.*, p. 164.

41 Grietje Dresen, Unpublished paper for symposium 'Over grenzen gesproken', Introduction, n. 4 above, p. 3.

42 Teresa de Lauretis, 'Signs of Wa/onder', in *The Technological Imagination*, ed.T. de Lauretis, A. Huyssen, K. Woodwards (Madison: Coda Press, 1980), pp. 159–74.

43 Influential in propagating this view has been Brian Aldiss (with David Wingrove), *Trillion Year Spree: The History of Science Fiction* (London: Paladin Grafton Book, 1988).

44 See for instance David Seed, ed., *Anticipations: Essays on Early Science Fiction and its Precursors* (Liverpool: Liverpool University Press, 1995), in which such founder stories are balanced by theories of a gradual convergence of different genres and processes of influence between writers.

45 Ellen Moers, *Literary Women* (London: The Women's Press, 1978). See also Juliann Fleenor, ed., *The Female Gothic* (Montreal/London: Eden Press, 1983) for a variety of illuminating essays on the female Gothic in both the Romantic age and the twentieth century.

46 Anne Cranny-Francis, *Feminist Fiction; Feminist Uses of Generic Fiction* (Cambridge: Polity Press, 1990), p. 41.

47 Robin Roberts, *A New Species: Gender and Science in Science Fiction* (Urbana and Chicago: University of Illinois Press, 1990).

48 Roberts, above, pp. 36–7.

49 *Ibid.*, p. 45.

50 Aldiss (with Wingrove), n. 43 above, *Trillion Year Spree*, chapter 12.

51 Cranny-Francis, n. 46 above, p. 41.

52 *Ibid.*, p. 42.

53 The history of 'hidden' female authors, e.g. C.L. Moore, Leigh Brackett, Judith Merril, Andre Norton and Naomi Mitchinson, in the male-dominated science fiction genre *before* the explosion of explicitly feminist writers in the late 1960s and the 1970s, has been documented by Pamela Sargent in the introduction to her first anthology of science fiction stories by women, *Women of Wonder: Science Fiction Stories by Women about Women* (New York: Vintage, 1974).

54 For an overview of female and/or feminist science fiction writers cf. Sharon Yntema's annotated bibliography *More than 100 Woman Science Fiction Writers* (Freedom, Calif.: The Crossing Press, 1988), in which, besides North-American and British writers, writers from as many as possible other countries are included, and Roger Schlobin's *Urania's Daughters: A Checklist of Women Science Fiction Writers, 1692–1982* (Mercer Island: Starmont House, 1983).

55 Lefanu, Introduction, n. 11 above, p. 7.

56 An example of a long and extensive, non-American SF tradition is found in the Czech and the Slovak Republics (the fandom has not divided until now and meet in annual *Parcons*, binational conferences). Many people were able to earn their living by writing SF in the time before the 'velvet revolution'. Afterwards, it became much harder, partly due to the American SF with which the market is flooded, partly because SF ceased to function as dystopian or codedly critical comment on the communist society. It is interesting, however, that recently several writers of feminist science fiction have emerged, like Carla Biedermannóva and Eva Hauser. See Josef Nesvadba, 'The Future That Just Ended: What happened to Central Europe and SF there', *Makropulos speciál*, Parcon 93, 33–44 and Eva Hauser, 'Science Fiction in the Czech Republic and the Former Czechoslovakia: The Pleasures and the Disappointments of the New Cosmopolitanism', *Science Fiction Studies* 21 (1994) 1, 133–40. I want to express my gratitude to Ludmila Freiová for introducing me to this community.

57 Lefanu, p. 4.

58 Aldiss (with Wingrove), n. 43 above, p. 465.

59 Marleen Barr *Feminist Fabulation: Space/Postmodern Fiction* (Iowa City: University of Iowa Press, 1992). Like McFague's speculative fabulation, feminist fabulation was derived from Robert Scholes' concept of structural fabulation.

60 I have employed Barr's feminist fabulation to connect novels as divergent as Marlen Haushofer's *Der Wand (The Wall*, 1983), Ingeborg Bachmann's *Malina* (1971) and *The Wall Around Eden* (1989) by Joan Slonczewski. Inez van der Spek, 'Voorbij de muur. Feminisme, apocalyptiek en science fiction', in R. Braidotti, *Poste Restante: Feministische berichten aan het postmoderne* (Kampen: Kok Agora, 1994), pp. 127–47.

61 Jenny Wolmark, *Alien and Others: Science Fiction, Feminism and Postmodernism* (Hemel Hempstead: Harvester Wheatsheaf, 1994), p. 25.

62 About male-authored SF Lefanu has remarked: 'While the cannier

writers of the late 1970s and early 1980s were hastily inventing some more active role for their female characters than simply a sexual one, that tokenism has been superseded by a serious attempt, amongst some writers, such as Robert Holdstock and Colin Greenland, to deal with issues of sexuality and sexual politics'. Sarah Lefanu, 'Sex, Sub-atomic Particles, and Sociology', in Lucy Armitt, *Where No Man Has Gone Before: Women and Science Fiction* (London/New York: Routledge, 1991), p. 178.

63 Lefanu, Introduction, n. 11 above, *In the Chinks*, p. 87.

64 Wolmark, n. 61 above, p. 21.

65 In Harold Bloom's *The Anxiety of Influence*, this scenario appears as a description of the struggle younger writers are involved in with their literary 'fathers'. Freud, Roland Barthes and Peter Brooks displace the Oedipal scenario in the first place onto the structure of narrative and tend, as Marianne Hirsch notes, to 'universalize an Oedipal textuality modeled on male sexuality and psychology' (see next note).

66 Teresa de Lauretis, *Alice Doesn't: Feminism, Semiotics, Cinema* (Bloomington: Indiana University Press, 1984); Marianne Hirsch, *The Mother/Daughter Plot: Narrative, Psychoanalysis, Feminism* (Bloomington: Indiana University Press, 1989), Cranny-Francis, n. 46 above, *Feminist Fiction*.

67 Cranny-Francis, p. 15.

68 Peter Brooks, *Reading for the Plot: Design and Intention in Narrative* (New York: Alfred A. Knopf, 1994).

69 Cranny-Francis, p. 15. Think also of the utopian project of the *écriture féminine* of French writers/theorists like Luce Irigaray and Hélène Cixous, who seek to explore a different, feminine libidinal economy by means of radical writing practices.

70 Lucy Armitt, 'Your Word is My Command: The Structures of Language and Power in Women's Science Fiction', in Armitt, *Where No Man has Gone Before. Women and Science Fiction* (London/New York: Routledge, 1991), p. 136.

71 Lies Wesseling, 'De genetisch bepaalde hartstocht van een zeeanemoon: feministische science fiction als damesroman', *Lover* 18 (1991) 4, 229–34.

72 Roberts, n. 47 above, *A New Species*, p. 7.

73 Nell Tenhaaf, Paper in the section 'Perfect Bodies', in *Virtual Seminar on the Bioapparatus*, ed. M. Moser (Banff, Alb.: The Banff Centre for the Arts, 1991), p. 47.

74 Compare e.g. the simplistic interpretation by Roberts of Vonda McIntyre's novel *Dreamsnake* about a female healer in a post-holocaust world with the fairly more sophisticated interpretation by Wolmark, *Alien and Others*, n. 61 above, pp. 56–72.

75 Nathalie M. Rosinsky, *Feminist Futures: Contemporary Women's Speculative Fiction* (Ann Arbor: UMI Research Press, 1984), p. 105.

76 *Ibid.*, p. 106.

77 Haraway, Donna, 'Cyborg Manifesto', n. 18 above, p. 173.

78 Ursula Le Guin, *The Language of the Night: Essays on Fantasy and Science Fiction*, ed. and with intr. by S. Wood. (rpt. New York: Berkley, 1985), p. 97.

79 The Canadian writer Candas Jane Dorsey, on the other hand, has provided a fine parody of cyberpunk in her story '(Learning About) Machine Sex', in *Machine Sex and Other Stories* (London: The Women's Press, 1990).

80 Scott Bukatman, *Terminal Identity: The Virtual Subject in Postmodern Science Fiction* (Durham and London: Duke University Press, 1993), p. 308. See also

Anne Balsamo, *Technologies of the Gendered Body: Reading Cyborg Women* (Durham and London: Duke University Press, 1996), pp. 116–132: 'The Virtual Body in Cyberspace'.

81 Wolmark, n. 61 above, p. 110.

82 Samuel Delany in an interview with Takayuki Tatsumi in *Science Fiction Eye* 1 (1988). Quoted in Wolmark, p. 110.

83 Bukatman, n. 80 above, p. 21.

84 James Tiptree, Jr, 'The Girl Who Was Plugged In', rpt. in *Warm Worlds and Otherwise* (New York: Ballantine, 1975).

85 Lies Wesseling, *Writing History as a Prophet: Postmodernist Innovations of the Historical Novel* (Amsterdam: Benjamins, 1991), pp. 95–6.

86 Tom Moylan, *Demand the Impossible: Science Fiction and the Utopian Imagination* (New York and London: Methuen, 1986).

87 Ruby Rohrlich and Elaine Hoffman Baruch, *Women in Search of Utopias: Mavericks and Mythmakers* (New York: Schocken, 1984). Nan Albinski, *Women's Utopias in British and American Fiction* (London/New York: Routledge, 1988). Frances Bartkowski, *Feminist Utopias* (Lincoln and London: University of Nebraska Press, 1989).

88 Wolmark, n. 61 above, *Aliens and Others*, p. 91.

89 De Lauretis, n. 42 above, 'Signs of Wa/onder', p. 162. Michel Foucault, *The Order of Things: An Archeology of the Human Sciences* (New York: Pantheon, 1970).

90 De Lauretis, n. 42 above, pp. 165–6.

II: Sexual Universes

1 Michael Ondaatje, *In the Skin of a Lion* (Toronto: McClelland and Stewart, 1987).

2 In the second part of the text two more dreams of Aaron are described. Because they do not occur at the beginning of each part of the text and are of a somewhat different character, I do not deal with them here but in Chapter III.

3 Wolfgang Kayser, *The Grotesque in Art and Literature* (Bloomington: Indiana University Press, 1963). Mikhail Bakhtin, *Rabelais and His World*, trans. Helene Iswolsky (Cambridge: The MIT Press, 1968).

4 Anton Simons, *Het groteske van de taal: Over het werk van Michail Bachtin* (Amsterdam: SUA, 1990), p. 135.

5 Is the nose always a substitute for the penis? Although Bakhtin would think so, one may dispute this. In any case, I enjoyed very much the grotesque re-phallization of Gogol's nose in 'A sausage in a warm roll' by the Croatian writer Dubravka Ugresic (*Zivot je babajka:(métaterxies)*).

6 Hans W. Bakx, ed., *Raster* 30: 'Het groteske' (Amsterdam: De Bezige Bij, 1984), p. 9.

7 Margaret Miles, *Carnal Knowing: Female Nakedness and Religious Meaning in the Christian West* (New York: Vintage Books, 1991). For another early feminist critique directed especially at Bakhtin's view of the grotesque see Mary Russo, 'Female Grotesques: Carnival and Theory', in *Feminist Studies/Critical Studies*, ed. T. de Lauretis (Bloomington: Indiana University Press, 1986), pp. 213–27. Russo notes that, for instance, Bakhtin's description of ancient figurines of senile, pregnant hags as model for carnival language, is,

notwithstanding its exuberance, very ambivalent for the feminist reader. 'It is loaded with all of the connotations of fear and loathing associated with the biological processes of reproduction and of aging' (p. 219).

8 Miles, p. 151.

9 Miles, p. 152.

10 Throughout this book I use fantasy in the Freudian sense of a representation of a subject's desire. Fantasies—like daydreams, fiction and other stagings—have both manifest contents and concealed, unconscious scenes, fears and desires, which get expressed indirectly in the fantasy.

11 Miles, n. 7 above, p. 153. Bakhtin, n. 3 above, p. 329. See also the astute analysis of Bakhtin's use of maternal metaphor by Ruth Ginsburg, 'The Pregnant Text. Bakhtin's Ur-Chronotope: The Womb', in *Critical Studies* Vol.3 No.2–Vol.4 No.1/2, ed. David Shepherd (Amsterdam & Atlanta: Rodopi, 1993), pp. 165–76.

12 Miles, n. 7 above, p. 151.

13 *Ibid.*, p. 155.

14 In this study, I use 'penis' and 'phallus' interchangeably, as also in Aaron's dream phallus denotes in the first place the (erect) penis. This comes close to the Freudian account, in which the penis is also the sign of sexual difference, of what men have and fear to lose, and of what women are supposed to be lacking and desire to have. In Lacan's linguistic elaboration of Freudian psychoanalysis, the concept of the phallus is severed from its biological basis, and turned into the prime signifier in the social-symbolic order, which is rule by the paternal law. It is a metaphor of existential loss, and hence desire, which come into existence when the child enters the order of language, which coincides with its separation from the mother. Feminists, however, have questioned the suggested neutrality of the phallus and arbitrary relation between penis and phallus. Can metaphors be really separated from their roots? As it turns out, in fact the phallus is a privileged metaphor because the female subject lacks the penis. This would make both Freudian penis and Lacanian phallus metaphors of masculine power, while the fear of castration is understood to signify the denial of sexual difference as positivity.

15 See on this Mary Russo, *The Female Grotesque: Risk, Excess, and Modernity* (New York and London: Routledge, 1995).

16 Cooey, *Religious Imagination & the Body*, p. 98. For the notion of the *carcajada* Cooey refers to Hayden Herrera, *Frida: A Biography of Frida Kahlo* (New York: Harper & Row, 1983).

17 James Tiptree, Jr, 'With Delicate Mad Hands', in *Out of the Everywhere, and Other Extraordinary Visions* (New York: Ballantine Books, 1981).

18 Lefanu, *In the Chinks*, Introduction, n. 11 above, p. 109.

19 James Tiptree, Jr, 'The Earth Doth Like a Snake Renew', rpt. in *Crown of Stars* (London: Sphere Books, 1990), p. 272.

20 Mark Siegel, 'Double-Souled Man: Immortality and Transcendence in the Fiction of James Tiptree, Jr.', in *Death and the Serpent: Immortality in Science Fiction and Fantasy*, ed. C.B. Yoke and D.M. Hassler (Westport, Conn.: Greenwood Press, 1985), p. 164.

21 It is a view which merits to be levelled as a criticism at contemporary strivings in astrophysics to rehabilitate man as the centre of the universe. See e.g. John D. Barrow and Frank J. Tipler, *The Anthropic Cosmological Principle* (Oxford: Clarendon Press, 1986) and Frank Tipler, *The Physics of Immortality:*

Modern Cosmology, God and the Resurrection of the Dead (New York: Doubleday, 1994).

22 See on this Teresa de Lauretis, 'Desire in Narrative', in *Alice Doesn't: Feminism, Semiotics, Cinema* (Bloomington: Indiana University Press, 1984), pp. 123–4.

23 N. Katherine Hayles, *Chaos Bound: Orderly Disorder in Contemporary Literature and Science* (Ithaca: Cornell University Press, 1990).

24 Hayles, p. 39.

25 Hayles also presents the counter-position of Claude Shannon, an engineer at Bell Laboratories, who in a 1948 paper claimed that information and entropy are not opposites but even identical things. Although Shannon was rebuked for this appropriation of thermodynamic entropy for information theory, Hayles thinks that one cannot but admit that he anticipated contemporary insights on the entropic tendency of information. Nowadays people do not fear most immediately 'that the universe will run down, but that the information will pile up until it overwhelms our ability to understand it'. Hayles, p. 49.

26 Siegel, *James Tiptree, Jr*, Introduction, n. 20 above, p. 14.

27 Charles Platt, 'Profile: James Tiptree, Jr', Introduction, n. 20 above, pp. 46–7. In a story written just before her death, 'Our Resident Djinn' (in *Crown of Stars*), Tiptree has given an explicit shape to this idea in an allegorical black comedy on Lucifer after the death of God, visited by Physis (Mother Nature) and her mother Tyche (Chance). It says, in the depths of Hell's pit some 'immanent incarnation' of Entropy is stirring. The image of the devil in the pit must have been taken from the Book of Revelation 9:1 and 20:1–3, which refers back to Isaiah 14:12.

28 Siegel, *James Tiptree, Jr*, p. 14.

29 While in the 1970s the Maoist Third Way (besides Western capitalism and Russian communism) was still a popular option for revolutionary movements in Third World countries, just as for certain Western intellectuals (see for instance the French journal *Tel Quel* of, among others, Philippe Sollers and Julia Kristeva), the outcome of 'A Momentary Taste of Being' does not exactly promote Chinese socialism as the new paradise.

30 Klaus Theweleit, *Male Fantasies*. trans. S. Conway, E. Carter, C. Turner. 2 vols (Minneapolis: University of Minnesota Press, 1977–8).

31 Interesting discussions of the underpinnings of the cinematic cyborg (such as *Terminator* and *Robocop*) in terms of Theweleit's theory of the mental armour are offered in, e.g., Bukatman, *Terminal Identity*, pp. 303ff.

32 For the record, *blastomeres* are the first cells in which the impregnated ovum is cleft; a *zygote* is the result of the fusion of two *gametes* (the reproductive cells).

33 Ilya Prigogine and Isabelle Stengers, *Order out of Chaos: Man's New Dialogue with Nature* (London: William Heinemann, 1984). Prigogine was Nobel Prize winner for chemistry in 1977.

34 *Order out of Chaos* is the translation of *La nouvelle alliance* (1979), updated with new scientific information. The large exposition of Prigogine's model of dissipative structures, *From Being to Becoming: Time and Complexity in the Physical Sciences* (1980), and some earlier articles in English were specialized literature. David Porush, 'Prigogine, Chaos, and Contemporary Science Fiction', *Science Fiction Studies* 18 (1991), 367–86, discusses various North American science

fiction works written after 1984 in which Prigogine's model is explicitly used for the narrative: A.A. Attanasio's *Radix* (1985), Lewis Shiner's *Deserted Cities of the Heart* (1988), Bruce Sterling's *Schismatrix* (1986), William Gibson and Bruce Sterling's *The Difference Engine* (1991). Unfortunately he forgets to pay attention to Rhoda Lerman's beautiful novel *The Book of the Night* (1984).

35 Prigogine and Stengers, p. 19.

36 Hayles, *Chaos Bound*, n. 23 above, p. 113.

37 Prigogine and Stengers, p. 7. Italics in text.

38 Prigogine and Stengers, p. 12.

39 Siegel, *James Tiptree Jr*, Introduction, no. 20 above, p. 38.

40 Marleen Barr, *Alien to Feminity: Speculative Fiction and Feminist Theory* (Westport, Conn.: Greenwood Press, 1987), p. 23.

41 Bukatman, *Terminal Identity*, Chapter I, no. 80 above, p. 283.

42 See e.g. the statement of pro-life attorney Thomas Ford: 'The fetus might well be described as an astronaut in a uterine spaceship'. Cited in Mary Daly, *Gyn/ecology: the Metaethics of Radical Feminism* (Boston: Beacon Press, 1978), p. 58.

43 To mention only a few analyses of the representation of the free-floating foetus, in connection to new reproductive technologies, medical scopophilia, popular (SF-)cinema, and Christian pro-life discourses. Zoë Sofia, 'Exterminating Fetuses: Abortion, Disarmement, And the Sexo-Semiotics of Extraterrestrialism', in *diacritics* 14 (1984), 47–59; Rosalind Pollack Petchesky, 'Fetal Images: The Power of Visual Culture in the Politics of Reproduction', *Feminist Studies* 13 (1987) 2, 263–92; Rosi Braidotti, 'On Contemporary Medical Pornography', *Tijdschrift voor Vrouwenstudies* 12 (1991) 3, 356–71; Barbara Duden, *Disembodying Women: Perspectives of Pregnancy and the Unborn* (Cambridge, Mass.: Harvard University Press, 1993).

44 Sofia, p. 52.

45 Estella Lauter, *Women as Mythmakers: Poetry and Visual Art by Twentieth-Century Women* (Bloomington: Indiana University Press, 1984), p. 17.

46 Lauter, p. 219.

47 Alfred Tennyson, *In Memoriam, Maud and other Poems* edited, with an introduction and notes by John D. Jump (London: J.M. Dent & Sons, 1974). The initials A.H.H. refer to Arthur Henry Hallam, the husband of Tennyson's sister and his best friend, who died suddenly in 1833. The poem pertains to the ninth and last group of lyrics composing *In Memoriam*, in which Tennyson seems to have regained his lost faith in divine love. He rejects materialism as reductive, but does affirm evolution. 'Moreover, the evolutionary process moves towards the fulfilment of a providential plan; it is bringing into being "a higher race" ...,' as Jump explains in the introduction, p. xii.

48 'Put simply, the quintessential aim of Modernists has been to reconnect all that the Victorian moral dichotomy tore asunder—to integrate once more the human and the animal, the civilized and savage, and to heal the sharp divisions that the nineteenth century had established in areas such as class, race, and gender.' Daniel J. Singal, 'Towards a Definition of American Modernism', *American Quarterly* 39 (1987) 1, 7–26, p. 12.

49 In astronomy Centaur is a planetary constellation; and in NASA terms it is a special rocket, used for the launching of, among others, the Voyager 1 and 2 to Jupiter, Saturn, Uranus and Neptune.

50 Sigmund Freud, 'The "Uncanny"' (1919), *Standard Edition of the Complete*

Psychological Works of Sigmund Freud (London: The Hogarth Press), Vol. 17, pp. 217–56. Hélène Cixous, 'Fiction and its Phantoms: A Reading of Freud's *Das Unheimliche* (The "uncanny")', *New Literary History* 7 (1976) 3, 525–48.

51 Cixous, p. 543.

52 *Anna, Soror* ... (London: Harville, 1992), pp. 227–42. I am thankful to Nell Tenhaaf for informing me about this postscript. In her small essay Yourcenar aspires to list some literary works on brother–sister incest of at least the Western world. Oddly enough she does not mention some famous books of fellow-French authors, like *Les enfants terribles* by Jean Cocteau, or *Agatha* by Marguerite Duras.

53 To mention only one contemporary example, both themes are represented in a lucid way in the film *March Comes in Like a Lion* (1991) by the young Japanese director Hitoshi Yazaki. I was particularly affected by its play with literal and metaphorical meanings of blood.

54 Siegel, *James Tiptree, Jr*, Introduction, n. 20 above, p. 38.

55 Siegel, 'Double-Souled Man', Introduction, n. 41 above, p. 164.

56 No matter how delirious, this passage is full of allusions to the central issues of the story. They will return in other chapters.

57 Lilian Heldreth, 'Love is the Plan, the Plan is Death: The Feminism and Fatalism of James Tiptree, Jr.', *Extrapolation* 23 (1989) 1, 22–30.

58 Heldreth, p. 29. She quotes from George Bataille, *Death and Sensuality* [*L'érotisme*] (1962; rpt. New York; Ballantine Books, 1969), p. 55.

59 Bukatman, *Terminal Identity*, p. 280.

60 Bukatman, p. 281.

61 Elizabeth Grosz, 'Animal Sex: Libido as Desire and Death', in *Space, Time, and Perversion* (London/New York: Routledge, 1994), p. 204.

62 See Sigmund Freud, *Beyond the Pleasure Principle* (1920), *SE* Vol. 18, pp. 7–64.

63 Grosz, pp. 201–2. Let me, in addition, recall the discussion in the first chapter about desire in *narrative*, or narrative dynamics, in for instance Brooks' *Reading for the Plot* as likewise modelled on the masculine orgasm.

III: Father in Crisis, Mother Rises? (1)

1 Marianne Hirsch, *The Mother/Daughter Plot: Narrative, Psychoanalysis, Feminism* (Bloomington and Indianapolis: Indiana University Press, 1989), p. 3.

2 *Ibid.*, p. 9.

3 *Ibid.*, p. 11.

4 An interesting contribution to maternal discourse is Rosemarie Buikema's study *De loden venus* (Kampen: Kok Agora, 1995), in which she analyses five biographies of famous women (Milena Jesenská, Anzia Yezierska, Vanessa Bell, Margaret Mead, Alva Myrdal) written by their daughters, in order to explore the possibilities of unconventional representations of the story of mother and daughter.

5 Roberts, *A New Species*, p. 10.

6 Nancy Steffen-Fluhr, 'The Case of the Haploid Heart: Psychological Patterns in the Science Fiction of Alice Sheldon (James Tiptree, Jr)', *Science Fiction Studies* 17 (1990), 188–220.

7 Steffen-Fluhr, p. 216.

8 James Tiptree, Jr., 'Houston, Houston, Do You Read?', rpt. in *Star Songs of an Old Primate* (New York: Ballantine, 1978).

9 Steffen-Fluhr, n. 6 above, p. 206.

10 *Ibid.*, p. 207.

11 *Ibid.*

12 I realize that some contradiction may be involved as to the significance of the death drive, considering my criticism at the end of Chapter II. On the one hand, I do think the problem of the automatic linkage of the death drive to sexual desire needs further critical examination. On the other hand, however, as yet I know not of a better model to reflect upon the constitution of the subject than Kristeva's Freudian model of the ambiguity of the drives.

13 Let me recall that by fantasy is meant the representation of the subject's desire, i.e. both of its manifest contents and concealed, unconscious scenes, fears and desires, which get expressed indirectly in the fantasy.

14 Kaja Silverman, *The Acoustic Mirror: The Female Voice in Psychoanalysis and Cinema* (Bloomington: Indiana University Press, 1988), p. 101.

15 Tiptree, in *Khatru*, Introduction, n. 12 above, p. 18.

16 *Ibid.*, p. 19.

17 Julia Kristeva, *Au commencement était l'amour: Psychanalyse et foi* (Paris: Hachette, 1985), p. 14.

18 Julia Kristeva, in *The Kristeva Reader*, ed. Toril Moi (Oxford: Basil Blackwell, 1986), p. 93.

19 *Ibid.*, in Moi, p. 94.

20 *Ibid.*, in Moi, p. 95.

21 Marilyn Edelstein, 'Metaphor, Meta-Narrative, & Mater-Narrative in Kristeva's "Stabat Mater"', in *Body/Text in Julia Kristeva: Religion, Women, and Psychonanalysis*, ed. David Crownfield (Albany: State University of New York, 1992), p. 37.

22 Respectively, Jacqueline Rose, 'Julia Kristeva: Take Two', in *Sexuality in the Field of Vision* (London, NLB/Verso, 1986); Edelstein, 'Metaphor'; Elizabeth Grosz, *Sexual Subversions: Three French Feminists* (Sydney: Allen and Unwin, 1989), p. 49.

23 Kelly Oliver, 'Kristeva's Imaginary Father and the Crisis in the Paternal Function', *diacritics* 21 (1991) 3, 43–63.

24 A.O. Hirsch, *The Mother/Daughter Plot*; Domna C. Stanton, 'Difference on Trial: A Critique of the Maternal Metaphor in Cixous, Irigaray, and Kristeva', in *The Poetics of Gender*, ed. Nancy K. Miller (New York: Columbia University Press, 1986), pp. 157–82.

25 Kristeva, quoted in Hirsch, p. 172.

26 Silverman, n. 14 above, p. 102.

27 *Ibid.*, p. 107.

28 *Ibid.*, p. 123.

29 Judith Butler, *Gender Trouble: Feminism and the Subversion of Identity* (New York and London: Routledge, 1990), p. 87.

30 Kristeva, in Moi, n. 18 above, p. 205.

31 Silverman, p. 124. Italics added.

32 Sigmund Freud, *Totem and Taboo*, 1912–13. *SE*, Vol. 13.

33 The suggestion that this so-called murder of the archaic father, according to Kristeva, in fact veils the primary murder of the mother will return, in different terms, in Chapter IV.

34 As to the absence of the category of race in Freud and a great deal of psychoanalysis, see Mary Childers and bell hooks, 'A Conversation about Race and Class', in *Conflicts in Feminism*, ed. M. Hirsch and E. Fox Keller (New York and London: Routledge, 1990).

35 Nonetheless Foreman lost his world title to Mohammed Ali in the legendary fight between the two heavyweights on 30 October 1974 in Kinshasa. Ali called the fight 'Rumble in the jungle'. In 1994 Foreman, 45 years of age now, once more conquered—and lost again—the world title.

36 Roz Kavaney, 'The Science Fictiveness of Women's Science Fiction', in *From My Guy to Sci-fi*, ed. Helen Carr. See Chapter I n. 4 above, pp. 78–97, p. 81.

37 bell hooks, *Yearning: Race, Gender, and Cultural Politics* (Boston: Mass: South End Press, 1990), p. 58.

38 *Ibid.*, p. 60.

39 Oliver, 'Kristeva's Imaginary Father', n. 23 above, p. 51.

40 Rosi Braidotti, *Patterns of Dissonance* (Cambridge: Polity Press, 1991), p. 238.

41 Butler, *Gender Trouble*, n. 29 above, p. 86.

42 Steffen-Fluhr, 'The Case of the Haploid Heart', n. 6 above, p. 213.

43 One could recall Kristeva's idea of the 'father of the personal pre-history', introduced in *Tales of Love*, trans. Leon S. Roudiez (New York: Columbia University Press, 1987), which refers to a kind of conglomerate of the two parents, of the two sexes, which nevertheless should be conceived as a father, though not as a rigid Oedipal father but as a loving father. This idea has been found both approval and harsh criticism for its inclination to subsume just about everything under the sign of the father. It would lead too far astray from my argument, however, to further discuss this contentious notion.

44 The only interpretation I know of from the viewpoint of the sirens themselves, instead of their effect on the men, is Margaret Atwood's witty poem 'Siren Song', in which the siren reveals the secret of the song in exchange for being liberated out of the bird suit: 'Come closer. This song / is a cry for help: Help me! / Only you, only you can, / you are unique / at last. Alas / it is a boring song / but it works every time'. With thanks to Christien Franken.

45 Max Horkheimer and Theodor Adorno, *Dialectic of Enlightenment*, trans. John Cumming (New York: Continuum, 1972).

46 Maurice Blanchot, 'La rencontre de l'imaginaire', in *Le livre á venir* (Paris: Gallimard, 1959).

47 In his story 'The Silence of the Sirens' (1917), Franz Kafka thinks that the sirens might have had an even more terrible weapon than their singing— their silence—and he suggests that Odysseus made himself deaf to both of them.

48 Kristeva, in Moi, n. 18 above, p. 95.

49 Catherine Keller, *From a Broken Web: Separation, Sexism, and Self* (Boston: Beacon Press, 1986), pp. 10–11.

IV: Father in Crisis, Mother Rises? (2)

1 Luscious Jackson, 'Energy Sucker', from *Natural Ingredients*, Capitol Records, Inc., 1994.

2 Julia Kristeva, 'Lire la Bible', in *Les nouvelles maladies de l'âme* (Paris:

Fayard, 1993), p. 189.

3 For discussions of interesting examples see Thelma Shinn, *Worlds Within Women: Myth and Mythmaking in Fantastic Literature by Women* (New York: Greenwood Press, 1988); Roberts, *A New Species*, see Chapter I n. 47 above, pp. 90–116, in particular on Suzette Elgin's *Star Anchored, Star Angered*; and Lefanu, *In the Chinks*, See Introduction n. 11 above, pp. 50–2, on the novels of Gwyneth Jones.

4 In Chapter VI I will return to the actual 'theological' strategy offered in the narrative, which allows the reader to move beyond conventional meanings of the divine by employing the power of disruptive transformation with respect to the alien–human encounter.

5 Steffen-Fluhr, 'The Case of the Haploid Heart', See Chapter III n. 6 above, p. 206.

6 Julia Kristeva, *Powers of Horror: An Essay on Abjection*, trans. Leon Rudiez (New York: Columbia University Press, 1982), p. 62.

7 Rosi Braidotti, *Nomadic Subjects*, see Chapter I n. 20 above, p. 81.

8 Significantly, however, neither Kristeva nor Mary Douglas, on whose innovative study *Purity and Danger* she heavily relies, considers sperm to be dirty and abject. For a critical feminist analysis of the division between 'clean' male bodily flows (semen) and 'polluting' female bodily flows (menstrual blood, vaginal mucus) see Elisabeth Grosz, *Volatile Bodies: Toward a Corporeal Feminism* (Minneapolis: Indiana University Press, 1994), pp. 192 ff.

9 Kristeva, n. 6 above, p. 3.

10 *Ibid.*, p. 4.

11 *Ibid.*, p. 91.

12 Kristeva, 'Lire la Bible', n. 2 above, p. 179, p. 177.

13 Kristeva, *Powers of Horror*, n. 6 above, p. 107.

14 Barbara Creed, *The Monstrous-Feminine: Film, Feminism, Psychoanalysis* (London and New York: Routledge, 1993), p. 26.

15 In the sequel of *Alien*, however, the 1986 James Cameron release *Aliens*, the archaic mother, a monstrous Mother Alien, *does* appear. See Creed, pp. 50–2.

16 *Ibid.*, p. 25.

17 *Ibid.*, p. 27. Italics in text.

18 *Ibid.*, p. 28.

19 In Chapter II, I discussed Yellaston's defence system from a somewhat different, but largely compatible theoretical framework. It would be very interesting, moreover, to relate this metaphor of the fort with Kristeva's comparison of the borderline patient with a 'fortified castle' (in *Powers of Horror*, n. 6 above, pp. 46ff), who is nevertheless an 'empty castle, haunted by unappealing ghosts—"powerless" outside, "impossible" inside' (p. 49). This, however, would lead me too far astray from my present line of interpretation.

20 Kristeva, *Powers of Horror*, p. 63.

21 *Ibid.*, p. 106.

22 *Ibid.*, p. 100.

23 In her earlier deliberations on Judaism in *Des Chinoises* (1974), Kristeva even argued that 'no other civilization seems to have made the principle of sexual difference so crystal clear' (Kristeva in Moi, *The Kristeva Reader*, see Chapter III n. 18 above, p. 141). Between the two sexes lies an abyss, due to and causing at the same time their different relationship to the law, both

religiously and politically. The law does not want to have anything to do with the female body, precisely because the unity of the Word and the preservation of the community is dependent on its procreative powers.

24 Famous though very divergent representatives of the so-called Goddess movement in the US are Starhawk, Zsuzsanna Budapest, Charlene Spretnak and, connecting it to a critical 'thealogy', Carol Christ, and to object-relations theory, Naomi Goldenberg. Foundation-stones have been works on mythology and history of the Goddess by Merlin Stone and Heide Göttner-Abendroth. See Carol Christ, 'Why Women Need the Goddess: Phenomenological, Psychological, and Political Reflections', in *Womenspirit Rising: A Feminist Reader in Religion*, ed. C. Christ & J. Plaskow (San Francisco: Harper and Row, 1979), pp. 273–87.

25 'Many of Sheldon's male figures are "Dons", perhaps because the name means "sir" or "lord" and thus stands for patriarchal maleness in general', Steffen-Fluhr, see Chapter III n. 6 above, p. 218.

26 Catherine Keller, *From a Broken Web*, see Chapter III n. 49 above, p. 83.

27 I derive this information from Susan Niditch, *Chaos to Cosmos: Studies in Biblical Patterns of Creation* (Chico: Scholars Press, 1985) and Keller, *From a Broken Web*, who refer to the comparative studies of E.A. Speiser, *Genesis*, A. Heidel, *The Babylonian Genesis*, H. and H.A. Frankfort, *Before Philosophy*. The tabulation is cited in Keller, pp. 80–1.

28 Northrop Frye, *The Great Code: the Bible and Literature* (London: Routledge & Kegan Paul, 1982), p. 146. I do not agree with Frye's model of apocalyptic, but for the topic of apocalyptics see the next chapter.

29 Hayles, *Chaos Bound*, see Chapter II n. 23 above, p. 100.

30 *Ibid.*, p. 100.

31 Keller, *From a Broken Web*, pp. 77–8.

32 J.A. Philips, *Eve: the History of an Idea*, cited by Keller, p. 83. At several other places in the Hebrew Bible the Deep/Tehom as the monster of the sea reappears explicitly: Psalms 89; Isaiah 27:1 and 51:9–10; Job 3:8 and 26:12. She also re-emerges in the Christian biblical Book of Revelation (Apocalypse), which I will discuss extensively in Chapter V.

33 Kristeva, *Powers of Horror*, n. 6 above, pp. 116–17.

34 *Ibid.*, p. 124.

35 *Ibid.*, p. 119.

36 Cleo Kearns McNelly, 'Art and Religious Discourse in Aquinas and Kristeva', in *Body/Text in Julia Kristeva*, ed. Crownfield, pp. 111–23, p. 116.

37 *Ibid.* My italics.

38 And yet, Kristeva reminds us, sin is a double-edged reality. Precisely because sin points at the repressed fusion with the maternal body, at the fluxes of the drives and overflowing desire, sin is also the requisite of beauty and *jouissance* (a doubleness which Kristeva detects also in the different modalities of the flesh in Pauline theory, see *Powers of Horror*, p. 124). Although it would be very possible to develop a view on sin and *jouissance* in relation to the Lory-figure as well, this is not the point I seek to make here.

39 For a thorough and creative reading of *Tar Baby* from this perspective see Susan Corey Everson, 'Toni Morrison's *Tar Baby*: A Resource for Feminist Theology', *Journal for Feminist Studies in Religion* 5 (1989) 2, 65–78.

40 Marina Warner, *Joan of Arc: The Image of Female Heroism* (London: Weidenfeld and Nicolson, 1981), p. 157.

41 *Ibid.*

42 *Ibid.*, p. 158.

43 Kristeva, *Powers of Horror*, n. 6 above, p. 122.

44 Remember the discussion of both the spaceship *Centaur* and Captain Yellaston in relation to Theweleit's theory of the mental armour, the defence machine against the female body in Chapter II.

45 Grietje Dresen, *Onschuldfantasieën: Offerzin en heilsverlangen in feminisme en mystiek* (Nijmegen: SUN, 1990), p. 32/English summary. In her study, Dresen assesses a 'psychohermeneutic' reading of the writings of two exemplary women, Alijt Bake, a Dutch mystic from the reform movement of the Modern Devotion, and Gertrud Bäumer, leading woman in the right-wing women's movement in Germany in the first half of the twentieth century.

46 *Ibid.*, p. 41.

47 *Ibid.*, p. 40.

48 See Warner, n. 40 above, chapter 13, 'Saint or Patriot?', p. 268: 'It is astonishing how many of Joan's apologists like her dead. Without this badge of blood, this self-obliteration in the ideal, her glory would be the less.'

49 Dresen, p. 256.

50 Kristeva, 'Women's Time', in Moi, see Chapter III n. 18 above, p. 209.

51 Toni Morrison, *Tar Baby* (New York, Alfred Knopf, 1981), p. 245.

V: (Counter) Apocalypses

1 Nelle Morton, *The Journey is Home* (Boston: Beacon Press, 1985), pp. 202–9.

2 Catherine Keller, 'Why Apocalypse, Now?', *Theology Today* 49 (1992), p. 184.

3 Catherine Keller, *Apocalypse Now and Then: A Feminist Guide to the End of the World* (Boston: Beacon Press, 1996), p. 11.

4 Keller, ''Why Apocalypse, Now?', see n. 3 above, p. 189.

5 The last section (22:6–21) is a confirmation by John of the authenticity of his vision and the power of God's words. This is in accordance with the concentric pattern of the book ABCDC'B'A', derived from Elisabeth Schüssler Fiorenza, *The Book of Revelation: Justice and Judgement* (Philadelphia: Fortress Press, 1985), p.175:

A 1:1–8/ B 1:9–3:22/ C 4:1–9:21; 11:15–19/

D 10:1–15:4/

C' 22:10–22:21/ B' 19:11–22:9/ A' 22:10–22:21.

6 Louis-Vincent Thomas, *Civilisation et divagations: Mort, fantasmes, science-fiction* (Paris: Payot, 1979), p. 8.

7 Thomas, p. 65.

8 Stanislaw Lem, *Phantastik und Futurologie*, 2 vols, trans. Edda Werfel (Frankfurt a/M: Suhrkamp, 1984), II, p. 9.

9 Lem, II, p. 48.

10 Lem, II, p. 39.

11 Without problematizing the relation between literature and reality, however, Lem also draws a direct analogy between the fantasies of de Sade and the real atrocities of Nazism, a very complicated matter which I consider far beyond the scope of this study. See also Lem's story 'Provokation' (*Forum* June/July 1983, 55–62, & Aug/Sept 1983, 52–7), a review of the fictitious book

Horst Aspernicus: Der Völkermord in which the *Endlösung* is discussed as staging of the Last Judgement.

12 Thomas, p. 86.

13 Brewer mentions, for example, Bernard Malamud's *God's Grace*, which represents God as the author of the solitary male survivor of a nuclear holocaust who is involved in a Oedipal triangle with a female chimpanzee named Mary Madelyn and his adopted son, the monkey Buz.

14 Mária Minich Brewer, 'Surviving Fictions: Gender and Difference in Postmodern and Postnuclear Narrative', *Discourse* 9 (1987), 37–52, p.44.

15 Roberts, *A New Species*, p. 113.

16 Compare Marie-Blanche Tahon's finding that: 'The catastrophe forms a means to make a clean sweep with the relations of the past and to invent new ones. Sometimes worse, sometimes better. In both cases, one is often less far from home than it seems.' M.-B. Tahon, 'S.F. et l'après-catastrophe ou avant Adam et Ève', *Les Cahiers du grif* 40/41, 151–61; p. 151.

17 Brewer, see n. 14 above, p. 46.

18 Brewer, p. 48. Brewer refers in particular to writers such as Doris Lessing, Marge Piercy, Joanna Russ, Ursula Le Guin, Margaret Atwood and Christa Wolf. Many could be added of course, science fictional and others.

19 Frederick Kreuziger, *Apocalypse and Science Fiction: A Dialectic of Religious and Secular Soteriologies* (Chico: Scholars Press, 1982).

20 Theologically, Kreuziger's study must be situated in the so-called 'political theology' of the late 1960s and 1970s (with theologians as Dorothee Sölle, Jürgen Moltmann, Johann-Baptiz Metz, and to a certain extent also Edward Schillebeeckx), which has been inspirational to Latin-American liberation theology as well as North American and Western European feminist liberation theologies.

21 Kreuziger, p. 1.

22 Unfortunately, Kreuziger ignores other than North American origins of science fiction, like the British and Eastern European traditions of science fiction writing, which have had a different character and *Sitz im Leben*. See Chapter I.

23 Kreuziger, p. 50.

24 David Ketterer, *New Worlds for Old: The Apocalyptic Imagination, Science Fiction, and American Literature* (Garden City, NY: Anchor Press/Doubleday, 1974). Of course Ketterer has not been the only one to consider the apocalyptic tendencies in North American literature. Not many critics, however, have recognized that the apocalyptic imagination, as Ketterer puts it, found its purest outlet in the gothic tale and its 'granddaughter' science fiction.

25 Ketterer, p. 13. Italics in text

26 Ketterer, p. 91.

27 Kreuziger, *Apocalypse and Science Fiction*, see n. 19 above, p. 2.

28 *Ibid.*, p. 3.

29 *Ibid.*, p. 164.

30 *Ibid.*, p. 147.

31 *Ibid.*, pp. 86–7.

32 *Ibid.*, pp. 79–80.

33 *Ibid.*, pp. 127–8.

34 Compare to this, however, Bukatman's objection that it 'is a commonplace of critical approaches to the [SF] cinema that special effects

constitute an unfortunate sideshow … I would join those critics who hold that special effects in fact constitute a privileged locus of meaning. The reflexive spectacularity of special effects challenge many paradigms of film theory, derived as they are from theories of narrative.' Bukatman, *Terminal Identity*, see Chapter I n. 80 above, p. 13.

35 Ketterer, *New Worlds for Old*, n. 24 above, p. 333.

36 *Ibid.*, p. 91.

37 Kreuziger, *Apocalypse and Science Fiction*, see n. 19 above, p. 89.

38 *Ibid.*, p. 181.

39 *Ibid.*, p. 5.

40 Hermann Häring, 'De redding komt alleen van God: Het laatste oordeel bezien vanuit de apocalyptiek', *Tijdschrift voor Theologie* 33 (1993) 4, 348–70, p. 354.

41 Häring derives the notion of apocalypse-blindness from the work of the Jewish German-American philosopher Günther Anders.

42 Kreuziger, see n. 19 above, p. 366.

43 Walter Benjamin, 'Theses on the Philosophy of History', in *Illuminations* (New York: Schocken Books, 1964). Quoted in Häring, p. 69.

44 This formulation clearly recalls the famous and, indeed over-commented first words of Melville's *Moby Dick*, 'Call me Ishmael'. Consequently, we might think that Aaron is as lonely in the spaceship as Jonah was in the whale's belly.

45 Elsewhere: 'She's like a play, Aaron thinks. If a brontosaurus stubbed its toe, Soli would go *Oooh* in sympathy. Probably do the same at the Crucifixion, but he doesn't hold that against her. Only so much band-with for anybody; Soli is set low' (A85).

46 Laura Mulvey, 'Visual Pleaure and Narrative Cinema', *Screen* 16 (1975) 3, 6–18; p. 14.

47 Teresa de Lauretis, 'Desire in Narrative', see Chapter II n. 22 above, p. 133.

48 *Ibid.*, p. 119.

49 *Ibid.*

50 Jann Ruyters, 'Horror-heldinnen: Een feministische interpretatie van "The Silence of the Lambs"', *Tijdschrift voor Vrouwenstudies* 13 (1992) 4, 461–76.

51 Donna Haraway, 'Situated Knowledges: The Science Question in Feminism and the Privilege of Partial Perspective', in *Simians, Cyborgs, and Women*, see Chapter I n. 18 above, p.198.

52 Mieke Bal, *Verkrachting verbeeld: Seksueel geweld in cultuur gebracht* (Utrecht: HES, 1988), pp. 26–7. My translation.

53 I am in serious doubt, however, about the extent to which certain developments of the last decade with respect to sexual abuse by relatives—the media-hyped coming-out stories in the United States and Western Europe, spectacular lawsuits in the US, sensational debates between False Memory Associations and their opponents—really help women to articulate their *own* story instead of fitting them into yet another public scenario that posits women as either powerless victim or cunning schemer.

54 Liesbeth Eugelink, 'Een engel met een tweesnijdend zwaard: Broer en zus in de Nederlandse incestroman', *Lover* 23 (1996) 4, 60–5. It refers to Nanne Tepper, *De eeuwige jachtvelden*, Renate Dorrestein, *Verborgen gebreken*, Christine Otten, *Blauw metaal.*

55 Lowry Pei, 'Poor Singletons; Definitions of Humanity in the Stories of James Tiptree, Jr', *Science Fiction Studies* 6 (1979), 271–80; p. 278.

56 *Ibid.*

57 As in so many texts of fantastic literature, science fiction and others. Only think of Mary Shelley's *Frankenstein*, Anna Kavan's *Ice*, Ursula Le Guin's *The Left-hand of Darkness*, as well as Tiptree's own story 'The Earth Doth Like a Snake Renew'.

58 Catherine Keller, 'Die Frau in der Wüste: ein feministich-theologischer Midrasch zur Offb 12', *Evangelische Theologie* 50 (1990) 5, 414–32. See also Keller, *Apocalypse Now and Then*, n. 3 above, pp. 64–73.

59 I want to refer in this context to Michèle Roberts' intriguing novel *The Wild Girl* (London: Methuen, 1984), which is composed of a fictive Gospel according to Mary Magdalene, Acts of the female Apostles and Mary Magdalene's revision of the Book of Revelation. Roberts' novel can be very well read as a feminist Midrash on the Christian Bible (or New Testament) in its entirety. For further theoretical exploration of the topical meaning of Midrash from a variety of angles, see also Geoffrey H. Hartman and Sanford Budick, eds, *Midrash and Literature* (New Haven and London: Yale University Press, 1986).

60 Keller, 'Die Frau', n. 58 above, p. 418.

61 Rosemary Radford Ruether, 'Motherearth and the Megamachine', in *Womanspirit Rising: a Feminist Reader in Religion*, ed. Carol Christ and Judith Plaskow (San Francisco: Harper & Row, 1979), p. 43.

62 Keller, p. 422.

63 *Ibid.*, p. 420.

64 Another moment in which woman and snake, traditionally partners, are turned into each other's enemies is of course in Genesis 3, when God expels Adam and Eve from the Garden of Eden after they have been seduced by the snake into eating the fruits of the tree of knowledge.

65 Catherine Keller, 'Women Against Wasting the World: Notes on Eschatology and Ecology', in *Reweaving the World: the Emergence of Ecofeminism*, ed. I. Diamond and G. Orenstein (San Francisco: Sierra Club Books, 1990), pp. 256–7.

66 Keller points out the agreement among biblical scholars that this martial child is not to be identified with the historical figure of Jesus, no more than the woman with Mary. Rather it can be seen as a mythologizing interpretation of the Jewish Messiah in Christian perspective.

67 Frank Kermode, *The Sense of an Ending: Studies in the Theory of Fiction* (New York: Oxford University Press, 1967).

68 Such as is the stance of Lee Quinby's *Anti-Apocalypse: Exercises in Genealogical Criticism* (Minneapolis: Minnesota University Press, 1994). Quinby offers a far-reaching and original critique of the millenarian and apocalyptic rhetoric in North American culture from Henry Adams to jeans adds, eugenics and Baudrillard. Her rejection of apocalypticism as a 'regime of truth' largely coincides with Keller's condemnation of the masculinist and absolute slant in biblical and secular apocalypse.

69 Keller, 'Why Apocalypse, Now?', see n. 2 above, p. 190.

70 *Ibid.*

71 *Ibid.*, p. 191.

72 *Ibid.*

73 The last notion she proposes in 'The Breast, the Apocalypse, and the Colonial Journey', *Journal of Feminist Studies in Religion* 10 (1994) 1, 53–72, a fine essay on Christopher Columbus' apocalyptic self-understanding as founding aspect of modernity, and more fully works out in her brilliant and evocative study *Apocalypse Now and Then* (see n. 3 above).

74 Donna Haraway, 'The Promises of Monsters', in *Cultural Studies*, ed. L. Grossberg and P. Treichler (New York: Routledge, 1992), pp. 295–337.

75 Keller, 'Die Frau', n. 58 above, p. 415.

76 Stanislaw Lem, *Solaris* (Utrecht/Antwerpen: Spectrum, 1972), p. 190. Quotation is my translation from the Dutch.

VI: A Momentary Taste of Being

1 Bataille, *Death and Sensuality* (New York: Ballantine Books, 1962), p. 268.

2 Julia Kristeva, *The Kristeva Reader*, see Chapter III n. 18 above, p. 157.

3 *Ibid.*, p. 158.

4 *Ibid.*, p. 150.

5 *Ibid.*, p .145.

6 *Ibid.*, p. 144.

7 *Ibid.*, p. 158.

8 Pei, 'Poor Singletons', see Chapter V n. 55 above, p. 278, referring to an interview in *Phantasmicom* 6 (June 1971), quoted by Robert Silverberg in the Introduction to James Tiptree, *Warm Worlds and Otherwise* (New York: Ballantine, 1975), p. xiii.

9 Pei, p. 278.

10 Jame Tiptree, Jr, 'Mama Come Home', in *10,000 Light-Years from Home*. Introduction by Harry Harrison (New York: Ace, 1973), p. 83.

11 James Tiptree, Jr, 'The Psychologist Who Couldn't Do Awful Things to Rats', in *Star Songs of an Old Primate*, p. 244.

12 Pei, 'Poor Singletons', p. 278.

13 *Ibid.*, p. 279.

14 Elisabeth Bronfen, *Over Her Dead Body: Death, Femininity and the Aesthetic* (Manchester: Manchester University Press, 1992), p. 403.

15 Bronfen, p. 432. Besides texts of Virginia Woolf, May Sarton and Anne Sexton, Bronfen more thoroughly discusses Sylvia Plath, *The Bell Jar* (1963); Fay Weldon, *The Life and Loves of a She-Devil* (1983); Margaret Atwood, *Lady Oracle* (1976); Angela Carter, *The Infernal Desire Machines of Doctor Hoffmann* (1972). Because Tiptree's 'A Momentary Taste of Being' moves about in the same context of white Anglo-Saxon female writing of the 1960s and 1970s as these texts, I consider Bronfen's findings pertinent. One wonders, however, if extension of the focus to for instance comtemporary black American female authors would not have offered further different interesting narratives about femininity and death.

16 Bronfen, p. 407.

17 *Ibid.*

18 For discussions of canonical obstacles, prejudices and (self)censorship with respect to female authors and the literary system, cf. besides the scholarly works mentioned in earlier chapters also the many concrete examples in Joanna Russ, *How to Suppress Women's Writing* (Austin: University of Texas Press, 1983).

19 Haraway, *Simians, Cyborgs, and Women*, see Chapter I n. 18 above, p. 161.

20 Braidotti, *Nomadic Subjects*, see Chapter I n. 20 above, chapters 8–10.

21 Think of certain tendencies in Horkheimer and Adorno's *Dialectic of Enlightenment*, see Chapter III n. 45 above. Haraway e.g. points to its equation of the dark side of technological progress with the notion of 'dehumanization'. Nevertheless she highly values the insistence on negativity, i.e. 'the relentless commitment to show that the established disorder is not necessary'. And she feels that: 'Technoscience studies can inherit the bracing negativity of critical theory without resurrecting its marxist humanist ontologies and teleologies'. Donna Haraway, 'A Game of Cat's Cradle: Science Studies, Feminist Theory, Cultural Studies', *Configurations* 1 (1994) 1, 59–71.

22 I know myself also to be influenced by Joke J. Hermsen's study *Nomadisch Narcisme: Sekse, liefde en kunst in het werk van Lou Andréas-Salomé, Belle van Zuylen en Ingeborg Bachmann* (Kampen: Kok Agora, 1993), in which the notion of negative difference (*negatieve differentie*) is linked to the writings of the Austrian author Ingeborg Bachmann to denote an absolute deferment or decoding of the meaning of sexual difference.

23 Jean-François Lyotard, 'Si on peut penser sans corps' (Can Thought Go Without a Body?), in *L'inhumain: Causeries sur le temps* (Paris: Galilée, 1988), p. 24–5. My translation.

24 Lyotard, p. 30.

25 *Ibid.*

26 *Ibid.*, p. 31.

27 Rosi Braidotti, 'De dood van de zon, de verduistering van de maan en de nieuwe constellatie van de planeten: Een dialoog met Lyotard over het seksuele verschil', in R. Brons and H. Kunneman, eds, *Lyotard lezen: Ethiek, onmenselijkheid en sensibiliteit* (Amsterdam/Meppel: Boom, 1995), p. 226.

28 *Ibid.* However, one may argue about whether Braidotti does fully justice to Lyotard's attempts to transcend traditional sexual identities. His vision that sexual difference generates endless thinking may leave open more space for the radically new than suggested. For a different view on 'Can Thought Go without a Body?' see Hermsen, *Nomadisch Narcisme*, n. 22 above, p. 304.

29 Feminist theologians use notions like 'radical immanence', 'transcendence in the finite', or 'immanent transcendence' to signify this. I am especially indebted to Maaike de Haardt's study *Dichter bij de dood: Feministisch-theologische aanzetten tot een theologie van de dood* (Zoetermeer: Boekencentrum, 1993), in which the careful scrutiny of progressive non-feminist and feminist theological visions of death forms the context for the deconstruction of the traditional pairs of immanence/transcendence, finiteness/infinity, matter (body)/spirit.

30 Amy Hollywood, 'Violence and Subjectivity: *Wuthering Heights*, Julia Kristeva, and Feminist Theology', in *Transfigurations: Theology and the French Feminists*, eds C.W. Maggie Kim, Susan St. Ville, Susam Simonaitis (Minneapolis: Fortress Press, 1993), pp. 81–108, p. 103.

31 Hollywood, p. 104.

32 Kristeva, 'Women's Time', in Moi, see Chapter III n. 18 above, p. 210.

33 Hollywood, n. 30 above, p. 107.

34 See Chapter V, where I discussed this in relation to the (theological) revaluation of apocalyptic thought.

35 Hollywood, p. 104.

36 Terry Otten, *The Crime of Innocence in the Fiction of Toni Morrison*

(Columbia: University of Missouri Press, 1989), pp. 3–4.

37 Toni Morrison, *Beloved* (New York: Alfred A. Knopf, 1987).

38 Katherine M. Sands, *Escape from Paradise: Evil and Tragedy in Feminist Theology* (Minneapolis: Augsburg Fortress, 1994), p. 13.

39 *Ibid.*, p. 174.

40 *Ibid.*, p. 11.

41 *Ibid.*, p. 10.

42 *Ibid.*, p. 11.

43 *Ibid.*, p. 14.

44 *Ibid.*, p. 15.

45 *Ibid.*, p. 15. On the theological–ethical implication of the 'scar' in postmodern narrative see also Mark Ledbetter, *Victims and the Postmodern Narrative or Doing Violence to the Body* (London/New York: Macmillan/St. Martin's Press, 1996).

46 Sands, p. 15.

47 *Ibid.*, p. 13.

48 Judith Plaskow and Carol P. Christ, eds, *Weaving the Visions: New Patterns in Feminist Spirituality* (San Franscisco; Harper & Row, 1989), p. 10.

49 Sharon Welch, *A Feminist Ethic of Risk* (Minneapolis: Augsburg Fortress Press, 1990), p. 178.

50 For another view on the immanent meaning of grace see Charlene Spretnak, *States of Grace: The Recovery of Meaning in the Postmodern Age* (San Francisco: Harper Collins, 1991), an interesting yet because of its misconceptions of postmodern thinking flawed attempt to reclaim wisdom traditions (Jewish, Buddhist, Native American and Goddess spirituality) for the recovery of meaning in the present age. Spretnak objects to the 'postmodern deconstructive' assumption that there is 'nothing but construction', and, in opposition to it, defends the possibility of pre-linguistic, authentic experiences and wisdom.

51 Welch, n. 49 above, p. 175.

52 *Ibid.*, p. 178.

53 *Ibid.*, p. 179.

54 Sands, n. 38 above, pp. 63–4.

55 As an opposite model from the Sf field Arthur Clarke's famous fable 'The Nine Billion Names of God' (1952) might be referred to, in which a computer program assists a group of monks in a Tibetan monastery to compile a list which contains all the possible *real* names of God. These are names which are, according to the lama, not just man-made labels, like God, or Jehovah or Allah. The accomplishment of this name-finding task coincides with the stars going out. But what's in a name, I would reply, isn't this megalomania, can any name definitely cancel out difference?

56 *Santa Teresa de Jesús, Libro de la Vida*, Edición, introducción y notas de Otger Steggink (Madrid: Castalia, 1986), Vida 29, 8.

57 See on the meaning of corporeality and the Divine in Teresa's mysticism, Harriëtte Blankers, 'Teresa of Avila: experience of God', in *Yearbook of the European Society of Women in Theological Research*, Vol. 2, ed. E. Green and M. Grey (Kampen/Mainz: Kok Pharos/Grünewald), pp. 92–6.

58 Virginia Woolf, *Moments of Being: Unpublished Autobiographical Writings*, ed. Jeanne Schulkind (London/Brighton: Sussex University Press, 1976), p. 70.

59 *Ibid.*, p. 72.

60 *Ibid.*

61 On Woolf's notion of moments of being see also Genevieve Lloyd, *Being in Time: Selves and Narrators in Philosophy and Literature* (London and New York: Routledge, 1993), pp. 147–61. Anne-Marie Korte, *Een passie voor transcendentie: feminisme, theologie en moderniteit in het denken van Mary Daly* (Kampen: Kok, 1992), p. 376, recalls the influence of Woolf's notion on Daly's pivotal concept of being and the creation of a self.

62 See e.g. Rebecca Chopp, *The Power to Speak. Feminism, Language, God* (New York: Crossroad, 1989), pp. 10–39, where she refers to Kristeva's notion of the semiotic to open up theological discourse about God. She quotes Kristeva, who wrote in *About Chinese Women*: 'God generally speaks only to men. Which is not to say that woman doesn't know more about Him ... But woman's knowledge is corporal, aspiring to pleasure rather than tribal unity (the forbidden fruit seduces Eve's sense of *sight* and *taste*' (in Chopp, pp. 26–7).

63 We may think in particular of the writings by Pseudo-Dyonisius Areopagite (5th or 6th century AD), *De divinis nominibus* (On divine names) and *De mystica theologia*, practices of 'negative theology', influential to Western theology and philosophy until the present day. In the interesting article 'Duister licht: Het verlangen naar God en de mystiek van Nietzsche', *Tijdschrift voor Theologie* 34 (1994), 385–406, Toine van den Hoogen recalls Jan van Ruusbroeck's similar image of the 'abysmal light' to express the experience of being touched by the divine.

64 Ben Okri, *The Famished Road* (London: Jonathan Cape, 1991), p. 229.

Index of names and terms